HOW
MAIL ORDER
FORTUNES
ARE MADE

HOW MAIL ORDER FORTUNES ARE MADE

4th EDITION

Alfred Stern

ARCO PUBLISHING, INC.
NEW YORK

Fourth Edition
Published by Arco Publishing, Inc.
215 Park Avenue South, New York, N.Y. 10003

Copyright © 1970, 1974, 1979, 1983, 1984
by Alfred Stern

Library of Congress Cataloging in Publication Data

Stern, Alfred, 1892–
    How mail order fortunes are made.

    1. Mail-order business. I. Title.
HF5466.S726   1984   658.8'72   84-462
ISBN 0-668-05988-5 (Cloth Edition)
ISBN 0-668-05990-7 (Paper Edition)

Printed in the United States of America

10   9   8   7   6   5   4   3   2   1

CONTENTS

A PREVIEW OF THE MAIL ORDER BUSINESS

The three most popular words in the English language are probably "Enclosed find cash (or check or money order)."

Now imagine yourself receiving stacks of mail every day—with each letter containing these three opening words.

What an exciting way to start the day!

You may wonder whether it is at all possible for you to achieve this delightful and profitable experience. Yes, you are no different from the countless mail order operators who started from scratch and who are now taking in more cash *daily* than they had previously received in a *week's* wages.

If it is as simple as all that, then why doesn't everyone make a huge success of the mail order business? That's the $64,000 question which this book shall try to answer for you. The author draws on 35 years of successful mail order experience to tell you what to do and what not to do. You should be able to steer a straight course and eliminate guesswork, because a workable plan will be provided.

However, no one has a magic formula for success. Much depends on the public's response to a given product in the face of changing times and conditions. Such factors as changing buying habits, competition, seasons, pricing, profit margins, economics, and world conditions alter situations. Experienced executives will tell you even with the use of computers for determining facts, their decisions are often based on hunches, intuition, and even ESP (extra-sensory perception). Yet you cannot get along without facts.

And of course a great deal depends on you—how you follow the rules and how you apply the knowledge you gain as you proceed. This book shall define in simple language all the essential ingredients that help to make a smooth-running mail order business. Although the book provides the recipe, you will be the chef to carry it out. Two bakers given the same recipe rarely obtain the same results. Personal considerations enter into the undertaking. Pardon the pun, but it is hoped you have what it takes to produce the "dough" you are after. Undoubtedly you have the interest and ability; otherwise you would not be seeking further information.

Broadly speaking, some of the things covered in this book, which is virtually a study course, are:

How to Get Started Properly
What to Sell
Methods Likely to Get Results
How to Avoid Pitfalls
How to Organize Your Capital, Time, and Efforts
How to Expand Your Enterprise

Among all these "How-to's" there are many intricate details that must be mastered. Many questions that you have in mind will be answered. Of course this book contains some theory, but in addition it includes down-to-earth working principles and facts, the kind that you can get your teeth into. If, after a careful reading of this book, you still seek answers to your mail order problems, you are invited to write to the author.

Alfred Stern
33-45 92nd St.
Jackson Heights, NY 11372

HOW MAIL ORDER FORTUNES ARE MADE

THEY STRUCK IT RICH

Mail order sales have increased by 50 percent over the past ten years. Are you getting your share? Here are some top mail order enterprises which have cut a big slice out of the melon for themselves. These are but a few of the hundreds—perhaps thousands—which have had a huge success in this field.

- One quite well-known man made a million dollars selling some of the wierdest gadgets. He later wrote a book about his experiences. The book alone brought him over $25,000 in royalties. He was invited to appear on at least a half-dozen top, prime-time radio shows to tell millions about his marvelous success.

- A firm that produces two types of tablets for women—one for reducing, the other for gaining weight—grew from a small start to one bringing in a $50,000 yearly income.

- A firm selling man-made diamonds had been placing advertising amounting to several thousand dollars a month for years. Steady substantial earnings have been realized.

- For years, a mail order man has been enjoying outstanding success by selling live chameleons to boys. One ad alone brought in $2,000 in profits.

- Several concerns have been making substantial profits by selling various types of posters: historical, photographic blow-ups, and psychedelic, to mention a few. At least judging from the thousands of dollars they invest in advertising, it is reasonable to assume that these firms are doing a lucrative business.

A Case History of a Money Maker

One man made a small fortune selling Kennedy medallions. This came about only through his foresight, ingenuity, and courage. While John F. Kennedy was still a senator, this mail order firm sensed that the popularity of the man and his driving ambition would lead to greater glory. A sort of charisma or aura was already developing around John F. Kennedy, and later affected his brothers as well.

1

The mail order man decided to gamble on Kennedy's ascendancy to fame. First, he wrote to Senator Kennedy and received a letter in reply granting (to quote) "permission to engrave dies and strike Medallions bearing my likeness." On the strength of this letter a huge order was placed for Kennedy medallions. It was then decided to run a little test ad in the *Wall Street Journal*. That 4-inch ad cost about $200 and brought in an astounding $10,200.

Such spectacular results naturally inspired the mail order man to greater achievement. He immediately placed another and larger order with the manufacturer of the medallions, meanwhile running ads in over a hundred publications, including newspapers, magazines, and especially all the Catholic publications. This entailed an advertising expenditure of $35,000. It was well worth it. Business firms ordered medallions by the hundreds to give to their executives, and dealers sent in wholesale orders as well.

By that time the mail order man's premonition came true and Kennedy was elected President. With the inaugural and the ever-increasing popularity of the famous man, the demand for the Kennedy medallions knew no bounds. Out of respect for the President, the mail order firm wrote to Kennedy again for permission to sell medallions bearing his likeness. A reply was received from the White House, signed by Pierre Salinger, Press Secretary to the President, granting permission again.

Alas, as everyone knows and as history records, Kennedy was subsequently assassinated. The mail order concern recovered from the painful news, as everyone else did in time, and then felt compelled to take fresh measures. A commemorative memorial piece was then promoted. It took the form of a block of lucite in which a Kennedy coin was imbedded. It sold as fantastically as the medallion. Finally, to make a long story shorter, this extraordinary enterprise realized an overall profit of $150,000, a fine example of what mail order can accomplish with judicious planning and perseverance. This points up the fact that there is still opportunity in the good old U.S.A. for individual initiative that leads to outstanding success.

How a Woman Made a Fortune

Here's the success story of a woman who started a mail order business with her $100 a month veterans allowance and then step by step, over a period of 19 years, the business developed to such a point that she draws an income of $9,000,000 from it.

She began by advertising a new type of rodent poison, which drew a substantial response. She then took on a line of vitamins and health aids. This activity all took place while raising children and running a household.

In eight years, sales shot up 2000 percent. Her husband, who operated a chain of drug stores, soon realized that he would be better off to sell his stores and pitch in with his wife to develop her business further. The health food market fortunately grew larger, so dietetic foods were added to the line. This led to the creation of a multitude of new items. Exotic foreign foods were among the novelties and subsequently a catalog was created to feature housewares and gifts as well as food delicacies. At last report, the business was still expanding.

Success Reported by Publishers

A publisher of a group of eleven magazines, of the true story-romance-movie-confession-radio-TV type, reported that a large number of the advertisers who had started small, began to use full pages when they became successful. The full pages used by these advertisers cost between $4,537 and $11,540 per issue at that time, depending on whether one magazine or all eleven titles in the group were used. The type of advertisers varied; for example:

A School for Training Women to Become Medical and Dental Assistants and Technicians
A Glamour Exerciser
A Course in Shorthand
A Bronzer of Baby Shoes
A High School Training Program
A Wig Stylist
A Speaking and Writing Course

The same publisher reported that scores of its advertisers insert ads of various sizes all 12 months of the year.

Another magazine, catering to women in home-owning families, stated that 110 of its advertisers use 12 issues of a year, which is indicative of successful enterprises. Since the minimum cost of space in this publication was $450, each of these 110 advertisers spends at least $5,400 per year in this publication alone. The ads are keyed so that the mail order houses know precisely where the business emanates.

WHAT MAIL ORDER MEANS

Make sure that at the very beginning you understand what is meant by "mail order." Some people confuse it with "direct mail." Surprisingly enough, many experienced advertising executives, who should know better, use the terms "direct mail" and "mail order" interchangeably, even though each phrase might express an entirely different method of operation. It is not just a matter of semantics. Unless one holds the distinctions clearly in mind, he is liable to use one loosely when he actually means the other. The result: confusion and fuzzy thinking.

It seems elementary but let us get the record straight: Mail order simply means conducting a business without personal contact—in such a way that orders are solicited either through publications, direct mail, radio, or television advertising. The merchandise is shipped by any means of suitable transportation, and the money is generally sent by mail. The term direct mail might include mail order but not necessarily. Many firms use mailing pieces, not to get direct orders, but as institutional advertising, or to entice customers to an establishment, or to pave the way for salesmen, or for fund raising, public relations, publicity, or other purposes.

As a mail order operator, you are concerned only with buying and selling to customers (whom you may never see) by means of mailing pieces, ads, and other media as pointed out previously. In short, you are bent on getting an order. The advertiser might employ direct mail primarily but not always. On other occasions, publications are used to far greater advantage in stirring up orders direct from the advertisements. On still other occasions, a combination is used: publications to get leads, and direct mail to follow up leads and to close the sale.

Many are attracted to the mail order busines because it requires little investment. It can be operated either full- or part-time at home or from a small desk-space office. No large stock of merchandise is required, no high office or warehouse rent, no wages to pay, and no credit risks. Countless mail order concerns started on a shoestring, and today they invest thousands in advertising that pays a substantial return.

The most well-known example is Sears-Roebuck, which was started by Richard W. Sears to sell low-priced watches. He merged with A.C. Roebuck and expanded their watch and jewelry business to a nationwide operation. Other merchandise was added and a catalog was produced to feature each item in the line attractively.

Montgomery Ward and International Correspondence School had equally interesting beginnings. These multimillion dollar businesses did not mushroom overnight. The process was gradual. The same successful principles of mail order selling which they used many decades ago are still valid today.

WHO IS QUALIFIED TO START A MAIL ORDER BUSINESS?

Any Businessperson

The normal intelligent person, who can follow certain guidelines presented here and in other publications on the subject, can make a success of the mail order business. His progress, of course, will depend on the degree of effort and skill he puts into it as well as the amount of money available for adequate testing. Perseverance—the patience and will to keep trying despite possible early failures—is also a very important quality.

Housewives

This type of business is the salvation of the woman who is fed up with housework and seeks more satisfying activities than bridge games, gossiping, or social gatherings over coffee, sewing or TV watching. It also appeals to the woman who seeks extra pin money to buy things she could never otherwise afford. Another type of housewife uses this convenient method to raise money for her church. In many cases, the husband, who has more business experience, starts the operation and then turns it over to his wife to keep it running.

Manufacturers

Countless manufacturers, who are not satisfied with sales emanating from normal dealer-distributor channels, turn to mail order as an effective additional outlet. By selling direct to consumers and eliminating the middleman they earn a far greater profit on each unit produced; moreover they are assured of immediate sales and thus avoid accumulating inventory. Products sold through retail stores tend to become shopworn because the average dealer, handling countless items, does not as a rule push any one of them but waits for the customer to ask for it. It takes a costly national advertising campaign to create consumer demand to the point where folks are induced to go to a store and ask for a particular brand.

Dealers and Distributors

As in the case of manufacturers, dealers, distributors, and wholesalers find mail order is a convenient means of increasing lagging sales. Many consider it so profitable that they give up their long-established stores and turn to mail order exclusively. A case in point is a pharmacist who ran a successful drugstore on Fifth Avenue in New York City. He grew tired of working long hours seven days a week, and he was persuaded to start a mail order business on the side. This new activity showed such a substantial profit that he decided to close the store and devote all of his time to selling by mail. This business kept developing to such a point that he was able to spend $50,000 a year on mail order advertising, which raised his profits even more. And the beauty of it is that the new venture occupied only a few hours a week of his time. Much of the work he turned over to youngsters who filled orders after school. The rest of the time he spent playing golf or vacationing in Florida.

In contrast to the case cited, many firms reverse the procedure, by first using mail order advertising to create consumer demand and develop national distribution. Once this is accomplished, they then induce dealers and jobbers to carry their line.

Salesmen

This type of individual is also looking for ways and means to augment his earnings. He finds that he can make his normal calls by day and still run a mail order business at night and on weekends, with or without the aid of wife and children. He may be fed up working for someone else and seeks the satisfaction and the peace of mind of being his own boss. (In a later chapter on "The Specialty Salesman—A Mail Order Prospect," there is a discussion of methods to induce the specialty salesman to work for you.)

The Retired Person

Mail order is defintely the answer to the retired man's prayers. It is an extraordinarily rejuvenating mechanism—often the turning point in a man's life. Thousands upon thousands of men are forced into early retirement only to find themselves with too much leisure time. Most of them, during their working years, build up dreams of retiring under ideal conditions. Alas, when the time arrives to say goodbye to job or business, disillusionment comes quickly. Perhaps the first year or so after retirement they do a bit of traveling, take up a hobby, or just spend hours watching TV or reading. Soon idleness becomes boredom, parlticularly if they had previously led active lives in business.

Spending so much time around the home tends to create unexpected discord. Under such conditions a man is apt to get under the feet or into the hair of his wife who is not accustomed to having him around the house during the daytime when household chores must be done. It has been aptly stated that a wife, after a man's retirement commences, acquires "twice as much *husband* but only half the *income.*"

This can lead to bickering and disharmony. It frequently does. Then consider what goes on in the minds of the idle men under such circumstances. Alone with their thoughts, they often feel sorry for themselves. As a relief, they just sit and rock by the hour, wondering how long they must wait for the bitter end. This state of vegetation tends to deteriorate mind and body and to shorten the life span.

Fortunately, many retired people wake up in time to learn that they can still be useful and retain their self-respect. All they need is wholesome stimulation, worthwhile incentives, and pleasantly active involvement. Thus, a man loses himself in what he is doing, age is forgotten and life is renewed through the impetus of achievement. Men of 70, 80, and over frequently plunge into a fresh business with all the zest and eagerness of a 20 year old.

This is where a mail order business can play a major role. It seems made to order for such a situation because, as previously mentioned, little capital or space are required because the business can be operated in the home, and if necessary, merchandise can be drop-shipped (goods shipped directly from the manufacturer to the consumer). Finally, little exertion is required, the greatest effort consisting of addressing labels, sticking them on packages and carrying them to the mailbox. Opening mail and counting the checks and dollar bills can scarcely be considered work. Incidentally, a new interest also enters the home. The wife often pitches in with vim as an escape from household drudgery. She sees life from a new view-point thereby widening her outlook. A harmonious husband-wife relationship often results, and to cap it all, income is augmented to make life more enjoyable.

All this may sound like an over-simplication, yet it is true because it has been experienced by countless men. Of course, the successful ones observed certain basic principles of sound mail order practice such as locating salable, profitable products; selecting effective publications or mailing lists; preparing persuasive advertisements or mailing pieces, etc. Apropos of this, the author recently visited St. Petersburg, Florida—a city noted for its many retired inhabitants. On one suburban street I visited, I found almost every home was occupied by a retired couple. Conversation soon revealed that nearly all of them felt bored and even miserable for want of something worthwhile to engage their time.

Think of how well a mail order business could fill the vacuum!

HOW MUCH CAPITAL IS REQUIRED

The question which bothers many newcomers to the mail order field is: How much capital do I require to get started? The correct answer is two-fold: 1) Allow about 15 percent of expected gross sales; for example, on estimated gross sales of $5,000, allocate $750 for an advertising budget; 2) you can start an initial test of a product with a few hundred dollars, or with a few thousand. If you employ the smaller amount, however, the test might not be conclusive, because some products require testing in various fields to ascertain which is the most productive. One could test a single field at a time, but this would take many months. And if the first and second fields failed to bring in a satisfactory profit, the advertiser might become discouraged and drop the item, whereas if he waited for the results of the third test in a different field, it could possibly be highly successful.

Of course, not everyone possesses the wherewithal for testing a product simultaneously in various fields—as in the case of a certain manufacturer of an electronic bug killer who spent $25,000 during one summer month testing various markets, as well as advertising in the most effective publications in each field. He bought advertising space in Shelter Group magazines, such as *House Beautiful* and *House & Garden*; in farm papers, such as *Southern and Western Farm Units*; in small town publications, such as *Grit* and *Capper's*

Weekly; in weekly tabloids, such as the *National Enquirer* and in Sunday newspapers like the *New York Times* and the *Chicago Tribune*. This advertiser, of course, possessed the funds to do it and he was willing to gamble because he knew he had a better product than his competitors, who were already doing a big business selling a similar item and advertising it extensively. However, his test proved successful.

This case might be considered unusual because of the large amount of money involved. It is cited merely to point up the value of testing various markets. The man who has only a few hundred or even a few thousand dollars, and who is introducing a new product without knowing how the public will respond to it, need not invest so heavily in his initial testing program. However, too many small firms make the mistake of placing all their available funds in a single test, when they should have enough remaining for at least another test of either the same product or of another item. If the single test turns out to be a flop, the impatient advertiser often jumps to the wrong conclusions: that mail order does not pay; that the product is no good; that the advertising agency is inefficient; or that the wrong medium was used. All or part of this may be true but one test cannot provide a sound basis for judgment because of the meager evidence, no more than the sight of a swallow means that summer is near.

Most of the firms that have made a success of mail order advertising have tested several products before ascertaining which was the biggest producer. Even then, they did not hit the real jackpot until they tested the selected product in several likely fields. Furthermore, the successful firms never stop testing. Look at some of the advertising of leading mail order houses. They run multiple product ads, featuring up to a dozen or more articles, in the hope that public response will reveal one or two surprisingly hot items. It is true, however, if a product is advertised in an accepted logical medium, with extremely poor results, it could be an indication to drop the item and try another rather than spend more funds testing a failure.

Some products, by their very nature, require fewer funds for testing If the product manifestly lends itself to newspaper advertising, the test might cost less than if it required ads in large circulation national magazines. Moreover, some items can be successfully tested with relatively small space, while others require more room for illustrations and detailed description.

Many a mail order product starts off on a wrong footing, either because of timidity, parsimony, or just plain lack of funds. The advertising agency that tries to do a conscientious job is often stymied before it can get underway properly. The agency might recommend a certain size ad in a specific publication. The advertiser then responds by telling the agency to cut the ad down to half its size and use a cheaper publication to save money. As a result: 1) The ad is too small to illustrate and describe the product adequately or to make a forceful impact on prospects; 2) the medium selected is the second or third best for the purpose. Under such circumstances if the advertising is successful, it would be an exception. If it does poorly, the last one the advertiser blames is himself.

Bear in mind that a $50 ad could be expensive if it produces little or nothing, while a $500 ad might be a bargain if it shows a huge profit. In any case, it is better to wait until more funds are accumulated than to start an undercapitalized business and end with regrets. Of course, one can begin with as little as $20 which would pay for a tiny classified ad. Even if the ad showed a profit, this type of snail-pace operation is not recommended, for it would take a long, long time for the business—if you can call it such—to get on its feet and give the owner a feeling of achievement.

This statement may disillusion many mail order freshmen who had expected instant success in the glamorous mail order field, lured on perhaps by the extravagant claims of ads which promised a fortune overnight if their advice were followed. It is important to be realistic, although you may, as some have done, strike a rich lode immediately. On the other hand, it is wise to steel yourself against a possible initial failure while keeping in mind the ultimate success you can achieve if sound guidelines are patiently adhered to over a period of time.

IS MAIL ORDER SEASONAL?

Beginners in the mail order field are often in a quandary as to which months are best for advertising. Hot items know no seasons, it is the weak articles and those on the borderline that must be promoted with caution.

The timing can all be gauged to reach a predetermined audience at the height of its responsiveness. Experience, research, and instinct might give you the answer as to what is the critical moment. Much depends on the product and the conditions surrounding it. It is unwise to generalize. Some old-timers still stick to the false notion that summer is a dead period for mail order because people are vacationing.

But conditions have changed, and today many persons take fall or winter vacations. Besides, only a small percentage go away during the same week, and those that do read their mail when they return home. Bear in mind that business goes on all the time. Ask yourself: "Do I stop buying in the summer?" Ordinarily spring and fall are the best seasons for sales, yet there are many products that sell better in summer and winter. Suntan lotions, bathing suits, and insecticides obviously sell well in summer, while boots and windshield de-icers are better winter sellers. There are preschool, prevacation, prewedding items, and many others designed for special occasions in all seasons. This means that you must tailor your message to the occasion and plan your schedule accordingly.

Housewares are traditionally promoted in February and September, but if you have an item that is novel and fills a need, it can sell year-round—even as a gift.

Men's Gifts ordinarily sell better in December but there are many other good occasions: Father's Day and birthdays, which might be at any time of the year, are examples.

Reducing Items do very well in the summer, along with those mentioned above. They are weakest during October through December, the Christmas gift-buying season, because they are products that people buy only for themselves.

Gifts in General are undoubtedly most active duing the Christmas season when the world seems mesmerized by the spirit of the yuletide. However, gifts are presented for countless other occasions as well: birthdays, anniversaries, Mother's Day, Father's Day, and Easter, also as expressions of gratitude to a hostess or as surprises to children whenever they are visited.

Some advertisers regard January and August as slow months, yet others have found these months very active. Apparently, many persons receive Christmas bonuses which they spend in January. In August, mothers buy school supplies and clothes for their children in preparation for the opening of school after Labor Day.

As stated at the beginning of this chapter, if you have a good selling item, forget about seasons. One publication in the shelter group lists 110 mail order companies which are oblivious to seasons, as evidenced by their advertising in the magazine every month of the year.

Those mail order men overly concerned with seasonal selling would welcome a product that straddles summer and winter. Here is one that does it perfectly. The sale price adds extra punch to the ad.

FRESH GIFT HOLLY & MISTLETOE

Deck the Halls with fresh, choice treated sprays of glossy green, rich red berried English Holly. Boxes topped with sprig of Mistletoe. Gift cards enclosed. Money-back guarantee. Arrival about Dec. 16th unless otherwise requested. All boxes Prepaid.

H-2	An Armload of Holly	$3.95 via Air 4.75
H-3	Whopping Armload, sprays to 22" long.	$6.50 via Air 7.95
HG-6	Chalet Box. Bounty of Holly plus aromatic Mt. greens, pine cones and Variegated holly.	$8.95 via Air 12.95
HG-37	Loads of English plus Variegated Holly, giant pine cones, choice aromatic mountain greens.	$13.95 via Air 21.75

(Air suggested for deliveries to remote East Coast areas and Florida, and arrival wanted much earlier or later than Dec. 16th.)
Write for Free Gift Brochure

NORTHWEST CORNER STORE
Longview 2, Wash. 98632

A fine ad of a seasonal item. The firm selling it does not depend entirely on the pre-Christmas gift buying period, but the names acquired from holly sales are used for distributing a catalog of other items throughout the year. The ad appeared in *House Beautiful* and *House & Garden*.

In case one might forget that Christmas should be merry, this silvery bell has the reminder exquisitely engraved on its surface. It serves as a charming decoration or as a gift for the occasion, and was wisely advertised in *House Beautiful* just before the grandest holiday of the year.

Only $4.95 ea. ppd. 2 for $9.50

Ring in a

Memorable Christmas
With an Engraved
SILVER BELL

A touch of nostalgia for the old fashioned days for this coming Christmastide. A charming gift for a friend or relative—the perfect decoration for your own Christmas tree or table. Finished in gleaming silverplate, each lovely bell stands 3" high. "Merry Christmas" is engraved in the center at no extra charge. This thoughtful beautiful memento can be the start of a wonderful collection. Handsomely gift boxed. Give your loved ones a lasting Christmas wish of love and good cheer. Orders yours today.

SHOW and TELL GIFTS, Dept. HB
P.O. Box 6, Niagara St. Sta., Buffalo, N.Y. 14201
N.Y. State Res. add local sales tax.

How to Get Started

You will recall that Sears started with a single item, took on a few more, then branched out in all directions. Beginners would do well to follow this principle. Test out one or a few items either by running small ads in well-recognized mail order publications or by sending out small test mailings. If the ads pull, repeat them in the same publications—until they cease to pull—then gradually test the same merchandise in additional publications (or in the case of mailings, expand your list). As time goes on, also test new merchandise in this way. Ultimately, you will discover quite a number of "hot sellers" and you will be building up a responsive mailing list—all of which place you in a position to get out a catalog of diversified items.

Some find it more profitable to purchase ready-made catalogs, prepared by reputable firms which have already tested the pulling power of the items listed. (This is discussed in detail in a later chapter.) In an operation in which you start with a test of one or a few ads and develop into a catalog mail order house, all efforts to get business should be keyed or charted: list the name of the publication or mailing list; the size of the ad or the number of mailing pieces; the cost of the ad or mailing; the number of inquiries; the number of actual orders; the cost per order; the profit per order; the total profit, etc. In a subsequent chapter we shall provide specific methods of "keying" advertisements. By a process of elimination, ads or mailings are scheduled only in those publications that produce a profit. Thus, the more a person knows about his business—what makes it tick, what each component costs, and the kind of people who purchase this merchandise—the greater the chances for success.

So keep testing! You might hit the jackpot with your first try, but steel yourself for a second and third attempt. It takes patience, perseverance, and at least a little capital to insure success. Bear in mind that the International Correspondence School, after 75 years' experience in mail order advertising, is still testing new ads, to find fresh approaches, better ways to increase inquiries, and close sales at the lowest cost. Before undertaking such tests, it will probably be to your advantage to contact a conscientious mail order specialist, who can size up a product's potential, who knows media and advertising preparation, and who will provide objective advice.

From his long range of experience, he can save you from many pitfalls, minimize your risk, and guide you toward your objectives step by step. Even if he does not know all the answers, his assistance may not cost you more than your placing the ads directly with the publications.

What to Do First

To begin with, establish a mailing address—either at home, through a post office box, or from the office of a firm which is organized to receive mail for business people like yourself. Generally speaking, if you have a choice between a post office box and a street address, it is better to use the latter. People have more faith in a street address because it implies an established location. A "fly-by-nighter," living temporarily at a hotel, could easily rent a post office box for a month or so, and then skip with the money collected without delivering merchandise. Notwithstanding, many mail order businesses with post office addresses flourish. Fortunately, most people are trusting and will risk the chances of being victimized by a few frauds, knowing that federal law attempts to protect the unwary. If you live in a small town where the postmaster knows you, you are at an advantage. You can simply use your own town name, without a street address. After you establish your address, you will no doubt go through the usual procedure of providing stationery, labels, etc.

Assuming that you have lined up your products, the next step is to circulate information about them far and wide, to as many prospects as possible, and as economically as you know how. At this point, you will decide whether to circulate your literature or catalog through mailing lists or whether it is wiser to advertise for customers in publications. You may decide to do both. A case can be made out for either method as you will observe in the pages to follow.

Minimize Your Risk

Every business venture is a gamble, and this does not exclude mail order. The difference between this business and others is that you need not sink your life savings before you realize that you have made a bad move and, as in a checker game, if a bad move is made, you can still recoup. If you use your capital to open a store or a factory, over a period of time it would be necessary to spend a considerable sum for merchandise, equipment, fixtures, rent, etc., and even then there is always the possibility that your capital will not hold out until you can get the business on its feet. With mail order, as already pointed out; the risk is small and you keep it that way by constant testing and changing your tactics as the signals warn you.

In the beginning, it is best to confine your expenditures to bare essentials. Rent a typewriter instead of buying one if your capital is low. Type your own letters, do your own addressing, stuffing, stamping, and mailing. Keep your own records. Do whatever is possible without assistance unless your wife or other members of the family help you. It is not wise to skimp on literature because this is apt to reflect on the merchandise as well as you—the company. Cut corners in other ways. Your expenses are few except for stationery, literature, and advertising.

You can avoid carrying a large stock of merchandise. Many manufacturers will drop-ship for you. All you do is to send them your labels (addressed to your customers) plus the payments for the merchandise. The drop-ship manufacturer sticks your addressed label on his package, which is then mailed, However, if you possess the capital to lay in small stocks of goods, you can often make a larger profit because the manufacturer will offer you a better deal; besides, you will be ordering in dozens or gross lots. Moreover, you are protected against placing your customers' names (acquired by you at considerable expense) in other hands. You need not worry about this factor if a responsible house tells you it will keep such names in confidence and not use them for other purposes.

In this business as well as in all others, it is smart to hold a little capital in reserve for emergencies. However, if you are running the business part-time while holding down a salaried job, this outside source of income might serve as your contingency fund. Many job holders run a mail order business on the side until sales reach a point where this supplementary income warrants giving up the job and devoting full time to the development of one's own business. They are then in the position to say good-bye to bosses and to the troubles that come with job hunting.

WHAT'S IN A NAME?

Is the company name important? Can it be a liability or an asset? Draw or repel trade? It all depends on a number of factors. While a name carries some weight, its influence on mail order sales is not as great as generally imagined. One should not to be too concerned about the company name because the mail order buyer is primarily interested in how the product will benefit *him* and what it will cost him. Many firms with commonplace names are leaders in the mail order field today.

Your own name will produce almost as many sales as a more catchy, assumed name. The only advantage of using your own name is that it need not be registered. Most states require that assumed or fictitious names be registered at the county clerk's office. A small fee is charged and the procedure is simple. You fill out a form naming the principals of the company along with their home addresses. No attorney is required.

This registration is necessary to protect the public against fraud, so that if a customer has a claim against a company, he can trace the owner. There have been a few cases where a dishonest mail order advertiser, using a fictitious name and a hotel address, skipped with the money he received. Of course, since this is a federal offense which carries heavy penalties, few try it.

When choosing a company name, here are a few points to bear in mind:

1. Choose a name that reflects the prospect's benefits rather than your own. For example, House of Economy Gifts is better than Smith's Sales Enterprises. The latter suggest only the sales aspect and further indicates the items may be overpriced.

2. Select a name that is both easy to pronounce and to remember such as, Regal Gift Co. This is better than Wallcoverings Innovations Co.

3. Choose a name that is descriptive of the merchandise you are selling or the type of business you operate, such as All-American Post Co.

4. It helps to select a name that is alliterative, such as Helpful Household Products or Handy Hanger Co., these are more euphonious than Useful Household Products.

5. Avoid using the name of a well-known company. For example, if your name is Moore and you are selling paint, avoid the name Moore Paint Co. because there is a well-known company by that name. The name, The George Moore Company, would be safer. If you are not sure that the name you have chosen does not already exist, consult *Standard and Poors* or *Moody's* listings in directories at your library or at least check the local phone books. If you are advised by an attorney that your company name is in conflict with another organization's, it is easier and less costly to change your name than make a court case of it.

6. If you are selling to consumers by mail at the same time that you sell to dealers, it is wise to use different names for each type of operation in order to keep the two separate.

7. If there is any likelihood you will develop from a one-product firm to one offering diversified items, it is advisable to select a general name instead of one that is specifically descriptive of a

single product. For example, why be stuck with a name like The Novelty Jewelry Co. when before long you will be selling automotive accessories as well as jewelry? It would be better to protect yourself initially with a multiproduct name, such as The Plain and Fancy Gift Co. or some other name of a similar general nature.

In conclusion, the wording of a name has some value, yet a name is *what you make of it*, which means how much intelligence and energy you put into your business, how discerning you are when choosing products to sell, how compelling your advertising message is, and how well you treat your customers. All these factors contribute to your public image and ultimate success.

AVOID "CANNED" MAIL ORDER PROPOSITIONS

The cheaper mail order magazines are chock full of fly-by-night, get-rich-quick schemes to separate you from your hard-earned savings. You can generally recognize them by their extravagant claims. Do not be fooled by "free" or low-priced offers, for they are often come-ons. Be sure that you deal with a responsible firm—one that has been in business a long time—and proved reputable. Just bear in mind that no matter how little or how much you pay for a so-called mail order package plan, you will still have to pitch in yourself to achieve your own success. It's a mistake to rest entirely on a cut-and-dried proposition. The more you know about how a mail order enterprise functions and the more you work out the details yourself, the less your risk will be. Above all, you will achieve an inner satisfaction in feeling that most of the results were realized through your own efforts and ingenuity. In time, you will see a pattern of success forming; you will strike a faster pace, and go on to greater accomplishments.

When you really get your feet on the ground and look for wide-scale expansion, it may be wise to consult a reputable advertising agency specializing in mail order accounts. Such an organization, staffed with professionals of mature experience, can point out new methods and markets that you never realized existed. They will charge you nothing, as a rule, for the services of laying out and writing ads. You pay only the regular publication rates. The publishers pay the agency a commission for placing the ads. If there are any fees, it would be for extra assignments, such as preparing circulars, publicity, surveys.

SEVEN APPROACHES TO THE BUSINESS

Persons entering the mail order business generally fall into the following categories:

1. Inventing Your Own Product

If you have invented a product and possess the means to manufacture it yourself, all well and good, but do not make the common mistake of putting all your funds into equipment, dies, tools, and so on, and leave nothing over for mail order promotion and advertising. When you get into that position, you will be forced either to sell out your brainchild or give someone else most of the profitable sales rights. Unfortunately, many a good inventor lacks both the capital to manufacture his own product and the means of distribution to the public. In this case, it is advisable to contact manufacturers in the same field who will assume production costs and sell the item on a royalty basis. Names of such manufacturers can be secured from *Thomas' Register*, available at many public libraries.

Experience shows that it is advantageous to contact as many manufacturers as possible at one time because the more bids you receive the better your bargaining position. A mailing piece should be enclosed, describing and illustrating the product. A working drawing or photo of a pilot model can be shown. This mailing piece can be an inexpensive off-set job. A letter—preferably addressed to the individual manufacturers—should accompany the printed piece. If you do not feel capable of undertaking this mailing, consult a reliable advertising agency.

2. Buying Sales Rights

If you possess the wherewithal to purchase someone else's invention or the exclusive sales rights, you are in a strong position to make a substantial profit on each sale and ward off competition. It also provides leeway to sell wholesale to dealers and specialty salesmen. Of course, much hinges on selecting the right article and paying the right price for the invention or sales rights. The factors that contribute to the salability of a product are listed in a later chapter. You can find persons who offer patents, franchises, and sales rights by watching the Business Opportunity sections of large metropolitan nespapers like the *New York Times* or the *Chicago Tribune*, or you can run your own ads stating that you are in the market for such a deal. If you consider purchasing a franchise, make sure that you read the contract carefully and understand everything stated so that you will be fully protected. If necessary, engage an attorney. A liberal franchise permits the return for refund of all merchandise ordered at the start if the purchaser decides to give up the franchise for lack of sales. Generally, a franchise operation is not practical for mail order because the average franchise restricts the operator to a limited geographical area, whereas a mail order business is best operated on a national basis.

3. Buying from Manufacturers, Distributors, Importers, etc.

The easiest way of getting into the mail order business is by purchasing products already manufactured and tested. It means taking less profit on each sale and perhaps making fewer sales than if you completely controlled a product through invention or purchase of sales rights. However, to offset this, you have little capital risk. That is why there are a hundred people who choose this means for each person who approaches mail order by other routes. But even if you possess a single product through invention or purchase, you will find it to your advantage to take on other products as a hedge against the failure of your own product. Besides, the prospects and customers you acquire from advertising your own specialty can be converted with little extra expense, to customers for outside items—and vice versa. The same mailing list can be used for both.

When you order products in the open market, you will be concerned with novelty items that are not carried in stores or staples sold at a discount. You will also be concerned with markup and the sources of such merchandise are listed in detail in a subsequent chapter. Although the third approach to developing a mail order business is the most common and not necessarily the most profitable, it offers the widest range of products to choose from.

4. Buying from Catalog Houses

If you line up products from sources other than catalog houses, you will have to pay your own expenses for preparing sales letters, circulars, and catalogs. On the other hand, when you deal with catalog houses, such sales literature is ready-made for immediate mailing and is turned out in an attractive professional manner. You purchase the completed catalogs at a low rate—often for less than it would cost you if you produced them yourself because the catalog house prints hundreds of thousands and gives you the benefit of the quantity rate, even though you purchase only a thousand or so at a time.

And as indicated previously, you need not tie up your funds in merchandise. You order only as you receive orders. Before you decide to accept a proposition from a catalog house, make sure you are dealing with a dependable firm and not a fly-by-night. Ask your bank for a report on their financial history, find out how long they have been in business, whether they ever failed, etc. Make sure that they, or the manufacturers whom they represent, guarantee their merchandise and will make refunds cheerfully if complaints arise. Finally, settle on a clear written agreement regarding your costs, including merchandise, shipping, and literature, so that you will know the exact amount of your profit margin. It is also to your advantage to learn in advance whether you will benefit by a sliding scale of costs in case you build up volume sales. The major disadvantage of buying from catalog houses is that most of them do not allow a sufficient discount to insure a profit from mail order advertising. Watch this point!

5. Follow the Leader

Many who enter the mail order business reason this way: Why take the risk of introducing an unknown product to the market when I can profit by someone else's success? Such persons religiously follow, with product and media, the footsteps of those who seem to have been successful. They figure that a firm which has been in business over a period of time, constantly repeating the ads, must be making a profit or it would have quit. Then all that is necessary for the imitator is to find a similar item and advertise it in the same publications. This may work at times but not always. The leader you follow is ahead of you and firmly established. He had ironed out the wrinkles through testing. He probably has found an economical source of supply to allow him a wide profit margin. He knows the type of picture, headline, and copy to use, how large an ad to run, and which publications pull. So notwithstanding an imitative approach, some testing may still be necessary.

6. Seek a Repeat Product

Another kind of mail order operator starts off with the premise that products that induce repeat sales are more profitable than those that are bought only once. This is sound reasoning if you are fortunate enough to find such items. They are scarcer than the other kind.

A manufacturer of a reducing item sold to women claims his repeat business amounts to 35 percent of original sales. He nets a total of $50,000 a year from his mail order business.

A firm that sells live chameleons to Boy Scouts makes his biggest profit selling meal worms to his young customers who must feed their pet lizards regularly to keep them alive. His business has been going on successfully for years.

Items such as labels, stationery, rubber stamps, photo processing are also good for repeats. You will find concerns hammering away week after week in newspapers and magazines carrying mail order ads on such subjects. Such firms usually run one- or two-inch ads. The market is so immense that competition is not a serious factor. They figure, no doubt, that if they make as little as $10 on a single ad which appears in 100 publications, their potential is $1,000 per week. Of course, the more beguiling the offer and the more selective the medium, the greater the sales.

Even if a product is not inherently a repeat item, the additional sales can come by sending a stuffer along with each order filled. The stuffer will feature other items that customers can order, thus giving you the opportunity to make extra sales without advertising expenses.

7. Fill a Crying Human Need

The author was acquainted with a man who called himself a "bathtub chemist" because with little knowledge of this field he concocted various useful products. He made it a practice to look around daily for little unexpected occurrences that irritated the average person. For example, a drawer or a window that gets stuck when you are in a hurry; a car door that produces a continual rattling noise from road vibrations; a rung of a chair that drops off when you least expect it, and so on. So, he devised, sometimes with the aid of a chemist, the necessary remedies to correct such nerve-racking nuisances—all low in price. He bottled and labeled the solutions and then offered the collection, a dozen or more different types of remedies, in kit form to agents to sell door to door.

This is but one example. Such items need not be of a chemical nature. They can be strictly mechanical. Products of this kind appear constantly on the mail order market. You may have seen collar extenders that bring relief to the man whose shirtband has become chokingly tight—methods for correcting a noisy toilet flush—for guarding a phone from use by unauthorized persons—for fixing emergency tire flats—for fastening Venetian blind slats that break loose—for collecting the mess dropped by house pets. The list is endless. The point to remember is to be alert to discover the common bothersome occurrences, and find an easy inexpensive solution. It will pay you in the long run. The person who is forced to swear, either audibly or under his breath whenever confronted with a nuisance that cannot be corrected on the spot, will welcome anything you offer to remedy the situation and relieve his distress. He is not likely to be deterred by price as long as it is within reason. Such items are not generally available at retail stores. They are strictly mail order business.

HAVE FAITH IN YOUR PRODUCTS

An important factor to consider is your own attitude toward the product. Is it something you believe in, something you would offer to a member of your own family? Something you know represents fair value? Your own faith in the merchandise is soon reflected in your ads and literature. You cannot be hypocritical for long and get away with it. Your prospects, sooner or later, detect your insincerity or lack of enthusiasm. Even if they are not on the alert in the beginning, after they begin using the article, they soon discover that it is not as was represented. They are apt to turn on you and lose respect for your offerings—and look elsewhere for future purchases. So, in the long run, you would be the loser. Certainly, it is better to start off on the right foot. Deal only in honest-value merchandise and don't rush into an arrangement with manufacturers. Make haste slowly.

Success Depends on Your Choice of Products

It is generally agreed that 50 percent of mail order success hinges on the product selected; about 30 percent on the choice of effective media, and only 20 percent on the preparation of the advertisement. So do not underrate the importance of the product you select. Wherever possible, obtain an actual sample—test it out yourself—show it to members of your family and to friends to get their reactions. Ask them if they would buy the product should it be offered at such-and-such a price. Try selling it door-to-door, if you have the time. In short, satisfy yourself, beyond a shadow of a doubt, that the article has merit—even if no one else thinks so. If the majority you question feel that it is desirable, that should be sufficient to risk your mail order effort to sell it. That is the time to make your first test.

Win Customer's Confidence

One of the first things to learn in selling is *win the customer's confidence*, and mail order advertising is nothing more than salesmanship on paper. When you win the customer's confidence here, you have a chance to make several sales grow where only one grew before. This is important to remember because many an advertising or mailing campaign just barely breaks even or shows only a small profit. However, the man who looks ahead realizes that each customer's name he acquires is a valuable adjunct to his list—that he will send this same customer additional mailings of circulars and catalogs, ultimately producing many sales at the cost of a single effort.

Besides having faith in your merchandise, it is also essential that you know all about it: what it is made of; how it operates; what it can and what it *cannot* do. Thus, you will be able to satisfy customers by answering their questions intelligently and you will avoid making exaggerated claims. In short, speak about your products with authority—let your statements ring true. That is what instills confidence. If you cannot obtain the facts off-hand, ask the manufacturers or do the necessary research yourself.

How to Impress Manufacturers

Many mail order tyros seem to delight in telling the world that they are naive beginners. Frankness, modesty, and an open attitude are indeed admirable traits, but it is hardly necessary to make a display of unbusinesslike thinking. Just state that you are operating (not beginning) a mail order business—that you seek new products and would be interested in his terms either on an outright purchase or on a drop-ship arrangement; also ask whether he carries stock on hand to fill orders promptly.

Some beginners even make the mistake of sending a letter to a manufacturer on informal stationery, written in longhand. He is liable to ignore such a letter. The first thing to do is to have your printer run off some letterheads. They may cost you about $10, but are well worth it. Then buy or rent a typewriter, new or used. Most manufacturers wish to deal only with businesslike persons. So by all means, give the impression with the appearance and tone of your correspondence.

HOW TO FIND SALABLE PRODUCTS

Can you tell the temperature of your products? Hot, cold, or just lukewarm—*before* you invest in advertising? Few persons can. You can hire top advertising brains, but they can only approximate salability. The million-dollar national advertisers often spend more than $50,000 making countrywide house-to-house surveys before launching a new product to ascertain whether Mr. or Mrs. Average Consumer likes it enough to buy it.

You can promote your offering with the most elaborate circular or the best written advertisement, but if you lack a salable product you will land behind the 8-ball. People often ask what makes a product sell by mail. No one knows the complete answer. If he did, he could make a fortune overnight. The reason is that public tastes differ—markets change—new competitive conditions arise—and there are other unexplainable factors. Yet we know that certain broad requisites are needed to insure worthwhile results.

Leading department stores hire high-salaried buyers who are expected to register the pulse of the buying public, yet they constantly misjudge the market and are compelled to run sales to unload their mistakes.

How Does a Mail Order Novice Know What Products to Look for?

At least he should become familiar with the correct approach to the problem before plunging into an unknown abyss. What are the characteristics of good mail order products? This can only be stated in the most general terms unless the so-called "expert" wishes to stick his neck out. There are too many surprises, too many exceptions, too many unknown factors to contend with. Such imponderables include market saturation, competition, pricing, profit margin, seasons, fads, buying trends, economic conditions, and even world disruptions.

Broadly speaking, a mail order product has a chance to survive if it fills a human need and does not have to contend with too much store competition. If it actually fills a crying need, rest assured you have landed a hot item.

There are two avenues that can be explored before venturing out to locate mail order items:

1. Items Familiar to the Public with a Fairly Well-Known Market Value

Since such items are usually carried in stores, the only way to outsell them is through drastic price reductions. Not many newcomers in mail order are in a position to do this because they do not have access to low-cost sources of supply. Firms dealing in odd lots, distress merchandise, government surplus, and imports can more readily handle such an operation. In addition, manufacturers making large quantities at low cost and major book publishers are also in a position to sell on price inducements. However, those companies outside this limited area follow the more normal procedures.

2. Novelty Products with Price Only a Secondary Factor

If the item is entirely new, much can be said about it to intrigue the buying public. If not new, it should at least have some outstanding feature or improvement over items in its product line.

The following are some other characteristics to look for:

1. Products Appealing to the Masses

Consider whether your product will appeal to the general public, although this does not necessarily rule out the success of all merchandise that attracts a limited group. Yet a market of millions is manifestly more profitable than one of thousands—especially on a low-priced article.

2. Practical Merchandise

A practical product is generally better than an ornamental or gift-type article for year-round selling, because such an article is primarily bought for the buyer's own use although also purchased for gift-giving. In short, articles that place the emphasis on the practical applications generally fill a greater need than those appealing only to one's aesthetic sensibilities. Labor-saving, time-saving, and money-saving items impress many persons. Articles such as household aids and automotive accessories are in demand. This does not exclude ornamental objects such as jewelry, which seem to satisfy a strong feminine desire.

3. Lightweight Products

They are easy and inexpensive to ship. There have been notable exceptions, however. Heavy furniture, and large electric and electronic equipment have been sold successfully by mail.

4. Moderately Priced Items

Such products because of their novelty need not be offered at bargain prices. A fairly new article will sell at a price comparable to what is asked in better-class stores because folks are willing to pay a reasonable price for something which they cannot conveniently purchase anywhere else. Some products are termed "blind articles" because the consumer cannot guess their value. In such cases, there are no comparable items and no way of determining the value of parts or ingredients to serve as a price estimate. Items that fall into this category, for example, certain mechanical devices, books, and cosmetics. In any case, be careful not to price yourself out of the market, and conversely, the only time to employ bargain prices is when you are selling staples, the regular price of which is well-known to consumers who see the items sold constantly in retail stores. It is up to you to determine whether the selling price is competitive or too high to attract buyers and whether you must adhere to the price established by the manufacturer. You might inquire about the price to you on a drop-ship basis, as well as prices if bought outright in various quantities. The drop-ship arrangement obviates the cost of carrying stock, storing, packaging, and shipping. Be reasonably sure that your

source of supply is reliable and that there will be a sufficient stock
on hand at all times to fill immediate orders.

5. *The Article Should Be Profitable*

Satisfy yourself that the item offers a sufficient markup or differ-
ential between your cost and selling price. Be realistic. Do not fool
yourself into believing that you can operate a mail order business
successfully on a retailer's 33-1/3 percent profit off list price. Your
very minimum should be 50 percent off list price, but try for a larger
spread if you can. A markup of 2½ times cost is recommended for
items selling for a dollar or two. The higher the selling price, the less
markup is needed. Too many beginners go astray on this point. Divide the profit on a single unit sale into the cost of the ad (or mailing)
to establish how many you must sell to get beyond the break-even
point. The only time it is safe to work on a low markup is when you
possess a proven hot item or, in the case of a follow-up mailing in
which you offer a catalog of many diversified items, all of which
increase the chances of producing multiple sales. Frankly, half the
folks operating in the mail order business, alluring as it is, would be

Ideal Christmas Gift

Colorful Stenciled MINIATURE GRAND-FATHER'S CLOCK

$8.85 *from W. Germany*
postpaid

From the enchanted forest of
The Tyrol comes this delightful
wooden pint-size Grandfather
Clock. It is hand painted with
gay sprigs of wildflowers. Clock
stands 8¼"; pendulum with 36
hr. spring movement, solid brass
weights & chains, and peek-in
compartment with door! In red,
blue, black or ivory. State 1st &
2nd color choice.

Money-back guarantee. Send
check or money order to
ALAMAC CO., Dept. T
P.O. Box 346, Audubon Station
New York, N.Y. 10032

Imported items have a fascination about them. They convey a message about people of another nationality. Prospects expect something exotic. Those who bought this clock, advertised in the *New York Times*, were not disappointed.

better off if they dropped out because they are attempting the near impossible by working on too small a margin to make a reasonable profit. The risks are too great and the costs too high unless the firms possess sufficiently ample resources to enable them to make constant product tests until they hit upon a jackpot item. A moderate priced item would cost no more than $35.00.

WHAT PRICE PRODUCTS SELL BEST

Once upon a time an item that was priced at more than a dollar or two was not considered good for mail order selling. Strange to say, many persons still stick to that old-fashioned idea. True, there are far more persons with a dollar to spend than there are people who can afford to spend $10 or more, without straining their pocketbooks. Yet one must consider that during a period of prosperity, inflation reduces the purchasing power of the dollar; therefore, most of the desirable products offered cost more. The public, by and large, recognizes this situation. During a period of employment and greater purchasing power on the part of most of the population, the tendency is for mail order houses to sell higher priced products. It is not uncommon to see products that cost well over $100. An analysis by *House Beautiful*, a leading national magazine that carries a mail order section replete with ads, shows that only 39 percent of the items offered for sale were priced below $5. The remaining 61% were priced up to $25 and over. The bulk of the 61% was in the $5 to $10 range.

Breakdown of Mail Order Products

Price	Percent of All Items
Under $5.00	39%
$5.00–$10.00	22%
$10.00–$15.00	10%
$15.00–$25.00	12%
$25.00 & over	17%

Yet, during periods of vast unemployment where inflation still prevails, the spending ratio varies very little. A markup of at least 2½ times cost is generally recommended for items in the under five-dollar category. As the selling price rises, one requires a smaller markup to make a profit, because fewer sales are needed to get beyond the break-even point; for example, a markup of 100 percent on a $20 item might be adequate. No matter how attractive an item is, it is better to drop it than to gamble on making a profit based on too small a margin between cost and selling price. True, there are exceptions. Some fast sellers have been known to make a big overall profit when costs were only 25 percent below selling price. Unless an item has already been proven popular, do not take a chance selling it at a price that leaves an insufficient margin of profit. Moreover, it is unsafe to accept the fallacious premise that a reduced price will increase the volume of business enough to offset the smaller profit margin. If you can buy a well-known product at below wholesale cost and offer it to the public at an alluring price, *without* denying yourself a decent profit, then such an operation can be profitable.

However, this principle rarely applies to a new item. The public is prepared to pay as much for such a product as it would to a good store, if it were sold through this outlet. The price angle sometimes operates in reverse. For example, one firm advertised an imported women's accessory in *Vogue* at a higher than normal markup. The company then lowered the price, thinking that it would increase volume, but they guessed wrong. Sales actually dropped. Apparently, women with high incomes regarded it as being too cheap to own.

Some mail order firms add the costs of overhead and advertising to the cost of the product to establish their total costs. This figure is then subtracted from the selling price to arrive at the amount of profit. This is an admirable policy but often complicates matters—especially when numerous items are involved each selling at a different price, with a different markup.

Other mail order houses let normal overhead stand by itself as the initial investment for operating a business. This simplifies matters by taking the unit cost of the item (including packaging and labels—sometimes mailing cost), then dividing the cost of the advertisement by the profit on a single unit. This figure establishes how many must be sold to break even. Any number of sales beyond the break-even point become "gravy"—the welcome profits one seeks.

If your advertisements do not make a direct bid for a sale but simply invite inquiries, you might figure the cost per inquiry along with the cost of the product, that is the cost of circulars, postage, mailing operations. Where follow-up mailings are required their cost must also be figured.

The question, "How many orders can I expect from a mailing piece or an ad?" is as long as it is broad because of the number of variable factors: The public's response to a given item is of first consideration. In the case of direct mail, the percentage of response is contingent on the price of the article, which might range from $1 to $100 or more. Then the attractiveness of the mailing piece, the effectiveness of the copy, the quality of the mailing list, the postage (first class or third class), etc. are weighed. All of these have a bearing on the expected response. Broadly speaking, with respect to an average product, a 2 percent return might be a split-even operation; 3 percent might show a little profit; 10 percent would show a satisfactory profit.

The subject of the response to publication advertising has already been discussed. Where the ads produce only inquiries, the conversion rate of inquiries into orders is of importance. Generally, a conversion of 10 percent is considered satisfactory. The percentage is frequently much higher when the follow-up literature is very convincing and persuasive.

As for pricing—aside from markup which has already been explained—a $1 article should be offered at an even dollar because the customer can drop a dollar bill in an envelope. This is more convenient than sending an odd amount in silver or a check. Anything over $1 could be offered to advantage at an odd figure, such as $2.95 or $2.98 rather than $2.50. The customer would be asked to send a check or money order because sending large amounts in cash is unsafe. Some newspapers, like the New York Times, do not allow advertisers to request cash.

The question of whether to follow the price with "prepaid" or "plus a charge for postage and handling" can be argued pro and con. Some people reason that if postage charges are hidden in the selling price, the customer does not feel that he is being penalized for buying by mail. Others argue that postage costs have increased so much that the customer is aware of this added cost factor and is willing to pay the charges. One must use his judgment in such matters. If it is a low-priced or lightweight item, the inclusion of "prepaid" after the price would probably be better because the amount of postage is insignificant. However if the merchandise is familiar to the public or if the article is heavy and requires considerable postage, then it is recommended that this cost be mentioned in the advertisement. If the product purchased is shipped parcel post, better say "plus postage and handling." If you leave out "and handling" and the postage amounts to less than the charge in the ad, the customer might feel cheated.

To arrive at the amount to be absorbed for postage when shipping prepaid, first establish the weight of the package, then figure the postage charges for each of the 8 zones; add up these postal costs and divide by 8 to strike an average. The other way is to figure the cost of postage for the sixth zone as an average for the entire country.

What you lose in mailing to the seventh and eighth zones will be made up by your gains in the remaining zones.

The subject of C.O.D. shipments is discussed under "State Terms Plainly," page 170.

WHERE TO CONTACT SOURCES FOR MAIL ORDER PRODUCTS

1. Run a classified ad in the *New York Times* Business Opportunities section, somewhat like the ads below. This paper will require one bank and two business references:

> WANTED: NEW MAIL ORDER ITEMS
> What do you have? Y & R Sales
> 100 Broadway, Springfield, MA

> I NEED HOT MAIL ORDER ITEMS
> Send description, terms to
> Jones, Box 314, Dayton, OH

2. Send $2 to Jack Ward, Rutward Publications, Box 471, Georgetown, CT 06829 for his Drop-Ship Catalog of several hundred manufacturers. He also publishes a "Goldmine of Product Information" and a "Foreign Wholesale Directory" at $3 each, plus other manuals.

3. Subscribe to "World Gift Review," a monthly newsletter at $14 a year; 616-9th Street, Union City, NJ 07087.

4. Write to Bentley Gifts, Inc., 1331 Newbridge Rd., North Bellmore, NY 11710 for their catalog of items which they will drop-ship.

5. For a selection of mail order books write to:

ARCO PUBLISHING INC., 215 Park Avenue South, New York, NY 10003

PUBLISHING COMPANY OF AMERICA, Dept. 340, Miami Beach Federal Bldg., 407 Lincoln Road Mall, Miami Beach, FL 33139

SELECTIVE BOOKS, INC., P. O. Box 1140, Clearwater, FL 33517. Among other titles, Selective Books offers, "How to Write Mail Order Advertising."

R & D SERVICES, Box 644, Des Moines, IA 50303

WORLD WIDE BOOK SERVICE, Box 544, New York, NY 10010

WILSHIRE BOOK COMPANY, 12015 Sherman Rd., North Hollywood, CA 91605

EMERSON BOOKS, INC. Box 8618, Buchanan, NY 10511

LITTLE BLUE BOOK CO., Box 10, Girard, KS 66743

6. Attend business conventions such as gift shows, housewares shows, etc.

7. Check the "New Products" page in various magazines for products and write to the manufacturers of the items which appeal to you.

8. Make your own chemical products. There are many household and automotive items easily prepared from formulas. The ingredients, labels, and packaging can be obtained at low cost. Books on formulas are available from public libraries, or can be purchased.

9. If you have a good labor-saving, time-saving, or money-saving idea, construct a rough working model and then consult local manufacturers on costs. It may take a little capital to make the product, but it could produce big results and large profits if handled right.

10. Write to the consulates of countries such as West Germany and Japan for a list of manufacturers who have mail order items for sale. A list of consulates follows:

FOREIGN CONSULATE OFFICES IN NEW YORK CITY (insert New York, NY between street address and zip code)

AFGHANISTAN, 866 United Nations Plaza, 10017, (212) 754-1191
AUSTRIA, 31 E. 69th St., 10021, (212) REgent 7-6400
BELGIUM, 50 Rockefeller Plaza, 10020, (212) JUdson 6-5110
DENMARK, 280 Park Avenue, 10017, (212) 697-5101
DOMINICAN REPUBLIC, 1 World Trade Center, 10048 (212) 432-9498

FINLAND, 540 Madison Ave., 10020, (212) 832-6550
FRANCE, 40 W. 57th St., 10019, (212) 541-6720
GERMANY (West), 460 Park Ave., 10022, (212) 940-9200
GREAT BRITAIN, 845 3rd Ave., 10022 (212) 752-5747
GREECE, 69 E. 79th St., 10021, (212) YU 8-5500
INDIA, 3 E. 64th St., 10021, (212) 879-7800
IRELAND, 580 5th Ave., 10020, (212) 245-1010
ISRAEL, 800 2nd Ave., 10017 (212) 697-5500
ITALY, 690 Park Ave., 10021, (212) RE 7-9100
JAPAN, 280 Park Ave., 10017 (212) 986-1600
KOREA, 460 Park Ave., 10022 (212) 752-1700
LUXEMBOURG, One Dag Hammarskjold Plaza, 10017, (212)
    751-9650
MEXICO, 8 E. 41st St., 10017, (212) MU 9-0456
NETHERLANDS, 1 Rockefeller Plaza, 10020, (212) CI 6-1429
NORWAY, 800 3rd Ave., 10004, (212) 421-9210
PHILIPPINES, 556 5th Ave., 10020, (212) 575-7925
PORTUGAL, 630 5th Ave., 10020, (212) CI 6-4580
SPAIN, 150 E. 58th St., 10022, (212) 355-4080
SWEDEN, 825 3rd Ave., 10022 (212) 751-5900
SWITZERLAND, 444 Madison Ave., 10017, (212) PL 8-2560
UNITED KINGDOM, 150 E. 58th St., 10022, (212) 593-2258

DIRECT MAIL VERSUS PUBLICATION ADS

The person who plans to develop a mail order business is often in a quandary whether to: 1) send direct mail to lists; 2) depend on publications advertising entirely; 3) employ a combination of both. Some guidelines follow.

When to Use Lists

Broadly speaking, use lists only when they appear to be dependable. Get the facts about their history. Find out their source, how and when compiled. Consider the character of the names, bearing in mind such factors as age, income, habits, hobbies, locations—all viewed with respect to the nature of the product and how a person of that type would respond to it. The lists should be of recent origin and not overworked so that the recipient of the mailing piece will not regard it as "junk mail." In any case, test only a few thousand names on any list before you plunge willy-nilly into the entire list. Consumer mailing lists comprising millions of names are available, but those that produce well are difficult to find. You might have to test several lists before locating one that shows a profit. The exceptions are lists of professional men—lawyers, physicians, dentists, engineers, or specific kinds of industries and stores. Such lists are generally more dependable because more easily updated and the names can be found in reliable directories. For lists of mailing list houses and brokers, see your local classified telephone directory.

When to Use Publications

Use publications when: 1) reliable lists are unobtainable; 2) when you seek quick national coverage; 3) when the selling price or profit margin is too low to warrant a direct mail operation which entails such cost factors as printing, postage, and mailing operations.

When to Use a Combination

Use a combination of publications and direct mail on higher priced merchandise, especially when the advertising space is not large enough to permit you to describe the product and convince prospects to the point that they will order immediately. In such cases, the briefer ads are used merely to stir up leads by arousing interest, while the direct mail follow-up makes a massive effort to close sales. Direct mail is also employed here to expand business by offering the customer, acquired through publication advertising, additional items. Thus, the direct mail piece can serve as a stuffer to be sent along with the filled order or sent later as a follow-up. Once a customer is satisfied that he is receiving good value, further sales can be made without incurring additional advertising expense.

Sharpen Your Focus

The above points seem fairly obvious, but they are often overlooked. Every day firms are sending out costly mailing pieces to lists of uncertain value. The cost of a mailing piece to 5,000 names might, in many cases, pay for an advertisement reaching a million prospects. The experienced media man can often select publications that are sharply attuned to the product advertised instead of picking them in hit-or-miss fashion. The best way to approach the problem is with objectivity based on cold business facts, instead of being wedded to a particular method through long habit. Bear in mind that one product might sell better by direct mail while another lends itself better to publication advertising. So take each on its own merits and avoid generalizations.

THE MAILING LIST APPROACH

The mailing list approach is satisfactory when you are sure of the quality of the lists. Too often, however, the list you buy is out-of-date, most of the people may have moved without leaving a forwarding address, died, or gone out of business. Other lists fail to produce because they are not appropriate for the type of merchandise you are selling. For example, you may be selling an article suitable for yacht owners, but the list you purchase consists largely of factory workers. And there are still other lists that miss their mark because they have been overworked; that is, they have been used over and over again for various mail order propositions to the point that the prospects ignore all mail matter of this kind.

In the face of this, it is easy to see how mailing lists can be extremely wasteful—considering what you pay for the list, addressing of envelopes, printed enclosures, and postage. So look before you leap. Find out the history of the list you buy, and test no more than a thousand names on a particular list at one time.

Here are a few suggestions on what to look for when selecting lists.

1. Evidence that the persons are willing to buy through the mails; this evidence applies to all types of merchandise.

2. Evidence that the persons are willing to purchase merchandise in the same price range.

3. Evidence that the persons are willing to buy items of similar nature that fall within the same classification, such as the use of an automotive list to sell other automotive products.

4. Evidence that the persons are willing to purchase related items. For example: Persons who buy early American furniture would conceivably be amenable to an offering of colonial andirons or primitive American art.

5. Evidence that the person is willing to buy virtually anything from you regardless of its price or nature.

THE PUBLICATION APPROACH

Let's consider the other approach. Instead of using mailing lists, you decide to advertise in publications. In this way, you are sure to obtain all fresh, up-to-date names, and if you select suitable publications for your ads, your prospects, by and large, will be tailored to the kind of articles you offer. The persons who purchase your wares will then be the beginning of a new list that you can start building up for future business. In this connection, it is recommended that in the beginning you enter each customer's name on a 3-inch × 5-inch card, which will serve as a customer's ledger card as well as a mailing list. Here you will enter what was bought, when purchased, price paid, or any other pertinent facts. If you satisfy customers by providing merchandise of value, you'll win their confidence.

The advertising approach may be more costly in the beginning, but in the long run it generally pays bigger dividends than the "canned" mailing list approach. Many mail order operators use both methods. They generally find that the profitable mailing lists are few and far between so they augment lists with a certain amount of publication advertising. Advertising media will be discussed in detail later.

USE SELECTIVITY IN CHOOSING PUBLICATIONS

The dictionary defines "selectivity," when referring to radio, as the degree a circuit or apparatus responds to the desired frequency and not to others. This principle is especially true when applied to mail order advertising, in which large amounts of money are wasted because the right message is not directed at the right prospect, in the right medium, at the right time. One prominent businessman has said, "I know half of my advertising is wasted, but the trouble is I don't know which half."

Large manufacturers whose advertising is intended to motivate consumers to buy their brands can generally afford wasting this much money, but not mail order concerns. Newcomers to the mail order business usually read all the books available on the subject. Although the advice they get is, on the whole, helpful, the authors' generalizing can often be detrimental and lead readers to false and costly conclusions. As a philosopher once facetiously remarked, "All generalities are wrong, including this one."

TEMPERATURE WISE CUFFLINKS $5⁹⁵ per pair postpaid

Consult your thermometers "on the cuff" — one centigrade, the other fahrenheit, and both accurate. The collector of unusual cufflinks will get a kick out of them. They convert European into American temperatures, to the traveler's delight. A terrific conversation piece! An extraordinary gift! 22K Gold plated with black dial. Packed in a suede leather pouch.

SEND CHECK OR MONEY ORDER
CLIFF'S SPECIALTY HOUSE
Dept. P, 513 Yolanda Lane
Shreveport, La. 71106

These unusual cufflinks have been advertised a number of times in the Magazine Section of the *New York Times*. The advertiser reasoned that the supplement, read by both men and women because of its editorial content, would be a good medium to reach men who buy jewelry for themselves; as well as women who buy for the men they love.

Advertising men have learned from experience that a general offer of a free catalog is rarely effective because thousands of firms are doing the same thing, even mailing gift catalogs unsolicited. However, if the contents of the catalog as well as the ad are aimed only at the specified type of prospect who would be interested in that subject, the ad will accomplish its purpose, as in this case.

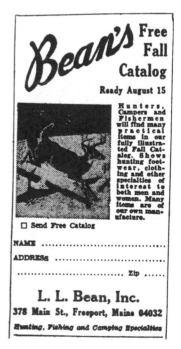

Bean's Free Fall Catalog

Ready August 15

Hunters, Campers and Fishermen will find many practical items in our fully illustrated Fall Catalog. Shows hunting footwear, clothing and other specialties of interest to both men and women. Many items are of our own manufacture.

☐ Send Free Catalog

NAME ....

ADDRESS ....

.... Zip ......

L. L. Bean, Inc.
378 Main St., Freeport, Maine 04032
Hunting, Fishing and Camping Specialties

The advertisement headlines the type of prospect wanted—"Women Who Love To Sew." The advertiser also selects publications aimed at his fixed target: *McCall's Needlework & Crafts, McCall's Pattern Book, Vogue Pattern Book* and *Workbasket.* The ad first appeared without a coupon. It was later found that the coupon increased sales.

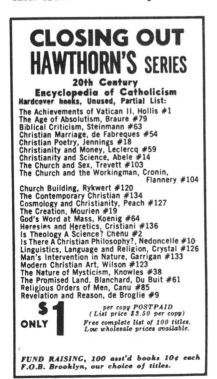

In this case, because of the nature of the books, the advertiser wisely confined his choice of media to Catholic publications. The campaign was successful. The very name of the advertiser suggests selectivity in outlook.

That is why this book does not make general sweeping recommendations about mail order publications, but lists separately the special ones to use for each market. However, even these lists should be analyzed further, and the publication that is geared to the product to be advertised should be hand picked. Such hand-picking can only be effective if one is familiar with each publication in a particular field, its distribution, the character of its readers, and its pulling power.

Gear Publications to Products

The choice of publications is as long as it is broad, and since you can waste a great deal of time and money groping for the right ones, it is best to enlist the services of a reliable mail order advertising agency. They can tell you at least in broad terms, based on considerable experience, which media are likely to produce. They cannot guarantee results because there are too many unknown factors involved. For example, much depends on the way the public reacts to a given product, buying habits, the timing of the insertion, price, competition, as well as the strength of headlines and copy.

As Mark Twain remarked: "The difference between the right word and the *almost* right word is the difference between lightning and the lightning bug." Frequently, two ads on a given item, each of which contains the same facts and price, will produce substantially different results. A change in headline or copy appeal often makes the difference between success and failure. Many examples can be shown where a single word substitution more than doubled sales.

Split-run Publications

That is why even the most experienced agencies will recommend testing ads in "split-run" publications. Certain newspapers and magazines, especially those with very large circulations, will let you run one ad in one half of their press run, and a different ad on the same product in the other half of the same issue, to determine the pulling power of each ad. You might also wish to ascertain the most profitable selling price in this way. For example, you can find out whether it would be advantageous to raise the selling price of a two-dollar article to three dollars. The three-dollar price might decrease the number of sales; on the other hand, the larger profit margin might more than make up for the reduced quantity. Test ads will settle the question, but test ads in different publications or in different issues of the same publication, but in different page positions might not provide a conclusive answer. Two different ads in a split run, of the same publication and in the same issue would be more convincing.

Watch that phrase "test ad." It is generally used too loosely. An ad in a single publication or one too small to tell a complete story might not be real test of the ad, the product, the publication, or the agency which prepared it.

Pinpoint Your Selections

Since there are literally thousands of publications, it is difficult to make a correct choice. However, experience has shown that specific newspapers and magazines have been more successful than others in conditioning their audiences to purchase articles by mail. Many of them set aside space—from a column to several pages—for mail order shopping. Some merchandise sells more effectively through the Sunday editions of metropolitan newspapers, others through home service magazines such as *House and Garden, House Beautiful,* and *Better Homes & Gardens,* others pull better in fraternal magazines, and still others in farm publications. Sometimes the very nature of the item can suggest the medium to use. If newspapers are employed which lack a designated mail order section, it is advisable to place the ad in the magazine section where it will be seen because of its proximity to reading matter. However, if the ad must be placed on one of the large pages in the body of a newspaper, it is wise to request a certain page, such as "radio," "woman's," or "sports" to avoid being lost on a page containing large department and specialty store ads. In any case, you might have to do some testing. An experienced advertising agency can, of course, avoid much guesswork.

Newspapers Versus Magazines

Newspapers are better for *quick* returns. A week after an ad appears in a Sunday paper, about half the total orders are in. The balance come in, generally, by the end of the second week. Magazines enjoy a longer life, and for that reason—if all other factors are equal—usually produce a larger return for the dollar invested. However, one must wait longer for results because the larger magazines go to press from six to eight weeks in advance of sale. A good magazine will generally produce about half its returns the first month and the balance will probably trickle in 30 days later. It is not uncommon, however, for an order to come in years after an ad has appeared. Many people hang on to old magazines indefinitely.

The larger the circulation of a magazine, the greater the cost of advertising space. In short, you pay a comparable amount for each thousand circulation, except in magazines with a quality circulation which ask a premium rate.

Media costs have increased from 15 to 100 percent over what they were ten years ago. They may rise higher due to increasing labor, paper, and overhead costs, so it is wise to think twice or seek the advice of a mail order consultant before you select a publication to carry your ad. Avoid all possible waste or, in other words, choose the media that has the highest concentration of readers who might be prospects for your merchandise.

CLASSIFIED VERSUS DISPLAY ADS

Many mail order operators are confronted with this problem: "Should I use *classified* ads or *display* ads?" The answer is that there is a place for both because much depends on what you are promoting and the extent of your advertising budget.

When to Use Classified Ads

Small mail order concerns, because of budgetary considerations, are prone to use classified ads exclusively, even when display ads would be more effective and no more costly. Classified ads can be successful in cases where the ad is used only to arouse interest and then followed up with sales literature. Where a classified ad is employed to make immediate sales, the article to be sold must be so familiar to the prospect as to require little description and no illustration. In the case of a book, the title must be so self-explanatory as to require only a few lines to distinguish the book from others. For example such titles as, *How To Lose Weight* or *Hypnotism—Self Taught.*

Classified ads lack prominence on a page filled with other classified ads because each one is set in the same size type and they all look alike. A person must be intent on seeking a specific object in the classified column to find the ad you have placed there. It will not be seen by the casual reader as in the case of a conspicuous display ad.

Classified ads are sold by the word or by the line of five or six words. Most newspapers and national magazines do not carry classified ads which sell products. The classified columns of newspapers are confined largely to help wanted and real estate ads. On page 45 is a partial list of magazines that carry classified ads. In cases where you wish to use a classified ad in a publication that does not carry this kind of advertising, it is wise to convert the classified ad into a one-inch (usually the minimum) display ad by adding a bold heading and placing a border around the ad. In some cases, a small display ad costs less than a wordy classified ad.

When to Use Display Ads

In the case of this kind of ad, the person preparing it can use all his skill, ingenuity, and imagination to make the ad stand out on the page and catch the eye of the casual reader. The description of your product should be compelling and convincing. Illustrations and strong headlines can be employed if necessary. Text or copy can be set in any size and style of type considered most effective. These points will be discussed in detail in a later chapter.

Not all newspapers carry special mail order sections. A partial list of those that do follows. It has been found that unless a paper carries a special mail order section, a page where readers are accustomed to look for such items, the mail order ads rarely pull well. This is especially true when small ads are placed in the body of a standard size paper and are lost among the large department and specialty store ads. In the Sunday magazine supplements of such papers, the mail order ads have a better chance to be seen because the supplement is smaller and the ad is usually next to reading matter. There are numerous papers that, as a matter of policy, reject all mail order ads because the newspapers are geared to local stores and consequently, their mail order advertising is "foreign" competition.

Most magazines carry mail order ads but not all of them provide special mail order sections. If the ad is placed next to reading matter, satisfactory results can usually be obtained. As in the case of the newspaper, the rate you pay for space is largely commensurate with circulation figures, but in the case of magazines another factor enters the picture. If it is a mass circulation publication such as *Family*

Circle the number of readers is the only thing that counts; whereas a class magazine like *Esquire,* aimed at a sophisticated group and generally printed on heavier glossy paper, charges rates in excess of the circulation figure. Among advertising men, a distinction is made between "pulp" and "class" magazines.

The distribution of a catalog is commonly regarded as a routine matter, not warranting any sizable advertising expense. Classified ads, rather than display ads, are generally employed. However, this firm considers the catalog the lifeblood of its business and runs display ads like this one steadily. This appeared in a popular science magazine.

Newspapers Versus Magazines

When a choice must be made between the use of newspapers and magazines, consider the timing, the closing dates, and the reading life of the publications.

An ad can be placed in a newspaper generally within a few days before it is off the press, with the exception of Sunday magazine supplements, which usually close about thirty days in advance of publication. However, the disadvantage of newspapers is their short life. They are leafed through quickly and immediately tossed away as trash.

Magazines, on the other hand, have a long life, especially the monthlies which are kept for weeks and months and passed on to others to read because the cover date is of no great consequence. Go into any doctor's or dentist's office and you will see patients reading back issues. The chief disadvantage in using magazines, particularly in the case of the monthlies, is the long wait after the ad is placed before it goes on sale. Closing dates of national magazines are generally six to eight weeks in advance. Weekly magazines might require about half that time.

By and large, magazines will give a greater return on the advertising dollar expenditure than newspapers. This is largely due to selectivity of readership (or less waste circulation) and the long life of the publication as stated before.

If the medium (whether newspaper or magazine) can be selected objectively, without inhibition imposed by budgetary considerations, maximum results are obtainable. But where you must use second or third best media because you beleive it necessary to stint, do not expect too much in the way of results. If sales are not up to expectations, do not blame the publication too quickly, or the one who prepared the ad, or the product itself.

Magazines Carrying Classified Ads

The following is a partial list of consumer magazines which carry classified advertising. Most of the national magazines do not take classified ads, as previously stated, in which case it is often advantageous to run display ads of minimum size.

Monthlies	Circulation
Ladies Home Journal	5,134,649
Redbook	3,864,417
Parade	21,460,054
Family Circle	7,795,975
Moose Magazine	1,296,490
MacFadden's Women's Group	2,592,439
Popular Mechanics	1,612,391
Popular Science	1,812,654
Mechanix Illustrated	1,619,242
Science & Mechanics	104,768
Woman's Day	7,007,909
Field & Stream	2,016,637
Sports Afield	527,085
Outdoor Life	1,537,015
The Retired Officer	317,819

Weeklies	Circulation
Grit	677,840
Capper's Weekly	650,522
National Enquirer	5,208,375
Army Times, Navy Times, and Air Force Times	373,583

The following are the leading national and regional farm publications that carry classified ads. A large number of state farm magazines also carry classified advertising.

Farm Magazines	Circulation
Progressive Farmer	625,977
Successful Farming	606,088
Farm Journal	1,012,030
Midwest Unit Farm Publications	618,091
Prairie Farmer	1,971,031
Wallace's Farmer	113,802

Newspapers With Mail Order Pages

NOTE: Many other papers accept mail order ads besides those listed below, but not in special mail order sections or pages so designated.

California	Circulation
Los Angeles Herald-Examiner (Magazine)	326,046
Los Angeles Times (Magazine)	1,270,538
San Francisco Examiner	659,950
San Diego Union (Magazine)	325,055

District of Columbia

Washington Post (Magazine)	762,825

Florida

Miami Herald	483,095

Illinois

Chicago Sun Times (Magazine)	677,681
Chicago Tribune (Magazine)	1,101,615

Iowa

Des Moines Register	371,542
Des Moines Register Magazine	371,542

Maryland

Baltimore News American	248,528
Baltimore Sun (Magazine)	307,707

Massachusetts

Boston Herald Examiner (Magazine)	227,452
Boston Globe (Magazine)[1]	628,758
Christian Science Monitor	212,000

Missouri

Kansas City Star	401,148
St. Louis Post Dispatch (Magazine)	436,391

New Jersey

Newark Star Ledger	604,986

New York

National Enquirer	5,119,382
New York Daily News (Country Edition)	863,845
New York Daily News (Metropolitan)	2,641,985
New York Times(Magazines)	1,586,151
New York Times (Shopping Guide)	1,498,673

Pennsylvania

Grit (National)	677,840
Lancaster Sunday News	137,101
Philadelphia Inquirer[1]	1,031,231
Philadelphia Inquirer (Magazine)	1,081,231

Texas

Houston Post (Magazine)	436,659

[1]Does not have special mail order section but carries a considerable amount of mail order advertising.

LARGE VERSUS SMALL ADS

To be effective how large must an ad be? The answer depends on many factors: the budget; the nature of the product; the size and type of publications to be employed, and their circulations.

In general, a large ad has greater impact than a small one which may be lost in a voluminous publication. On the other hand a smaller ad is spotted easily in a tabloid-size newspaper or in a magazine. Moreover, if the publication carries a special mail order section, a small ad will get attention. Sometimes, therefore, the large ad will only retain the advantage of impact value.

The terms "large" and "small," as used here are, of course, relative. Disregarding for the moment the importance of a forceful impact, an ad should be large enough to tell the prospect the following: what the offering can do for him; what it consists of; how much it costs and how he can send for it. If an illustration is necessary for visualization, then by all means supply it. But an advertisement that provides only a prosaic description of the product rarely does an effective selling job. Extra space is generally required to create desire through fresh copy with a personal appeal, and dramatizing the product so that it makes a deep impression in the mind of the reader. A dynamic layout and a large, bold heading contribute much to this objective.

Generally speaking, a large circulation publication is better for mail order, but only if the preponderance of readers are the type likely to buy the product. The percentage of response to mail order ads is small as compared with a publication's total circulation so that it is generally necessary to use those with considerable circulation to achieve worthwhile results. Yet, as already stated, the nature of the readers must be taken into consideration in relation to the product. For example, if you are trying to reach camera fans, it might be more economical to advertise in photography magazines than in the mass media publications where you would be paying for considerable waste circulation.

If your budget requires that you make a choice between placing large ads in fewer publications or small ads in many, *first* decide how large an ad is required to do an adequate selling job; *second*, make a list of the most appropriate publications from the standpoint of both circulation and readership; *third*, establish the cost of placing the ad in each publication selected, considering size and rate; *finally* add them all up, and if the total exceeds your budget, eliminate as many of the less important publications as necessary.

MAKING CLASSIFIED ADS PAY

Can money be made with classfied ads? The answer is "Yes." Can every product be sold through classified advertising? The answer is "No." Many mail order men—and unfortunately, this includes some professional consultants—are so classified-ad minded that they take a one-sided view of the subject. This bias prevents them from being objective about the question of classified versus display ads in relation to the product that is being sold.

If your offering is such that your prospects can visualize it without a lengthy description or a picture, it might be sold profitably through classified ads. For example, there are a number of firms which spend from $500 to $1,000 or more a month advertising information on how to get a good-paying job in foreign countries. Their identical ads appear month after month in a host of magazines.

When Not to Use Classified Ads

If an item requires further explanation before a sale can be completed, then the classified ad should be employed chiefly "to whet the appetite" and arouse interest to the point that prospects are induced to inquire for further details.

A classified ad that features a low-priced item, requiring little explanation can be so worded as to persuade prospects to send money immediately. Items in this category include rubber stamps, stationery, stamps and coins, photo-finishing, books, fishing, and sporting goods.

Bear in mind that the average reader of a publication does not run his eye down the long gray columns of classified ads in the hope of finding something that interests him. Only those intent on seeking some particular item or service, which they know is generally advertised in the classified columns, will look through the ads; for example, a person looking for a money-making opportunity or a job as a salesman would be expected to search the classfied columns. However, most novel mail order items are not being sought after by consumers. Such items, unknown to the general public, must be advertised boldly in display ads so that the casual reader will suddenly stop to admire the article as his eyes are arrested by a picture or a headline. He then reads what is said about the product, becomes convinced that it will benefit him, and is persuaded to order it.

Don't Waste Words!

Classified ads should be written without wasting words, just as though one is writing a telegram confined to a specific word count. Start by stating all the essential facts about your offering. Then prune your ad by taking out unnecessary words or rephrase the copy so that the same thought can be expressed in fewer words. Finally, you might show it to your wife, relatives, or friends to see whether you left out some essential point and if your offering sounds desirable to them. The following tells how to cut down costly words:

1. Instead of "Complete information will be supplied without cost on request" say "Free details" or words to that effect. Thus 7 words are saved.

2. Use numerals instead of words where possible. Instead of 25 cents, say 25¢. The one word saved is money in your pocket.

3. Often your name and address can be condensed. L.A. Crosley &

Co. can be shortened to Crosley, which saves 4 words, or to Lawrence Crosley, which saves 3 words.

4. Post Office or P.O. in front of a box number can be dropped to save 2 words and, in many cases, when keying ads, Dept., followed by a key number, can be dropped and the key placed after the box number, as in Box 24-H2.

Since most publications charge by the word instead of by the line, check your word count carefully. There is no need to abbreviate under such circumstances. For example, why say Phila., PA, when you can write Philadelphia, Pennsylvania, and make your ad deeper without extra expense.

Answering Inquiries

Inquiries are received in the form of postcards and letters—both short- and long-winded. In most cases, there are more postcards than letters. Many newcomers in the field are inclined to disregard the postcard inquiries and make no attempt to answer them. The reasoning behind such an attitude is that if a person does not think enough about what is offered to take the trouble to write a letter, why bother with mere "curiosity seekers." However, experience has shown that a postcard writer can develop into just as good a customer as a letter writer. Picture the tired businessman looking over a publication at home when he spots an ad that strikes his fancy. If he were required to get up out of his easy chair to write a letter on the subject, he might never get around to it, for inertia holds many back from exerting themselves. Instead the reader grabs a postcard and scribbles a few lines, asking for particulars.

Oftentimes it is advisable to run more than one classified ad in a publication on the same subject. This is usually done for one of two reasons: 1) It is a means of testing the pulling power of differently worded ads; 2) by placing two ads under different subheads, you can appeal to different kinds of prospects. For example, an ad under "Business Oportunities" is not likely to appeal to the same person if it were listed under "Spare Time Home Work," yet what is offered in both cases might amount to substantially the same thing. Where more than one ad on the same subject is run in the same publication it is advisable to select a publication that carries a full page of classified ads; otherwise the ads will be too close together, and the similarity would be noticeable. However, do not expect to double the number of inquiries on the strength of two such ads.

The above ad is one that can settle the question: "Do people read lengthy copy?" This advertising was successful notwithstanding its abundant wordage and the high cost of space required. People will generally read an ad if you offer a solution to something that bothers them. This ad is also unique in the way it employs a timely, human-interest and biographical sketch to win attention.

How to Stimulate Response

The response to your classified ads can be stimulated in various ways:

1. Offer a free booklet, a free trial of the product for a specific number of days or a premium.

2. Your low-price appeal can also be restricted to a limited time.

3. State that the supply is limited.

4. Include a strong guarantee.

5. Use a "leader" or even a "loss-leader" to get a larger volume of inquiries.

How to Distribute a Catalog

Although it is sometimes necessary to charge for a catalog, especially when it is costly, it is generally advantageous to offer it free; otherwise put a minimum price on it to discourage curiosity seekers. The idea of issuing a catalog in the first place is to get it into the hands of as many potential prospects as possible and at the lowest cost. For example, one jewelry house put out a catalog which cost them $1 and offered it for 50 cents. However, later they found that it was more economical in the long run to offer it for 25 cents, which meant taking a greater loss on the catalog, because they sold more jewelry as a result of wider catalog distribution.

EXAMPLES OF CLASSIFIED ADS

1

SALESMEN & AGENTS WANTED

EARN Big Commission Full or Part Time. Show America's largest line Low Priced Business Printing and Advertising Specialities Plus calendars in season. No experience. No investment. No collections or deliveries. On-the-spot commissions. Big Free Sales Kit samples hundred items used daily by businessmen. Merchandise bonuses for you. Build profitable repeat business. Start now.

SPARE Time Cash—Sell Advertising Book Matches—every business a prospect—no investment—no experience needed to build steady repeat business. Daily Cash commission in advance. Write today—We'll send your sure-fire selling kit by return mail.

MAKE extra $25 to $75 spare time! Take orders for double air cushion Bronson Shoes. Amazing comfort. Terrific men's women's line for dress, work, play. Highest commissions. Shoes for yourself. Big outfit FREE. Write

WANT TO MAKE UP TO $100.00 A Week spare time, and get free shoes for life, too? No investment. Rush card for free details.

2

BUSINESS OPPORTUNITIES

EARN BIG MONEY OFF SEASON Repairing. Reupholstering Furniture. Enormous year 'round demand. Earn to $5.00 hourly. Husbands-Wives Learn-Earn for secure future. We supply EVERYTHING! Build BEAUTIFUL FURNITURE while learning. Use home-garage-barn as workshop. No experience or high-school necessary. FREE BOOK! APPROVED FOR VETERANS.

SPORTSMEN! Make big profits buying low cost imports abroad, selling friends, stores, mail order. Plan reveals suppliers hundreds foreign bargains like Spinning Reels 98¢, Rifles $3.24, Flies 1¼¢, Binoculars $2.40. Free home business details.

VENDING Machines—no selling. Operate a route of coin machines and earn amazing profits. 32 page catalog free.

MAKE big money growing ginseng! $3,000-$30,000 annually. We buy your crop. Send $2 for seed sample and information.

PIANO Tuning learned quickly at home. Tremendous field. Musical knowledge unnecessary. GI approved. Free information.

3

OF INTEREST TO WOMEN

TYPE Manuscripts at home for authors. Immediate earnings. Complete instructions $1.00.

$100 WEEKLY POSSIBLE—Home Typing. Immediate earnings! Employers list, complete instructions. Details 25 cents.

$75.00 THOUSAND. Home Addressing! Longhand. Typewriter. Information. Send Stamped self-addressed envelope.

$500-$800 MONTHLY. Raise small laboratory-breeding stock for us. We supply equipment, breeders, and instructions.

MAKE Money at Home . . . Addressing and mailing our sales letters! Everything furnished!

$350 MONTH ADDRESSING! Companies furnish everything. Mail $2.00. Moneyback guarantee.

EARN $100.00 Fast Lacing Beautiful Products! Write:

HOMEWORKERS! $85 weekly addressing mail for firms. Start immediately! Details, send stamped self addressed envelope.

$400.00 MONTHLY POSSIBLE . . home Typing! Guaranteed Profitable Methods. Instructions, $1.00.

DO Profitable Home Typing. Addressing. $400.00 Monthly Possible. Details, 25¢.

4

MAGIC TRICKS, CRAFTS & HOBBIES

WORLD'S Finest professional magic tricks. Joker Novelties, Giant Illustrated catalog 10¢.

HOUDINI'S GREATEST MAGIC! Giant Illustrated Deluxe Catalog . . . 164 pages! 10¢ Gift certificate Free.

42 PAGE illustrated joke and novelty catalog. 25¢.

5

BUY IT WHOLESALE

MEN's Rubber Goods Guaranteed—43 for $4.00. Gross —$10.00. Lubricated 72—$8.00.

GOVERNMENT SURPLUS

JEEPS Typically From $53.90   Trucks From $78.40 Airplanes, Typewriters, Boats, Clothing, Camping, Sporting, Photographic, Electronics Equipment. Wide Variety, Condition. 100,000 Bid Bargains Direct From Government Nationwide. Complete Sales and Surplus Catalog $1.00 (Deductible First $10.00 Order).

JEEPS From . . . $52.50. Typewriters From $4.15. Cars from . . . $31.50. Walkie-Talkies. Motorcycles, Airplanes, Boats, Typical "As Is" Bid Bargains From Uncle Sam. Tremendous Variety. Exciting Free List. Write

GOVERNMENT Surplus—How and where to buy in your area. Send $1.00 to

ARMY & Navy surplus illustrated catalog 25¢. Southwestern.

GIANT FREE Catalog. Nearly 4000 Scientific bargains. War Surplus! Astronomical and spotting telescopes, binoculars, microscopes, magnifiers, sniperscopes, lenses prisms, project kits. Request Catalog.

RUVEL & Co. 1969 Army-Navy Store 32 Page Illustrated Catalog. Bayonets, Helmets, Field Equipment. Packs, Sleeping Bags, Survival Foods. Field Phones, Rubber Boats, Tents, Etc. All in Stock! Hundreds of other items. Send 25¢ refundable first $5.00 order to:

6

FRANCHISES

56 ACTIVE Franchise opportunities available all over U.S.A. Brochure details 56 franchise chances for you to have your own business tied with successful national companies. Send name, address to

7

HELP WANTED

OVERSEAS Jobs—Europe, South America, Australia, Far East, etc. 2000 openings all trades. Construction, Office, Engineering, Sales, etc. $400 to $2,500 month. Expenses paid. Free Information. Write

HIGH Paying Overseas Jobs. Construction, other projects. Bonuses, travel expenses, extras.

8

COINS

UNITED STATES Specials; Half Dime before 1873, $3.00; Large Cent before 1857, $3.00; 1893 Columbian World's Fair Half Dollar, $3.00; Old style Large $5.00 bill, $12.00; All four offers $20.00. Moneyback Guarantee.

50 MIXED "S" cents, includes uncirculated 1955S, new 1968S, 1969S. Only $1.95.

SILVER DOLLARS. 1883-84-85-99-1900-01. O Mint $3.50 Each. Coin Catalogue 50¢.

PRICE list of U.S. coins. Send 10¢.

LINCOLNS: 22 "S" including 1955S, $1.60. 26 1909-1939, $1.60. 10 "S" Jeffersons, $1.60. 10 "S" Roosevelts (1946S-1955S Complete) $3.25. All different. All four $7.75. Silver Dollars $2.45 each. Pricelist 10¢.

9

STAMPS

225 STAMPS For Only 10¢! Airmails, Pictorials; stamps from strange countries cataloging up to 25¢ each!! Plus unusual stamps to examine. Buy any or none, return balance, cancel service anytime.

BSOLUTELY Free 25 Different United States Commemoratives When Requesting United States Approvals.

"AFRICA" 25 Beauties, 10¢ when requesting our Worldwide Approvals.

FREE! Big Bargain Catalog—New Edition listing thousands of bargains including U.S. & B.N.A. stamps, packets, albums, accessories and supplies. Also, fine stamps from our approval service which you may return without purchases and cancel service at any time.

10

EDUCATIONAL & INSTRUCTION

ACCIDENT INVESTIGATION career training. Train at home for position that includes new car furnished, expenses paid, free benefits. No selling. Free Placement Service. Men urgently needed. Write for FREE booklet. No obligation.

COMPLETE YOUR HIGH SCHOOL at home in spare time with 72-year-old school. Texts furnished. No classes. Diploma. Information Brochure free.

LEARN Civil and criminal investigation at home. Earn steady, good pay. State age.

AUCTIONEERING Write:
                               Free Catalog.
Term soon.

HYPNOTISM, Sleep-Learning! Astonishing details strange catalog free!

MISSOURI Auction School. GI Approved. Free Catalog!

LEARN Auctioneering . . . Term soon. Free catalog. World's Largest School.

FINISH HIGH SCHOOL at home. No classes. Texts furnished. Diploma awarded. If 17 or over and have left school, write for FREE information and booklet.

11

CAMERAS & PHOTO SUPPLIES

GIANT Free Catalog. Nearly 4,000 unusual bargains. War Surplus! Lens, projects, shutters, filters, viewers, lamps, magnifiers, accessories booklets, kit. Many hard-to-get items. Request Catalog

FREE! FREE!—Photographic and optical bargain book.

12

BOOKS
AND MAGAZINES

DEER Hunting stories. '27 thru '67. $1.50. '68 "Trophy Buck" Story, $1.00.

"UNUSUAL Books"! Best Sellers! Adult Reading! Catalogue Free!

INCREASE your income. More confidence and personality helps you get ahead. Low cost books tells how. Free circular.

13

GOOD EATING

GENUINE Kentucky Hickory Smoked Country Hams. 12-20 Pounds Each. Shipped C.O.D. $1.05 Pound.

HICKORY FARMS OF OHIO BEEF STICK.

4 lbs. of world famous, Hickory-smoked, all-beef summer sausage. Easy to carry and keep. Provides welcome variety to meals on hunting, fishing, camping trips. In sandwiches or cooked with eggs or potatoes. At your local Hickory Farms Store. If you need address, write

FREEZE-dried dinners. Undergoing tests for astronauts. Sample $1.00.

SMOKE Fish, Game, Sausage. Build Electric Smoker. Instructions, Recipes, $1.00.

MAKE Jerky from beef or game. Four recipes, $1.00

MEXICAN Cooking Is Simply Delicious! $1.00 for Authentic Recipes.

14

MUSIC

POEMS, Songs, Wanted For New Hit Songs and Recordings by America's most popular studio.

SONGS. Poems Wanted For Publishing. Recording Consideration! We Pay Above Costs! ! ! !

POEMS set to music, Songs recorded. Send poems, songs.

OLDIES—45 RPM—Original Hits Over 4,000 Available. Catalog 25¢.

A Discussion of the Foregoing Classified Ads

[1]

The recruitment of salesmen and agents is a job in itself. The competition is very keen. Classified ads sometimes run to considerable length in order to convince the specialty salesmen and agents that the line offered will enable them to make a substantial, steady income easily. Many firms go further and run large display ads—even full pages—to recruit an army of salesmen.

[2]

Columns listing "Business Opportunities" appear in virtually every publication that contains classified ads. Similar headings are "Money-Making Opportunities," "Spare-Time Income," and the like. Such ads appeal to the countless individuals who want to go into business for themselves.

[3]

Strange as it would seem, items "Of Interest to Women" appear in many men's magazines, as was the case with the ads listed here. This means that the husbands spot ads which they think would interest their wives or else the wives look through their husbands' magazines for ads. Most of the ads in this category offer work that can be accomplished at home.

[4]

The hobbyist is always on the alert for new and fascinating pastimes and for equipment to pursue his current hobby. Fishing and hunting equipment are also often listed under this heading. Note that each of the three advertisers asks a small amount for a catalog, either to cover its costs or to discourage curiosity seekers.

[5]

These two headings are aimed at those constantly on the alert for bargain merchandise, and it stands to reason that a host of individuals are drawn to ads of this type.

[6]

There is a marked trend to franchise selling. Generally, a substantial investment by the purchaser is required; therefore franchises are considered good money-makers for the firms offering them. Although the buyer is usually protected with an exclusive territory arrangement, he should be sure of the salability of the merchandise and the reliability of the company offering the franchise.

[7]

Ads offering overseas job opportunities are becoming quite common. Most ads do not ask for money in advance, but some do, and these companies have been successful selling the information in the form of low-priced booklets.

[8], [9]

Stamp and coin collectors are accustomed to buying by mail and make the most of their purchases in this way. Note that some of the advertisers make a bid for sales direct from the ads, while others employ low-priced leaders to acquire prospects' names for followup.

[10]

Home-training courses have been sold for ages and will continue to sell as long as people have the urge for self-improvement, for culture, entertainment, or to learn a trade or profession which leads to higher earnings.

[11]

Camera fans, by and large, are concerned with the cost of developing and finishing the pictures they take, as well as with the accessories that are required for their hobby. A host of firms have entered this field and run ads steadily, both classified and display, to meet the heavy demand.

[12]

Book ads generally produce better results if the type of reading matter offered is specific rather than general. There are too many competitors offering book catalogs to make any one stand out. The first ad shown here offers deer hunting stories, which is good because it specifically appeals to the outdoor man. The third ad is effective in that it appeals to those trying to increase their income. How-to books usually sell well.

[13]

The ads in this column manifestly appeal to the gourmet. It is surprising that classified ads are effective in this category. It means that those with a passion for exotic food search hard for new delicacies to appease their epicurean palates. Display ads are used more often in this respect because the picture of a mouth-watering dish will stop gourmets more readily.

[14]

Such ads are meant for those who possess musical souls—song writers, musicians, poets, record hunters, and music lovers in general. The market is big!

The classified ad categories listed here represent only the more common ones. A glance at the pages devoted to classified ads in popular publications will reveal a far greater variety of merchandise. Many magazines will create a special heading for an advertiser for a small extra charge.

How to Gauge Response

Monthly magazines—Inquiries received during the 30 days following distribution date might total 50 percent of the ultimate amount to be expected. Because of the long life of most monthlies, inquiries are likely to come in 6 months or even a year later.

Weekly magazines—They might produce from 25 to 35 percent of the total amount during the first week. The remainder are likely to come in over a ten-week period.

Sunday newspaper supplements—These will produce about one-third of total results within four days but, in the case of the *New York Times*, figure about seven days because it has a longer life than most supplements. The remaining replies will arrive within a two-month period.

Many newcomers enter the mail order field by starting with classified ads because of their low cost. This is sound up to a certain point. As intimated, at the beginning of this chapter, it is often advantageous to avoid making the initial cost your primary motive; think in terms of the product to be promoted in relation to the return on your advertising investment: namely, is it the kind of item best suited for classified advertising, or would display ads sell it more effectively? This is a question to ponder or to seek the advice of a seasoned professional who can provide a logical answer.

THE MARKET IS BIG

The potentialities for mail order selling are tremendous. With over 226,000,000 people in the United States, you can figure on almost that many prospects for the average household article. Add to that the prospects for automotive accessories, jewelry, gifts, books, and countless other items. True, there are thousands of mail order operators already established in the field. But most of them just scratch the surface, and you need not worry about that kind of competition. There are probably not more than 50 sizable mail order concerns, and even they cannot reach the entire market. As small as your start may be, it is very likely that you will offer merchandise that the rest do not carry—and that includes the biggest of your competitors. Hence, as an independent operator, you can stand on your own feet, look your competition squarely in the eye, and say: "My business is as sound as yours. There's plenty of business for each of us. You go your way, I'll go mine. And let us all prosper."

MY FAIR LADY: A MAJOR MARKET

When statisticians tell us that women control three-fourths of the nation's total wealth, that women take part in or influence nine-tenths of all consumer spending, it is time for mail order concerns to study more intensively the fair sex as prospective buyers. Should we not concentrate on the problem of how best to persuade the ladies to buy our merchandise?

Yes, indeed, women have almost taken over the wealth of the United States. They garner the lion's share of inheritances. Add this to wages earned now that they represent 33 percent of the working force. And lest you forget, the wife is the acknowledged boss of the spending that takes place in households throughout the land. She even influences her husband's purchases of suits, socks, shirts, and ties.

Now, how can we handle this mighty dictator of the purse strings? She is no amazon, but a complex, delicate mechanism that has puzzled mankind throughout the ages.

To come a little closer to her effect on mail order problems, the distaff side of the family is not especially concerned with technical features of a product or manufacturing processes. She is inclined to brush over them or to ignore them completely. What she wants to know is what benefits are to be derived from an article she considers purchasing. Will it save time, labor, money? Will it make her more beautiful, more desirable, happier?

The only time you can catch her unawares is when her intuitive defenses are down. Under such conditions you can motivate her buying impulses by creating such a keen desire for the things she wants that emotions hold sway over intuitions, provided that your appeal is not spoiled by flagrant insincerities. Talk benefits in terms of her own interests. If features must be stated, reverse the procedure by stating first that the benefits are only possible because of certain features. For example, "This vacuum lightens housework and saves you from back-breaking bending to pick up nails and other heavy objects because of its powerful motor."

Up to this point all women have been lumped together. This is a tendency that must be guarded against if you aim for maximum sales. Moreover, consideration must be given to changes taking place in the thinking and buying habits of women as they grow older and evolve from adolescence to full maturity, when their social and financial status usually improves.

Publishers are cognizant of these factors and put out magazines aimed at specific segments of the female market, according to type, age, buying habits, income, and vocation. For example, each of the following magazines is directed at different age levels:

Magazine	Age
Teen	16
Mademoiselle	23
Harper's Bazaar	35
Seventeen	17
Glamour	25

Thus, you link the nature of the product with the wearing and buying habits of the age group concerned. If an item is designed specifically to appeal to teenagers, it would be a waste of money to advertise it in a magazine read mainly by women of thirty-five.

Other groupings will also show a high degree of specialization among publications. From the standpoint of income, magazines such as *Harper's Bazaar* manifestly reach women in higher financial brackets than those magazines in the romance, confession, true-story, movie, or TV-radio fields, all of which are aimed at a mass market. If you were trying to sell something in the home improvement line, you would advertise in a Shelter Group type of publication such as *House Beautiful* and *House and Garden*. And if you want to sell fabrics or knitting needles, you would use a magazine on needlecraft such as *Workbasket* or *McCall's Needlework and Crafts*. You certainly would not employ *Glamour* which contains mostly women's beauty tips and fashions.

Thus, great selectivity must be exercised to make sure that the mail order ad is placed in the publication attuned to the interest of the woman prospect. It is one thing to recognize that the female is distinctly different from the male in her thinking, feelings, and actions, it is still another thing to place women in specific categories and to know which sort of product will make certain types of women respond. All this seems fairly obvious, yet much money is squandered in buying wasteful circulation. This requires considerable patient study. If a mail order operator lacks time and ability to undertake such a project, it will pay him to engage an expert who is familiar with the editorial content and readership of most publications. A woman may always be a fascinating mystery, but fortunately, many vital facts about her consumer preferences and buying power have been amassed—data that leads to sales.

Mail Order Magazines Read by Women

Magazines Best for Higher Priced Items	Circulation
Harper's Bazaar	687,633
Vogue	1,206,581
Glamour	2,119,242
Mademoiselle	1,283,510
House Beautiful	817,062
House & Garden	1,000,518
Soap Opera Digest	647,850
Better Homes & Gardens	8,098,226
Sunset (West Coast, Hawaii)	1,429,685
Southern Living	1,433,620
Redbook	3,864,417
Seventeen	1,525,594
New Woman	1,053,090
Parent's Magazine	1,511,665
Good Housekeeping	5,489,934
Cosmopolitan	2,926,060
Ladies Home Journal	5,134,149

Magazines Aimed at a Mass Market	Circulation
MacFadden's Womens Group	2,592,434
US	800,000
True Story	1,592,629
Playgirl	672,489
McCall's Magazine	6,267,489
People	2,425,000
Viva	392,148
Weight Watcher's Magazine	749,235
Sterling Women's Group	1,000,000

Family Type Magazines	**Circulation**
Family Circle	8,498,517
Woman's Day	7,607,909
Family Weekly	11,438,435
Parade	21,460,054
Sunday	22,378,111
Family Health	17,214
Grit	677,040
Capper's Weekly	413,707

Magazines for Brides	**Circulation**
Expecting	1,007,235
Bride's Magazine	346,687
Modern Bride	294,000

Magazines of Needlework	**Circulation**
Workbasket	1,774,322
McCall's Needlework & Crafts	1,998,312
Handmade	74,849
Simplicity Today	560,871
Vogue Patterns	74,849

HOW SELLING HOUSEHOLD ITEMS STRIKES HOME

In a previous chapter, "My Fair Lady: A Major Market," some mention was made of advertising items in the home improvement line. In view of the fact that every housewife is involved in this category, the vast potential in this field warrants further discussion.

If you have a product that saves a woman steps, labor, time, and money, this is the ideal market. The average housewife today is no longer a kitchen drudge; she has many other time-consuming duties besides cleaning, cooking, and training her children. A large number are engaged in business, civic, and social activities. Hence, the so-called housewife has become a sort of home engineer who depends on mechanical contrivances to speed up things in the realm where she holds sway. Many already possess washing machines, dryers, vacuum cleaners, electric toasters, electric can openers, even electric

Here is an ad that "Makes it easy to buy"—the accepted precept of salesmanship and especially so of mail order practice. The three advantages of Aerobic Time Wear are brought forward dramatically with pictures, succinct descriptions and prominent prices. The ad gets the message across *pronto* to the woman who scans the pages of a magazine hurriedly. She can quickly grasp the credit card inducements, the ordering details, and the easy-to-read coupon.

Pioneer Historical Society, Box 433, Harriman, Tenn., *Catalogue offers*. History in one of its most fascinating forms an unusual collection of old, rare, and valuable posters, pictures, prints, playbills, paintings, advertisements, handbills, broadsides, maps, drawings, all in exact reproductions. (10¢.)

WILD GAME COOK BOOK

More than 350 exciting recipes how to change wild game and wild fowl into tempting dishes. Also secrets of barbecue, stuffings, gravies, sauces, dressing game. Only $1.

Box 433, Harriman, Tenn.

Women never seem to tire of investigating new cookbooks. There is now a vast variety to please every conceivable whim. A cookbook club-of-the-month offers a new volume of recipes every 30 days. This ad promotes unusual outdoor menus.

NOW! CLEAN THOSE OUT-OF-REACH AREAS

With The All New

BACK WASHING SPONGE

Washes those normally "out-of-reach" areas of your back. Massages and relaxes tired and tense muscles! Use it as a headrest for the bath too! Jumbo natural color sponge attaches easily to any flat surface by means of 2 special large suction cups. Sponge always retains natural soft texture. Give yourself that extra bit of bathing luxury with the soothing, relaxing BACK WASHING SPONGE. Only $2.50 postpaid. Satisfaction guaranteed.

The Bourse Company, Dept. TG
The Bourse Company
Dept. TG 2 RD #5
York, Pa. 17402

One definition of a good mail order item is a novel product which fills a human need and does not encounter much retail store competition. This product fits that definition to the Nth degree. It has been advertised in the *Shopping Guide* section of the *New York Times*.

Spring-Summer—Needlework—1969

SEE BETTER INSTANTLY 3-D sight master

Marvelous aid for women who sew a lot! Non-glare lenses are optically perfect. Produces unique 3-dimensional effect as details stand out crystal clear; eliminates eye strain. Sight Master helps protect the eyes . . . errors and accidents vanish! Easily used over regular glasses, even bifocals. Magnifies 2¼ times. You'll wonder how you ever got by without it. Rush check or money order today. Money back guarantee.

$6⁹⁵ add 35¢ for postage

Calif. Residents Add 5% Sales Tax
ANDERSON'S ENTERPRISE
Dept. MC, P.O. Box 4468, San Jose, Calif. 95126

This ad was directed to women who sew and appropriately was placed in *McCall's Needlework & Crafts*. The device is equally useful to men who need keener vision for performing fine work. In that case special masculine copy is written and the ad placed in men's magazines.

carving knives. All of these laborsavers, or "wife savers," as some
call them, are still not enough for a modern woman whose time is at
a premium and who finds it difficult or too costly to employ domestic help. She still seeks shortcuts; gadgets like egg slicers, clam and
oyster openers, electric knife sharpeners, cabbage slicers, and electric broilers, to mention just a few.

The housewife is not only seeking laborsaving devices but she
also is interested in any object that will make the home more attractive or that will contribute to its smooth day-to-day operation.

The following products were advertised in a recent issue of a
magazine and show the diverse number of household products
available. There are countless others.

Cake and pie server	Espresso coffee pot
Linen hamper	Door knocker
Steam-iron covers	Towel holder
Door chimes	Portable bar
Cookbook rack	Fiberboard furniture
Butcher block tables	Toilet roll dispenser
Cat litter cleaners	Ladderback chairs
Salad plates	Dessert plates
Candy dishes	Comforters
Salt, pepper, sugar shakers	Shelving
Candles	Monogrammed glass oven
Hurricane lamps	Pigeonhole space savers
Calorie counting scale	Calfskin rugs
Delft tiles	Personalized soap
Treasure box	Sewing organizer
Cocktail set	Fur bags
Bedspread	Fondue set
Rug hug tape	French recipes
Tub tape	Candelabrum
Rose jar	Ironing aid
Rolling serving cart	Fringe curtains
Closet light	Figurine lamps
Ceramic mugs	Sheets and pillowcases
Refuse burner	Cookbook
Monogrammed baskets	Homespun draperies
Cast-iron wall oven	Hand embosser
Crystal bulb covers	Giant roasting forks
Window garden	Gravy serving set
Air freshener	Wall mural
Card table spacer	Southern recipe cookbook
Watch display domes	Wood screens

Toast rack
Egg separator
Nutcracker
Toothpaste dispenser
Children's furniture
Appetizer dish
Coasters
Floral afghan
Personal sauna bath
Twin bed bridge
Marble stain remover
Hostess set
Rosewood stands
Door peeper
Telephone shower
Cheese bowl
Daisy calendar towel
Tray holder
Embroidered doorstop
Folding end table
Menu calendars
Welcome mat
Coffee mug racks
Cranberry server
Globe bookends

Typewriter desk
Tie hangers
Window grilles
Ironstone pitchers
China mender
Window sill garden
Wrought-iron fernery
Crystal vases
Pillow top stitching
Home calculator
Needlecraft sampler
Personalized pot holder
Baby bear rugs
Scale planter
Willow storage chests
Family phone amplifier
Magazine racks
Book holder
Basement toilet flusher
Engraved trivet
Clock thermometers
Silver wine cups
Milk can dairy set
Wine making set

The mail order man who sees the possibilities in this field should be on the alert for products of the kind described in the preceding. They are not hard to find. A little classified ad in the Business Opportunity section of a paper like the *New York Times*, stating your interest in this kind of merchandise, is bound to bring many replies from manufacturers who produce them.

Magazine supplements of newspapers are good media for introducing labor and time-saving devices for women; also such magazines as:

Good Housekeeping
Parents Magazine
House Beautiful
House & Garden
Ladies Home Journal
Family Circle
Grit

Metropolitan Home
Better Homes & Gardens
Sunset
Southern Living
McCall's
Woman's Day
Capper's Weekly

The circulation figures for most of these publications are given in the chapter entitled "My Fair Lady: A Major Market."

Cash In on the Home Sewing Boom

With constant variations in the economic picture, buying habits are bound to change too. The higher cost of ready-to-wear garments during a period of skyrocketing inflation has forced countless women to make their own clothes. Another factor that has engendered home sewing has been the steady growth in leisured society. The resulting extra unused time encourages creative activity and satisfies the desire for individuality. The upshot of all such factors has been a booming home sewing market, estimated at three billion dollars. This includes the sale of fabrics, patterns, yarns, precut garments, sewing machines, notions, and accessories such as thimbles, needles, and scissors.

One man stated the situation this way: "A few years ago, if my wife made a dress, the neighbors would think we were in financial difficulties. Today she shows it off to everyone." Some 600 million, or two out of every five garments worn by women and children, are now made at home. Close to 45 million women sew creatively— make new garments rather than mend or remodel. Auguring well for the near future is the fact that they are young; nearly half under 30. On campuses, sewing is beginning to outrank the guitar as a youth symbol and the greatest group percentage is in the 15 to 19 year-olds. In addition, more than six million girls are taking sewing lessons in home economics classes or under sponsorship of youth clubs.

Consider the billions of yards of material sold for home sewing at an average price of $4.00 per yard. Look about you in buses, trains, subways, as well as in living rooms and observe the multitude of females, from teenagers to grandmothers, indulging in knitting, crocheting, stitching, macrame, needlepoint, etc., using up tons of yarn and thread, and enriching those businessmen who sell them their supplies for making garments, shawls, sweaters, afghans, caps, bags.

The mail order operator is tapping this spectacular three billion dollar market and enjoying his slice of the pie. (For further details of the home sewing market, write to the author of this book. A survey will be sent to you gratis.)

Some of the leading publications in the mail order home sewing field are listed on a previous page. A number of mail order concerns encourage women to make garments for resale as a means of augmenting their incomes. They not only advertise in the publications discussed in the preceding but also in door-to-door selling magazines such as Spare Time, Income Opportunities, and Money Making Opportunities. See the chapter entitled, "The Specialty Salesman—A Mail Order Prospect."

This item appeals to the woman who wants to enhance the appearance of her bathroom. It was considered so novel that the mail order house ran a publicity program featuring it simultaneously with its *House Beautiful* advertising. Over 100 editors of appropriate media were supplied with photos and releases.

Place mats might be considered commonplace articles, but not if they are made with genuine butterfly wings. This mail order man realized that he had something beautiful, different, and appealing, so he advertised the items in *House & Garden* during the pre-Christmas season.

Special!

REGULARLY $198.

NOW only $150.

while the supply lasts!

GENUINE AFRICAN

LAY ONE
ACROSS
YOUR BED

GREAT
HEARTH RUG

HANG ONE
ON THE WALL

ZEBRA SKIN RUG

A virile decorating accent for den, bedroom or executive suite

AT LEAST
7 FEET LONG
...PLUS TAIL!

ACROSS
A COUCH
...WOW!

Our current catalog lists these breath-taking zebra skin rugs for $198. (And they're a bargain at that. You'll find they sell most places for $250.) Now —and while the supply lasts —you can get one for just $150! Imported by us from East Africa, they are all select-grade sleek adult zebra skins, the kind that last "forever." A truly spectacular, excitingly different decoration for home or office. If you have some important business gifts coming up, it would pay you to order several. Sent postpaid. Satisfaction guaranteed.

Send for FREE color catalog of unique gifts for men.
A MAN'S WORLD—Dept. HL-99,
7 Delaware Drive
Lake Success, N.Y. 11040

A MAN'S WORLD

Dept. HL-99, 7 Delaware Drive, Lake Success, N. Y. 11040

Please send me_____genuine African Zebra Skin Rug(s) at the special price of $150 each. If not 100% delighted, I may return for full refund or cancellation of charges.

☐ Check or money order enclosed. We send postpaid.
☐ Extended payment plan. Enclosed is $50 down, plus $3.00 postage & handling charges. I will pay the balance, $50 per month, for the next 2 months.

Name_____

Address_____

City_____State_____Zip_____

When a product appeals to both sexes, almost equally, the choice of media creates a problem. The zebra skin rug depicted here can be used in den, bedroom, or executive suite. It could be advertised effectively in household type publications, such as *House Beautiful* and *House and Garden* as well as in a typical man's medium, such as *Esquire* and *The Wall Street Journal* or in both types if the budget permits.

This chair, advertised in *House & Garden* magazine, meets the current demand for unusual and artistic furniture to harmonize with modern decor. The heading quickly establishes 3 points: it is Danish; it is full size; it is a comfortable lounge chair.

These clever and practical devices fill the householder's need for extra telephones without increasing his monthly bill. The above offerings capitalize on this situation effectively. Observe how the broken rule border enhances the ad which appeared in *House & Garden*.

BEAUTY—LIKE SEX—IS HERE TO STAY

Ever since Cleopatra, women have been concerned with cosmetics. During the Victorian age, it was considered vulgar for any woman, besides actresses, to apply paints, powders, creams, and the like. My, how conditions have changed! Virtually all females today, from teenagers to grandmothers, would not think of leaving the house without first studying themselves in the mirror and applying the necessary makeup.

For a long time, large national concerns have been making the most out of this demand. They spend millions of dollars annually in advertising special brands to win the favor of women, and to induce them to go to their favorite store to purchase their cosmetics and perfumes.

This means that the mail order man must approach the cosmetic field with extra caution. Standard cosmetics and beauty preparations are not usually profitable for mail order purposes. The store and brand competition are too tough to overcome. The exceptions are special preparations that correct specific facial blemishes or accomplish a new beautifying effect. Such items have been know to get results. Wigs, curls, braids, and the like, while not exactly cosmetics, are nevertheless beautifying items which are big sellers because they are in high style.

Some cosmetics, especially the corrective kind, border on health products (discussed in another chapter). Ads promoting such products should be carefully worded to avoid "cure" claims, which governmental authorities frown upon. It is safer to state that they help to relieve or overcome a certain condition.

Magazines, mentioned previously in the chapter entitled, "Classified Versus Display Ads," such as *Glamour*, *Mademoiselle*, *Harper's Bazaar*, *Seventeen*, *Redbook*, and *Cosmopolitan* are particularly appropriate. There are many others.

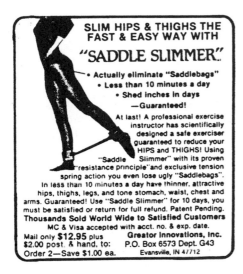

This ad exemplifies the principle that heading, picture, and text should be so unified as to make the salient appeal sharply evident. In this case, "Slimness" epitomizes the objective of the product while it fills a prevalent, deep-seated longing.

Here is an ad the heading of which is an answered prayer to millions of women troubled with wrinkles. Such telltale signs of aging, once removed, tend to lift the spirit. No wonder the ad pulled! The results might have been better if the ad, instead of starting the text praising the product, began by getting the prospect emotionally involved with a heart-throbbing human-interest mental picture of a beautiful wrinkle-free face achieved after using the product.

HOW THE MALE RESPONDS

The man of the house is as complex as his wife although not quite as mysterious. In the middle and lower income groups, a man is concerned primarily with the economics of running a home, paying off a mortgage and installments on a car, a refrigerator, electric appliances, and a lawn mower. The upper income group with domestic help and plenty of cash in the bank is not so much concerned with such matters.

But besides basic home activities, most men have other interests—sports, hobbies, investments, entertainment, and reading. Therefore, if you have anything to sell to men, select a medium whose readers are the kind likely to purchase your offering. After all, the less waste circulation, the more sales you will make and, consequently, the greater the return on your advertising investment.

To choose the best advertising medium for your particular offering, ask yourself the ten questions that follow:

1. Is the product strictly for men, or is it one that a woman is likely to buy as well, such as a labor-saving electric appliance for the kitchen, a dishwasher, washing machine, toaster, or can opener, to mention a few.

2. If the item is strictly for a man, is the wife likely to influence the purchase or present it to her husband as a gift? Such articles as ties, handkerchiefs, belts, socks, fall into this category. The women's magazines listed in the preceding chapter would be effective.

3. Is this publication or section read exclusively by men? For instance, Sunday's *New York Times* offers two mail order sections. One is the "Shopping Guide" at the back of the Sports section. This is read largely by men who are more interested in sports than women. The other is the "Shopping Mart" in The Magazine Supplement, which is read by as many women as men because this section contains editorials on fashions, cooking, and interior decorating, as well as feature articles of general interest.

4. What is the age group? Mass media such as detective and mystery magazines have younger readers more than sophisticated publications, such as *Esquire* and *Playboy*. The mass media

cover a wide spectrum of male readers of every age. Several Presidents of the United States have been known to read detective magazines for relaxation.

5. If it is a sports item, is it used broadly in all types of sports or only in a highly specialized field? For example, *Sports Illustrated* covers a wide range while magazines such as *Field and Stream, Guns Magazine, Golf Digest,* and *Skiing* report on specific sports. Bear in mind also that only the inveterate fisherman will spend money for a fishing magazine, while the man who fishes only now and then, when he has time or when the spirit moves him, is not likely to buy a fishing magazine. To sell him fishing tackle or a fishing rod you would use a mass market publication that is read by men. The same principle applies to golf and other sports. A comprehensive advertising campaign would include both kinds of publications for maximum sales.

6. Is your prospect mechanically minded? The number of men who possess workbenches in basements or garages runs into the millions. They are constantly in need of tools, kits, nails, screws, ladders, wood, paint, etc. They seek "how-to" advice on repairing, designing, and building. The mechanical type magazines, such as *Popular Mechanics, Popular Science,* and *Science Illustrated* are the natural ones to use. However, general media aimed at the men's mass market can also bring worthwhile results.

7. Does he pursue a hobby? The world is full of hobbyists—stamp and coil collectors, miniature airplane, ship and railroad builders, etc. Here too, you can select a specific magazine read only by individuals engaged in a particular hobby, or employ newspapers aimed at a mass market, with consequently more circulation yet more waste circulation.

8. Are politics his prime interest? The newspapers, of course, keep him informed on city, state, national, and international developments, yet the man who is intensely concerned with such matters reads national news magazines, such as *Time, Newsweek, U.S. News & World Report, The New Republic.*

9. What are his reading habits? Besides newspapers, does he read other mass publications of a general nature, such as *Life, Look, Reader's Digest?* Or does he prefer more literary magazines, such as *Saturday Review, Harper's Magazine,* and *The Atlantic?* His education often has an influence on his literary tastes. It is wise to ascertain how many readers of a publication are high school and college graduates.

10. Is he concerned with investments? Then he is likely to read the financial pages of such newspapers as the *New York Times*, the *Chicago Tribune*, and the *Wall Street Journal*. He may also read the *Baron's Weekly, Financial World, Forbes, Fortune*. As a business man he is prone to read national political and news magazines (mentioned in No. 8), as well as business publications in his own industry or profession. Men in this category are likely to be in a higher income group. This factor, of course, has a bearing on the type as well as the price of merchandise offered.

In every income bracket there are men who belong to fraternal societies, such as the Elks and the Knights of Columbus. Many fraternity members read the magazines put out by these organizations.

In general, study the market and media in relation to the products so you will strike at the very core of your prospect's interests, or, to change the metaphor, if you are probing for business go where you know you can locate a rich vein at once. Weigh in the balance such factors as age, buying habits, education and income, and ascertain how each publication measures up to your product's requirements. This is the way to arrive at scientific media selection.

Major Publications Read by Men

The following are some of the leading publications recommended. Space does not permit listing all of them. The categories are based somewhat on the ten questions asked in the foregoing chapter:

Men's Mass Media Magazines	Circulation
CBS Magazine Network	1,837,398
Petersen Action Group	4,024,811
Hustler	1,129,306
Rolling Stone	780,715
Official Detective Group	900,000
American Legion Magazine	2,533,358
Esquire	652,863
Scientific American	707,854
Science 83	720,401
Saga	250,000

For More Sophisticated Men	**Circulation**
Oui	672,668
Penthouse	4,022,034
Playboy	4,851,368
Gallery	484,191
Signature	643,850

Business & Finance Publications	**Circulation**
Wall Street Journal	1,925,772
New York Times (Financial Pages)	1,461,673
Fortune	679,983
Financial World	163,345
Baron's Weekly	258,726
Nation's Business	970,601

Magazines for the Mechanically Minded	**Circulation**
Mechanics Illustrated	1,619,242
Popular Mechanics	1,612,351
Popular Science	1,812,654
Science and Mechanics	104,768
Family Handyman	1,110,860
Work Bench	787,168

What the Sportsmen Read	**Circulation**
Sports Illustrated	2,452,049
Field & Stream	2,016,637
Outdoor Life	1,537,015
Sport	905,702
Sports Afield	527,085
Guns & Ammo	452,023

For Those with Hobbies	**Circulation**
Model Airplane News	87,000
Popular Ceramics	57,736
Coin World	91,021
Creative Crafts	53,966
Lapidary Journal	50,418
Model Railroader	178,591
Linn's Stamp News	82,203
Newsmatic News Weekly	54,009
Popular Photography	872,097

For Those with Hobbies (continued)

Computer Electronics	403,127
Ziff-Davis Magazine Network	2,539,035

For Those Who Keep Up with the News

	Circulation
Foreign Affairs	60,003
The New Republic	95,538
National Review	98,495
People	2,245,000
Christian Science Monitor	144,833
Newsweek	3,024,503
Time	4,555,610
U.S. News & World Report	2,157,978

Fraternal and Civic Magazines

	Circulation
Columbia	1,373,233
Eagle Magazine	695,455
Elks Magazine	1,638,386
Future	274,181
Lion's Magazine	666,058
Moose Magazine	1,296,400
Rotarian	479,756
Kiwanis Magazine	279,147
Scouting	923,191
V.F.W. Magazine	1,879,699
Woodman of the World	495,810

For the Literary Man

	Circulation
Saturday Review	528,834
Harper's Magazine	150,803
Writer's Digest	180,860
The Atlantic	400,000
New York Times Book Review	1,461,473
New York Review of Books	126,786

Bear in mind that space does not permit listing every publication that men read—not even every category in which they are interested. There are literally thousands of publications from which to make appropriate selections.

A man's world is a realm of ruggedness, virility, strength, and undiluted down-to-earth facts. It is free from emotional hogwash. The above ad talks the kind of sense men expect. It appeared in a business man's weekly.

A chair is just something to sit on for most people, but when it takes the form of a British officer's chair, the subject acquires novelty—one of the ingredients of a good mail order product. The low price is another inducement to buy. The ad appeared in a businessman's weekly.

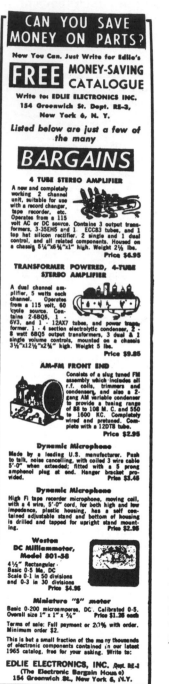

The old proverb that a picture is worth 1,000 words is true with respect to the above ad, which appeared in the Country Edition of the *New York Daily News.* The brief copy provides all the essential details to supplement the illustration.

The man who loves to tinker with electronic devices will read this ad which features bargain offers in odd parts. It appeals both to the experimenter and to the men who service radio-TV. The ad appeared in *Radio-Electronic Magazine.*

This advertisement catches the eye of the hobbyist and gun collector. The uniqueness of the antique pistol makes the ad stand out. Notice that a pen and ink drawing was employed rather than a photo. This was done because in a large reduction of a photograph details are inclined to blur.

GREEN LIGHT FOR AUTO ACCESSORIES

If cars could be shipped by parcel post, some enterprising mail order man would make an effort to sell them. Under the circumstances, the next best objective is to sell automobile accessories. Considering the millions of cars on the road, both new and used, the market is vast and worth tackling. Many mail order concerns are running a highly profitable business even with a single car acessory.

Since women also drive cars, they are considered good prospects in this field; however, men are regarded as the major market. Where mass media are employed, the ads could appeal to both sexes.

Car owners, as a whole, seek items that make their vehicle run more smoothly, provide greater convenience and safety, and that assist them in emergencies. New gadgets to fill the possible needs of car owners appear on the market weekly, if not daily. For example, here is a procession of accessories:

Radios
Air conditioners
Baby baskets
First-aid kits

Mirrors
Jacks
Emergency car flares and lights
Fire extinguisher

Road map holders   Portable garages
Windshield cleaners   Car phones
Coffee-making attachment   Antennas
Beverage holders   Heaters
Car covers   Horns
Writing-pad holders   Hi-fi attachments
Car locks

What Car Owners Read

Newspapers with mail order sections carry a considerable amount of auto-accessory advertising. Generally, these ads are effective because most papers feature both car and mail order advertising in the Sports Section, which is read largely by men. Moreover, the mail order section usually comes immediately after the car exchange columns. This is especially true of the *New York Times*.

In view of the fact that men who tinker with cars are mechanically oriented, they are inclined to read magazines like *Popular Mechanics* and *Popular Science*, both of which are excellent for auto-accessory advertising. They are listed in the chapter, "How the Male Responds."

Another market to consider is the one involving the car buff or fan who thinks enough about the subject to purchase a special magazine devoted to car news and mechanical developments. This group of individuals includes the "hot rodder." These auto enthusiasts are in a class by themselves and are generally younger than the average motorist. They are in the market not only for all sorts of accessory gadgets, but they also purchase special parts to "soup up" their racing engines. The following is a list of publications read by these car buffs:

What Car Owners Read	**Circulation**
Owner Operator	94,492
Motor Trend	733,225
Hot Rod	770,368
Street Rodder	97,010
Road & Track	656,763
Car Craft	308,317
Cars	91,882
Car and Driver	738,881
Cars & Parts	117,030
Motor Tech	94,492
Four Wheeler	85,111

What Car Owners Read (continued)

Popular Hot Rodding Magazine	262,658
Sports Car	25,846
Super Stock and Drag Illustrated	63,855
Auto Racing Digest	78,402
Autoweek	723,804
Hemmings Motor News	222,841

While newspaper headlines play up car accidents and fatalities, this advertiser offers a safety device in the same papers. An excellent tie-in as evidenced by the number of times the ad has appeared.

Motorists
New Thermos Bottle and Cup Holder Keeps Refreshments at Your Finger Tips!

New, handy holder provides a secure place under your dashboard to keep your quart size (or smaller) thermos bottle and cup while you're driving! A single clamp attaches the Holder under your dash. Made of sturdy, lightweight anodized aluminum with a satin finish. The perfect gift for someone "on-the-road." Add to YOUR motoring pleasure with the convenient, handy Thermos Bottle and Cup Holder. Only $2.50 postpaid. Satisfaction guaranteed.

THE BOURSE COMPANY, Dept. TG-I
RD #5, York, Pa. 17402

Here is another useful accessory. The car owner who acquires a thirst during a long trip welcomes such a convenience. The mail order house used wisdom in selecting the item. The ad appeared in the *New York Times*.

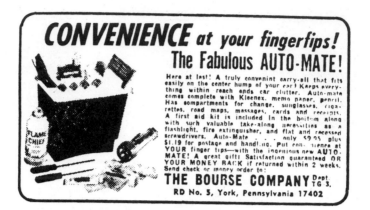

Can you think of all the items which car owners take along on extended trips? The chances are there is room for all of them in the Auto-Mate which fits nicely over the center hump of the car. It prevents the unpleasant disarray of odds and ends lying around in the car and holds them in one neat convenient container. If any article fills a need, it is this one.

THE SPECIALTY SALESMAN —A MAIL ORDER PROSPECT

House-to-house selling, which dates way back in American history, is still at its peak. Men and women have been ringing doorbells to dispose of merchandise for over a hundred years. Today, it is a two and a half billion dollar industry. Big names in this field—Avon, Fuller-Brush, Stanley Home Products—to mention a few, are getting their share by the simple process of persuading sales agents to comb their neighborhoods for sales, something any firm can do. It involves little risk because the sales representative buys wholesale from you, the supplier, for cash and resells at retail prices. He is virtually in business for himself.

This kind of business is still regarded as a mail order operation because agents must be rounded up and dealt with entirely by mail. Even a small company can succeed in this endeavor. It requires no more capital than a regular mail order operation in which one advertises and sells direct to the consumer. A major difference is that if you are selling through agents, your margin between merchandise cost to you and the retail price must be wide enough to allow a representative to earn a fair commission.

Make Money Faster as a Paperback Book Wholesaler

EVERY RETAIL STORE, PTA'S CLUB GROUPS CAN MAKE BIG $$$. BUY FOR FUND-RAISING, APPOINT SALES AGENTS TO COVER YOUR AREA.

REPEAT SALES ARE TERRIFIC. EVERYONE BUYS AGAIN & AGAIN. NEW TITLES ARE ALWAYS BEING PUBLISHED.

THOUSANDS OF TITLES IN NEW PAPERBACK POCKET BOOKS

HOW TO... MYSTERY ROMANCE WESTERN NOVELS LOVE EDUCATIONAL INSTRUCTIONAL

Lee Cusack, President.
ALL BOOKS WE DISTRIBUTE ARE FROM THE TOP NATIONALLY KNOWN PAPERBACK BOOK PUBLISHERS
START YOUR OWN WHOLESALE BOOK BUSINESS. GIVE AGENTS 25 TO 40%, MAKE 20% TO 35% YOURSELF.

UP TO **60%** DISCOUNT
TO YOU AS A WHOLESALER.

SEND FOR POSTPAID Assortment now.
Satisfaction Guaranteed.

retail **50¢**
your cost **20¢**
profit **30¢**

60% for you to work with

GIVE 25% to small dealers
40% to large buyers and make money

THERE'S MONEY IN BOOKS. STABLE, STEADY, PROFITABLE BUSINESS GOOD ALL YEAR AROUND BUT ESPECIALLY GOOD IN THE FALL AND WINTER.

If you are already a book wholesaler, better start buying from us and earn that extra money from our top discounts. If you are not now in the book business we will send complete instructions with your first order. But don't delay. This is the first time such an opportunity has been available for years. This is one of those once in a lifetime deals. Why! Simply because you need a source of supply for books if you want to be a wholesaler. Now we need new wholesalers in every corner of the country. If you are a sales producer and prove yourself we will give you an exclusive deal in your territory.

There's no need to tell you who your prospects are. Just everyone reads paperback books. They are low in costs, 50¢ retail. They can be sold by club groups interested in raising money they can be sold by door to door agents. And what's more you can let them make a NICE HIGH PROFIT and still make money for yourself.

Easy to sell, no sales pressure is required. Your market is already there. Line up 100 retail accounts and you've got yourself a terrific regular income. We tell you how to do it with your first order.

You can be a wholesaler in an exclusive territory with an initial investment of $1,000 o $3,000, depending on the size of the territory. There is no franchise fee. Your whole investment is safely invested in resaleable merchandise. Be an exclusive wholesaler in your area. Write today. Earliest postmark reserves the territory!

Make no mistake. These books are top quality paperbacks published by nationally known publishers. Your money back if you find any books in your assortment that are not up to top quality standard. THEY WILL SELL. THEY are selling every day. No need to bother selecting titles. New ones are always available, just let us give you a good assortment that will make money for you.

This order form will put you in business as a paperback wholesaler.

Lee Cusack, President, Book Distributors, Dept. SS-2,

☐ Please ship 500 assorted 50¢ retail paperback books. Enclosed is $100. I want to reserve the following exclusive territory.

☐ I enclose $25 for 100 assorted new paperback novels and selling plans.

☐ I enclose $7.50 for 25 assorted new paperback novels and selling plans.

☐ I enclose $1 for 2 sample copies and instruction.
($1 credit given on first order)

NAME

ADDRESS

CITY

ZONE   STATE

This full-page ad appeared in two colors, in both *Specialty Salesman* and *Salesman's Opportunity*. It represents the high-pressure dynamic approach which is needed in this field. The salesmen at whom this add is directed expect such tactics because they themselves sell in that manner.

Short-Range Versus Long-Range Approach

There are two broad approaches to this program: One is the short-range plan in which you will regard the whole operation as a mere test to find out whether you can sell your merchandise successfully through specialty salesmen or sales agents. This would impel you to be cautious and keep expenditures down to a minimum.

The long-range plan requires a different attitude. First try to establish your direct-selling business one way or another through persistent effort. If one approach does not work, try another; keep trying until you find the right method to acquire salesmen and build a business on a profitable basis. This may entail a larger initial outlay than the short-range plan.

How to Acquire Salesmen

Your first step is to advertise for specialty salesmen to handle your product. If you can offer a salable item at an attractive discount, you will encounter little difficulty in a least drawing inquiries. The most economical way to acquire representatives is to advertise in magazines that cater to specialty salesmen. Larger companies use not only such publications but others of a more general nature read by persons likely to make good prospects. Classified ads in newspapers can also develop leads, but the use of specialized magazines usually is more effective.

How to Convince Salesmen

One must be realistic enough to know that the man or woman who responds to an ad probably answers a number of others to see which offers the best deal. Therefore, your follow-up must be highly persuasive and convincing. Generally, a dynamic circular accompanied by a strong sales letter is required to get the prospect started. Bear in mind that most of these men are more concerned with earning money for a livelihood than anything else. You must convince them that there is a good market for your product and ample profit. You might ask for no money in the ad, merely using it to pull inquiries, and use the follow-up to close the sale. Or you might offer a sample at a low price to get the prospect started. In any case, you will point out to agents the extremely low cost and high profits when merchandise is purchased in quantities.

How to Hold Salesmen

It would be your aim to keep your salesmen from straying and to get as much business as possible out of each. This can be accomplished by a series of form letters:

1. To be sent to those who inquired but failed to respond to your initial follow-up.

2. To be sent to those who ordered a sample, yet failed to come through with additional orders.

3. To be sent to those who gave you a small wholesale order but have not sent additional orders; in general, to all who lag in their sales efforts and who could be needled to try harder.

From time to time, messages should be sent to all representatives, particularly to good producers, calling attention to new items you have added to your line as well as other company developments which might interest them.

Boosters

Most of the successful firms in this field offer incentive bonuses to their men. These might be special prices or discounts; bonus money or prize gifts which they earn after reaching certain sales plateaus.

House Organs

In time, you can acquire several hundred salesmen. The giants in the direct-selling field employ thousands of salespeople. When you reach this point it would be to your advantage to issue a house organ. This could start as a simple four-page paper and then gradually develop into a more substantial mailing piece. It should be both inspirational and instructive. Cite examples of the way your most successful men work; report new happenings and new products, offer selling hints, and perhaps conduct sales contests.

Potential

The road to success in direct selling is clear-cut, assuming that you possess one or more products which are highly salable. You may have to advertise steadily to acquire new men faster than you lose drifters, but as time goes on you will find yourself ahead. Such a program requires patience and persistence. You may start with a few hard-working men. One good producer sometimes brings in more than enough to pay a year's advertising costs. After a while, you will have a small staff of salespeople, enthusiastically promoting your products. If you have what it takes to develop a direct selling program, then proceed with it by all means—it can produce a sizable income.

A little guidance from an advertising agency specializing in the field will help select the most effective of suitable publications, prepare the ads, and develop mailing pieces. The chances are that using professional help will get you to your objective quicker, and may cost less in the long run.

Some of the magazines that cater to specialty salesmen are:

Publication	Circulation
Specialty Salesmen	300,000
Salesmens Opportunity	300,000
Money Making Opportunities	220,388
Spare Time	305,162
Income Opportunities	59,683
Agency Sales Magazine	13,910

YOUTH MUST HAVE ITS FLING

Bernard Shaw remarked once that youth is wonderful, but it is a shame that it is wasted on the young. He, like many others, was in rapport with youth. He had a nostalgic feeling for his own younger days and envied the buoyancy, ebullience, and exuberant spirit of youth, wishing that some of this uninhibited joy would rub off on him in his old age. The correct way then to approach this vast market is to try to place yourself on the thinking level of your young prospect. Look at his world of unfolding wonders, expectation, and promise which the years ahead offer boys and girls—all of whom are prospects for your merchandise.

In this chapter, we discuss the children who buy and not those oldsters who purchase articles for youngsters to wear, use, or enjoy.

The Very Young

This comprises those boys and girls who are about eight to seventeen and old enough to order their own merchandise—the age of

Boy Scouts and Girl Scouts. These youngsters read *Boy's Life*, and similar magazines. They also read the comics which, incidentally, are often read by their older brothers and sisters as well as by their fathers. Experience has shown that if an item is keyed to the mentality and habits of readers of *Boy's Life* or other youth magazines, the results are generally excellent. Youth is naturally enthusiastic. Once a Boy or Girl Scout exhibits at a club meeting a product he has just purchased, he or she is apt to shout, "Wow—Look what I bought!" (or another exclamation to that effect). His excitement stirs up his club mates. Enjoying his find, they probably will order the product for themselves. These sales snowball and the advertiser's profits pile up. Many firms feature a variety of items at one time in the publications mentioned, and the author knows of countless products that have been advertised for years. Of course, toys, bicycles, stamps, and coins are typical items in great demand. When a fad or a spectacular event such as landing men on the moon develops, the buying craze knows no bounds.

The Teenager

The outlook of the teenage boy is different from that of the teenage girl because the girl matures physically and socially faster than the boy. At fifteen to sixteen years he is still primarily concerned with sports and outdoor adventure, while the girl at that age has already become conscious of the opposite sex and does all in her power to make herself more attractive and desirable. All this has a bearing on the reading habits of teenagers and the selection of media that will be sure to influence sales.

A year or two difference in a youngster's age makes a vast change in his or her activities and outlook. A boy of eight might cast aside what amused him at seven. A girl of sixteen thinks and acts differently than one seventeen years of age. That is why there are a variety of magazines such as *Teen* and *Seventeen* which cater to fifteen- to eighteen-year-old girls.

Youth or Woman?

When a girl arrives at the age of seventeen, she enters the world of womanhood. She starts thinking like a young woman. Rate directories list the magazines read by such girls in both the Youth and the Women sections. For instance, a piece of jewelry or garment which a

A success story could be built around this *Boy's Life* ad which produced over $2,000 in profits. But that was only the beginning. The orders for live chameleons was followed by an avalanche of orders for meal worms to feed the pets. The repeat business never ended.

Every boy loves a circus, and the advertiser knows it. That is why he placed this ad in *Boy's Life.* The stimulating pictures and the exciting heading will make lads sit up and take notice.

Keeps Teeny-Boppers
Occupied For Hours

DOODLE DESK

On rainy days, long car rides, family visits . . . DOODLE DESK provides **4.98** postpaid endless hours of fun and education for the young scribbler and artist. Solidly constructed with Pine sides and Birch plywood surface, smoothly sanded for easy writing and drawing. 16"x15"x4", roomy drawer with assorted crayons. Paper roll easily renewed. Marvelous gift for birthday, Christmas or any other occasion. Satisfaction guaranteed. Send check or Money order.

RUDON COMPANY, Dept. TM
2522 Anniston, Houston, Texas 77055

*Texas residents add 4%
state and local sales tax.*

Youth must be served, entertained, and educated. This Doodle Desk was designed to keep those human bundles of energy happily occupied. The ad appeared in the *New York Times Magazine Supplement*.

HER VERY OWN
SEWING
MACHINE
"Just like Mom's"

Think of the delight a little girl will experience when she's able to make her very own doll clothes. This sewing machine is just right for any ambitious miss. It's your answer to the gift problem. Battery operated, it comes complete with switch light, foot pedal, and extension table. Educational, creative, your little homemaker will love making the same things **$7.00** only ppd. as Mommy!

SONIA STAR ASSOCIATES
286 Fifth Ave., New York, N.Y. 10001

This item evidently was designed with the thought in mind that youngsters are great imitators. As a matter of fact, thousands of toys are miniatures of articles used by adults. The sewing machine shown here is not actually a toy because it sews just like a large standard machine. The ad appeared in *House Beautiful* and *House and Garden*.

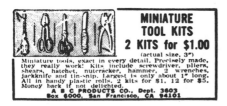

**MINIATURE
TOOL KITS
2 KITS for $1.00**
(actual size, 3")

Miniature tools, exact in every detail. Precisely made, they really work! Kits include screwdriver, pliers, shears, hatchet, nutcracker, hammer, 2 wrenches, jackknife and tin-snip. Largest is only about 1" long. All in handy plastic rolls. 2 kits for $1, 12 for $5. Money back if not delighted.
A B C PRODUCTS CO., Dept. 3603
Box 6000, San Francisco, CA 94101

An example of economical use of small space. This tiny *Boy's Life* ad pictures five different items, a heading large enough to make the reader take notice along with a complete description and sales message.

This *House Beautiful* ad offers gifts for youngsters from tiny tots to adolescents. The diversity is helpful to adults who must play Santa Claus for many youths. The descriptions under each item are well handled— plenty of verve and sell!

young woman of, say twenty-three, would be likely to purchase might readily appeal to one of seventeen also. Surveys show that today's teenager knows what she wants in merchandise. They generally use their own money (over seven billion dollars annually) and spend it on everything from sports to cosmetics. They look to Dad for the high-cost items such as cars. When cash runs out, they are apt to use Mother's credit cards and charge it.

The Student

Practically all boys and girls are attending grammar schools, high schools, or colleges. It is often necessary to sell them articles which they can use in connection with their studies. A number of publications are available that specialize in this field, such as those in the *Scholastic Magazine* Group, *Coed*, and the new *Student Weekly* issued by the *New York Times*.

Taken as a whole, the teenage market is tremendous. Think of it, about twenty-five million eager boys and girls are your potential market. Many mail order concerns take this market so seriously and consider it so lucrative that they spend all their time seeking products which youth will be likely to buy.

Magazines to Spark the Younger Element

For the Very Young	Circulation
Boy's Life	1,467,265
110 National 4-H News	66,000
Charlton Comics Group	2,460,058
Archie Comic Group	4,507,565
Harvey Comic Group	6,646,106
Marvel Comic Group	4,300,835
DC Comic Group	6,111,286
Young Miss	625,547

In addition there are countless newspaper comic supplements.

For the Teenager	Circulation
Seventeen	1,523,594
Teen	1,050,444
Campus Life	169,071

In addition many more movie, radio, TV, and romance magazines are read by teenagers.

For the Young Student	**Circulation**
Coed	719,036
Scholastic Magazine Group	2,113,306
Vica	226,000
Teen Beat—The Student Educator	420,854
Junior Scholastic	785,151

THE BABY MARKET IS WORTH NURSING

It is said a baby is born every minute. If true, it means that every sixty seconds one can virtually expect another mail order prospect. In spite of all talks about birth control, the United States population continues to increase, even if it cannot be called a "population explosion," a phrase applied to other countries. At this writing, the United States population has reached over 226,504,825.

You know what happens in a family when a baby arrives. All sorts of preparations take place even before the actual delivery. Layette, crib, bath supplies, nursing bottles, bedding, blankets, soap, powder, etc. are bought in advance. That is why there is a special magazine called *Expecting*. Then, scarcely has the infant made his or her appearance when a whole series of purchases are made: a carriage, toys, more bottles, more soaps, more powders, diapers, panties, sweaters. Babies grow fast. Each month they become taller and chubbier, which means that old wearing apparel must be discarded and replaced with new larger garments. The process goes on and on—from the creeping age through the toddling age to the running age—and right on up to the mischievous, rambunctious stage of irrespressible vigor. Then games, baseballs, bats, bicycles, and so on, must be provided to keep them under control.

Raising kids means raising money to keep up with the needs of the youngsters who outgrow and wear out things so fast. Much of this money is spent on mail order items. The magazines and newspapers carry countless advertisements in which children's items are featured. The mothers themselves buy innumerable articles for their youngsters, but probably more are purchased by proud and doting grandparents, uncles, aunts, cousins, and other relatives, as well as friends. In days gone by, about the only time a child received a gift was on his or her birthday and on Christmas. Today, customs have changed. Whenever a person visits a home where there are one or more youngsters, he or she is expected to bring a gift for each child. The youngsters count on it! If ill-mannered, they cry: "What have you brought me?" Otherwise, the thought is expressed only with their anxious eyes and disappointment.

To reach the mothers directly, one would do well to advertise in baby magazines. There are a number to choose from. All are similar except for the difference in circulation and commensurate rates. Most of the baby magazines are distributed through diaper services. The argument is sometimes advanced that if a magazine is received as a part of a service it is not regarded as seriously as one that is purchased at a newsstand or through a regular subscription. This may be somewhat true but should not discourage one from advertising in baby magazines.

Of course a mother reads other publications for pleasure and edification. She seeks information pertaining to her children, her home, and her own well-being. As a woman, she still wants to keep up with fashion trends and beauty hints because she wishes to look her best at all times. The kind of publications that she reads will vary, according to age, income, education, culture, tastes, as discussed in a previous chapter, "My Fair Lady: A Major Market."

Probably the magazine read most widely by mothers is *Parents Magazine*. With a circulation of 1,634,307 needless to say, it produces a volume of sales, if the product is appealing.

One of the best ways to influence the purchase of children's gifts by relatives and friends is to advertise in the Shelter Group magazines, which are read by women in home-owning families of medium and high incomes. Most of these women socialize and entertain a good deal. By mingling with many people, they encounter numerous situations in which they are expected to give gifts to youngsters. A list of the Shelter Group magazines will be found in a previous chapter, "My Fair Lady: A Major Market."

Here is a partial list of baby magazines and the circulation of each:

Magazine	Circulation
The American Baby	1,600,000
Baby Talk	928,502
Baby Care	500,000
Expecting	1,007,038
The First Year of Life	2,707,529
Redbook's Young Mothers	3,595,000
Mothers Today	904,020

Taken as a whole, the baby market opens up a continuous and lucrative field for aggressive mail order operators. It is big and important enough to deserve concentrated effort to the exclusion of everything else. Several firms offer catalogs that feature only baby items and most of them are novel, attractive, and useful.

Plump and Beautiful
Personalized

SILVER PIGGY BANK

An adorable and valuable gift with a purpose—to start the saving habit! Beautifully sculptured with one attentive ear cocked, this silverplated bank is tarnish-proof and has a plaintive face. Ideal gift for tiny-tots, teenagers, adults . . . everyone on your list. Gift-boxed. First name engraved FREE (Indicate name).

Only $6.95   plus 35¢ postage.

N.Y. residents add local sales tax.
Allow 2 weeks for delivery

SHOW AND TELL GIFTS
P.O. Box #6, Niagara Sq. Stn., Buffalo, N.Y. 14201

It's never too early or too late to start the saving habit. The silvery piggy bank, cute, attractive and useful, is designed largely for tiny tots but is utilized by adults as well. The fact that it is personalized with the name of the owner is an important sales feature. The ad appeared in *House Beautiful*.

ELECTRONIC BABY SITTER

Two transistorized units. One goes in the nursery, the other wherever Mom wants to be, kitchen, laundry, patio. Mom hears every sound baby makes "Loud and Clear." These units can also be an invaluable aid to those who must care for the sick or aged. Satisfaction or your money back. $14.95 pp.
Send check or money order to

SINBAD
Dept. HB1, 65 Alexander Dr.
Manchester, New Hamp. 03103
Please include your zip code.

How does a mother do it? . . . she must look after a baby's comfort while attending to a thousand and one household chores. She can manage very well if she uses the "Electronic Baby Sitter". The heading is appropriate and catchy. The ad ran in *House Beautiful*.

The above ad contains two buying motives: the gloves appeal to the housewife who is concerned with the appearance of her hands; the Sani-Pants appeal to the harried mother who is anxious to rid herself of the diaper problem.

Since little girls—and even little boys—like to play with dolls—Barnacle Bill pictured here makes many friends. It is the kind of gift one readily brings to a home where there is a child. It stands to reason that such a product would be a good seller. It has been advertised in the *New York Times*.

GIFT GIVING—A LUCRATIVE BUSINESS

What is a gift item? It is difficult to define because it could be virtually anything. Originally, according to the Oxford Dictionary, it means "payment for a wife." Now it is more apt to mean payment *to* a wife or anyone else. To the mail order man a gift is any object given as a token of love, friendship, or goodwill. This can range from a huge shiny Cadillac to a tiny plastic baby rattle.

Of course, here we are not discussing gifts of automobiles but only items that can be sent through the mails or by truck. This covers a multitude of products. Gifts are given for every conceivable occasion—for Christmas, birthdays, Mother's Day, Father's Day, weddings, bridal and baby showers, and countless other events. Consider also gifts to a hostess, housewarming gifts, and presents to young children when paying social calls to their families. In addition, there are gifts to retired employees and for special anniversaries.

Some objects are immediately categorized as gifts because of their "gift-like" appearance; regardless of gift wrapping, they are generally ornate novelties of the kind one is not likely to purchase for himself. In short, the gift hunter is prone to seek out-of-the-ordinary articles. He is also governed by the prices, the importance of the occasion, and his regard for the recipient. One puts a different evaluation on Christmas, brithday, and wedding gifts. The giver also bears in mind whether the gift is being presented to a member of his immediate family, a distant relative, an intimate friend, a casual acquaintance, a business associate, or a prospective customer. For example, it might do to give a new office receptionist a pound box of candy but a private secretary who had served faithfully for ten years would expect something more valuable.

Christmas is considered the greatest reason and season for giving. It has become a deep-seated custom that obscures the religious aspect of the holiday completely. When the Yuletide spirit pervades the realm, virtually everyone is mesmerized with a compulsive drive to give gifts to those thought worthy of being remembered, as well as undeserving persons to whom one feels obligated.

But the mail order operator should not make the mistake of putting all his effort into the pre-Christmas season and then lie down on the job the rest of the year when there are so many other occasions for gift-giving. Besides, any article that has merit can readily sell the year round. Many practical items which a person is likely to buy for himself can serve as gifts. All that is necessary is to add a sentence in the ad to the effect that the item makes an ideal gift too.

The mail order dealer who is in a quandary as to which articles to promote might look over the following list of items advertised in a single issue of a recent magazine. Although this will give you an idea as to what others are doing, it should not necessarily be followed as example of profitable products:

Doll kit	Night light
Astrology charts	Flatware
Hearing aids	Exercise suit
Christmas plate	Pet door
Car rear viewer	Ashtray
Decorative moulding	Figurine lamps
Collar extender	Lace
Oriental rugs	Collector's spoon
Primitive wood kit	Mugs
Fire protectors	Earrings
Mailbox name plates	Educational toys
Monogrammed glassware	Door knocker

Pigeonhole set
Coat of arms
Stickpin bracelet
Candies
Calfskin rugs
Corn pads
Personalized soaps
Outdoor incinerator
Valet chairs
Sewing organizer
Candles
Cologne
Eyeglass repairer
Pledge of Allegiance plaque
Fur storage case
Light fixtures
Typewriter stand
Desk lamp
Safety money holder
Pins and pendants
Child photos
Photo album
Colonial seat kits
Primping mirror
Pigskin cap
Deerskin gloves
Baking recipe
Curtains
Bronzed baby shoes
Candelabrum
Photo File
Sculpture
Cooking bags
Lamp kit
Zodiac paperweight
Briefcase
Men's wearing apparel
Ornamental pins
Men's tie tacs
Steaks
Sandals
Insoles
Knives, forks, spoons
Comforters

Canvas carryall
Light pulls
Napkin rings
Watch stands
Switch plates
Antique keys
Buffet stackers
Letter opener
Zodiac plaque
Bird feeder
Artificial diamonds
Photo jewelry
Chairs
Indian rugs
Bath rugs
Personalized pencils
Christmas labels
Pocket printer
Exerciser
Storage chests
Quilted dress
Crystal ball
Cuckoo clock
Towel holder
Doormat
Casual shift
Baton
Fiberboard furniture
Charms
Needlecraft
Medieval copperware
Personalized coasters
Handpainted shells
Handbag kit
Monogrammed basket
Letter seals
Auto back seater
Canning kits
Music box
Fruit cake
Embroidered crewel
Electric range
Electric bulb covers
Decorating book

Diet scale
Needlepoint
Love rings
Christmas tiles
Zodiac samplers
Art stamps
Cocktail sets
Hitching post
Rug-hug tape
Bedspreads
Steel drum
Doll
Scented soaps
Grandfather clock
Lithographs
Medal showcases
Tub tape
Closet light
Postage scale
Embroidery
Wall plaques
Portraits
Printed shirts
Trash burner
Electronic alarm
Cookbook
Homespun drapes
Stationery embosser
Riding boots
Personalized poems
Roasting forks
Fur coats
Wall murals
Candelesticks
Fingernail solution
Eardrum silencer
Tie hanger
Memo box
Window grills
Book shelf
Cake pans
Tree Brighteners
Director's chair
Chess sets

Greenhouses
Animal groomer
Christmas tree kits
Card table holder
Art sketches
Toy car
Glass watch domes
Occasional tables
Key ring
Odd-sized shoes
Trunk decorations
Photographic doll
Mailbox
Dog flea roll bed
Egg separator
Swimming pool covers
Console set
Ship models
High chair
Plastic jar caps
Christmas cards
Quilts
Decorative signs
Seahorses
Sheets and pillow cases
Home design book
Tropical plants
Tapestries
Food timers
Luau party kit
Coffee maker
Child's alphabet plate
Paperweight dice
Zodiac perfume
Monograms
Serving tray
Rings
Windowsill garden
Walnut bowl
Napkin holder
Space pen
Floral afghan
Tub shower treads
Genuine diamonds

Wetting preventors
Underwear
Cakes
Moon plate
Dried wheat
French police cape
Decorative phone
Cooking utensils
Silver draw pads
Dog "Train-O-Mats"
Twin bed bridge
Marble stain remover
Rosewood stand
Watchband calendar
Irish handkerchiefs
Fur scatter rugs
Turbans
Interior decorating course

Beauty bleach
Airplane kit
Photo blow-up poster
Dog deodorizer
Back brace
Marble accessories
Sauna bath
Bras
Pin cushions
Dress hangers
TV pole stands
Outdoor antenna
Door plaques
Door peeper
Cat litter box
Dinosaur skeletons
Personalized memo pads

About 225 items have been listed here—all taken from a single issue of one of the Shelter Group magazines. Think of the many additional products found in other issues and of the thousands of articles advertised in other publications. All this points up the tremendous range of items covered by the mail order field.

Gift items can be advertised effectively in many media. Like other products, the choice of publication is contingent on many factors: male or female; age; income; tastes. Unless a person has an intimate knowledge of the unique habits, preferences, individual outlook, and hobbies of the potential recipient of a present, he is likely to choose the wrong gift. This happens all too often and, consequently, countless gifts are never used. To play it safe, many persons give the man or woman "who has everything" something of a general nature. A man is likely to receive a necktie and a woman a box of candy or a bottle of perfume, but even such ordinary objects may not coincide with the tastes of the recipients. The necktie might be too flashy, the candy too rich, and the perfume too sweet.

The publications that carry the greatest number of gift items are the Shelter Group magazines like *House Beautiful* and *House and Garden*. As explained previously, they are read by women in the higher income brackets—women who entertain a great deal and lead active social lives. They are constantly under obligation to give presents on various occasions.

Since the deadline for most national magazines to accept advertising is six to eight weeks in advance of publication, it is sometimes expedient to advertise in Sunday newspaper supplements in order to catch pre-holiday business. These supplements, which can also be very effective, usually close 30 days in advance.

Business Gifts Sell in Quantity

Businessmen are obligated to give gifts to customers, especially at Christmas. The value of the gift is generally commensurate with the amount of business they receive, or expect, from certain clients. Some businesses divide their list into two or three groups—small, medium, and large customers. The mail order man can only handle this kind of business if he is in a position to sell gifts at wholesale prices or at a substantial discount on quantity orders. Such prospects might be industrial firms, publishers or service businesses, such as advertising agencies. Publications such as *Wall Street Journal,* and the *New York Times* (Business Section) provide good advertising media.

Banks are gift buyers, too, especially those offering presents to new depositors upon opening an account. Banking magazines would naturally carry such advertisements.

Consider also the free gifts that mail order firms, as well as retailers, so often offer in their ads. You can sell other mail order houses such gifts if you have the products and if your prices are low enough.

Finally, the house-to-house agent often uses the free gift as a door-opener. The Fuller Brush representatives have been doing this successfully for many decades. The specialty salesmen can be reached through those special magazines mentioned in the chapter on "The Specialty Salesman—A Mail Order Prospect."

The boom in C.D. Certificates has opened a tremendous market for gifts.

African wood carvings, especially novel ones, have been popular for years and make excellent gifts. Some are exotic and grotesque, others like these are more conservative and can fit harmoniously into virtually any decor. Naturally, the wider the possible applications, the greater the sales potential. The ad appeared in *McCall's Needlework & Crafts*.

The gift giver generally looks for something that will be appreciated because it is unusual—something that will be used over a long period—something that will serve as a beautiful reminder of the generous giver. This Firefly Lamp fills the bill nicely.

Some items fall into the gift category because the average person is not likely to purchase them for himself. This practical wallet is a year-round seller since it serves a dual purpose as a gift and as a product of everyday use. It was advertised in *House & Garden*.

Men's gifts that are different are more difficult to locate than novel gifts for women. To use the old cliche, the Pipe-smoker's dream is truly "for the man who has everything". The ad ran in *House Beautiful* as a tip to wives confronted with the tough problem of finding a gift which hubby would enjoy.

JEWELRY—A MARKET THAT GLITTERS

More than 200,000 people in the United States wear jewelry of some kind—men, women, children—even babies. The market is tremendous—almost three billion dollars in sales. Of course, they do not all order by mail because 25,000 stores sell jewelry.

In order to get around the store competition, one must either underprice them (which is not always difficult because most jewelry stores operate on a big markup), or you must offer prospects novel jewelry not usually found in stores.

When selecting items in this field, one must consider the class of merchandise. Is it made of metal other than gold or silver? If silver, is it plated or sterling? If gold, is it plated, 14 or 18 karat gold? If the jewelry features a stone, is it a genuine diamond or a rhinestone. If a pearl, is it real, cultured, or manufactured?

A mail order man must also consider the differences in tastes. The mass of women with small to moderate incomes will be inclined to purchase plated and cheaper costume jewelry, while others will wear nothing but the real thing. Some women are conservative while others go the opposite extreme and wear bold and flamboyant jewelry. Additional factors are age, social standing, and special occasions for wearing certain kinds of jewelry. For example, a pin that is worn on a plain tailored suit will not be appropriate on an evening gown. The jewelry market is also subject to style changes and trends which must be watched. When considering such merchandise, it is wiser to enter the market while the style demand is in its ascendancy rather than to take a chance advertising the style after it has hit its peak.

Many mail order men achieve success offering just one or two items, but the bigger operators take into consideration the wide range of taste, so they offer a diversified selection. Only a large ad can display an assortment of jewelry. Since this might be too costly for all but prosperous firms, smaller organizations have been solving this problem by featuring just a few items in a single ad. These serve as indicators of the types and prices of the merchandise. In the same ad, a catalog is offered, either free or at a small price. Even if the jewelry featured in the ad does not sell sufficiently to pay for the ad, the merchandise sold from the catalog generally shows a profit.

The author is familiar with several cases like this. One firm specialized in solid gold charms. Several leaders were advertised in better class women's magazines and 25¢ was asked for a catalog which showed over a thousand different charms. The catalog cost the firm $1 a copy. At first the catalog was offered at 50¢ and the firm took a 50¢ loss in order to get more catalogs into the hands of prospects. Later they reduced the catalog price to 25¢. They figured that it paid to take a greater loss on the catalog because it would be offset by the greater catalog distribution. The more catalogs in the hands of customers, the more sales would be realized and the greater the ultimate profit. Yet it was considered inadvisable to offer a free catalog. There are too many curious youngsters and "free loaders" who would write for the catalog.

Most of the cheaper costume jewelry worn by women is advertised in women's mass media such as the Romance-Confession-True Story-Radio-TV-Movie type magazines listed in the chapter, "My Fair Lady: A Major Market," also in weekly tabloids.

Better jewelry, on the other hand, is usually advertised in magazines such as *Glamour, Harper's Bazaar, Redbook, Mademoiselle, Seventeen,* the *Shelter Group,* and *Sunset.* Moderate-priced jewelry would also be advertised in such publications plus the more general kind of women's magazines such as *Women's Day* and *Ladies Home Journal.* In the case of artificial diamonds, it has been found that they sell best when the average age of readers of the publication is 35.

Jewelry for men and women has also been sold successfully in the magazine supplements of big city newspapers, which have wide national distribution, the best known being the *New York Times.* Such supplements are read by both sexes. Apparently the women buy jewelry for themselves and as gifts for others, including their husbands, or boy friends. The men are motivated the same way, buying for themselves, their spouses, and others.

Inexpensive men's jewelry would also be advertised in mass media, such as mystery, detective, western, and adventure magazines. Higher priced jewelry would be advertised in magazines such as *Signature* (published by the Diners Club), *Playboy, Esquire,* and *Gentlemen's Quarterly.* Specialized jewelry, such as fraternal rings and pins would naturally be advertised in fraternal magazines such as *Elks, Columbia,* and *Moose.* By the same token, jewelry designed especially for golfers would be featured in magazines such as *Golf Digest, Golf Magazine,* and *Golf World,* while jewelry of a religious nature would be advertised in religious magazines, such as *Christian Herald, Catholic Digest, The Lutheran* and *Presbyterian Survey.*

Thus, when surveying the jewelry market for items to sell by mail, take into consideration all the factors discussed such as style trends, who is likely to wear the jewelry, on which occasions and what he or she is willing to pay for it. Although the market is tremendous, it requires intensive study and discrimination to select profitable products.

What Mail Order Jewelry Item to Sell

Among the items broadly classified as jewelry by the trade are the following which can be sold through mail order:

Watches and **Watchbands**
Clocks
Diamonds (Genuine and synthetic)
Rings (Gold, Silver, other metals)
Earrings (Gold, Silver, Jeweled, other metals)
Necklaces (Gold, Silver, Jeweled, other material)
Pendants (Gold, Silver with genuine or synthetic stones)
Pins, Brooches (Gold, Silver, and other metals)
Tie Tacs and **Tie Clips** (Gold, Silver, and other metals)
Cuff Links (Gold, Silver, Jeweled, and other metals)

Watches and Watchbands

While retail jewelers do their greatest business in brand-name watches, mail order operators, on the other hand, are generally more successful with imported or off-brand watches. Such items are highly competitive pricewise. If the watches offered contain out-standingly novel features—always excellent drawing cards—the matter of price becomes less important. The same principles just stated for watches are equally true of watchbands.

Despite the glamour of the time-telling wrist computers and the superaccuracy of electronic watches, the inexpensive pin-lever wrist watch is still America's best seller. Between 50 and 70 percent of the approximately 46 million watches sold each year in this country are pin-lever types retailing for less than $25.00. Unlike more expensive watches with jeweled components, pin-levers have metal bearings and contacts at critical wear points. They are less accurate and wear out faster, but have kept their share of the market by taking on a new fashion note.

"For many women, and for some men as well, watches are a fashion accessory rather than just a straight timepiece," said the executive of a company making watches which retail from $15.00 to $50.00.

"Before the watch wears out," he said, "the fashion has worn itself out. Because of the rapid change in fashions in today's market, watches, like automobiles, have a built-in obsolescence."

"Over the past few years," he added, "the fashions for women's watches has changed from necklacelike pendants to oversized go-go watches to plastic bangle-type watches."

"The day when a company could do business with a plain round or square watch is long past," said another spokesman for a large watch company whose watches range from a $12.00 brand to the more than $2000.00 model. "Today," he continued, "watch cases come in all shapes and sizes, made of everything from tortoise shell to sterling silver to polished hardwood."

"These novelty watches, made with relatively inexpensive materials, are styled and bought primarily for look rather than function," he said.

A number of small companies have sprung up in recent years to capitalize on this swiftly changing market.

Clocks

For the same reason, clocks are highly competitive, unless they feature innovations. Cuckoo clocks; grandfather clocks, either large or miniature; the latest digital clocks, ceiling clocks, clock kits, and many other kinds have been sold successfully by mail.

Diamonds

Genuine diamonds are not commonly sold by mail because of the high price tag and the reluctance of many persons to purchase "sight unseen" objects that entail considerable expense. Nevertheless, there are some firms that sell genuine diamonds successfully by mail. Apparently, among the 226 million U.S. inhabitants, there are a sufficient number with the wherewithal and the craving for real diamonds who will risk large sums through the mail. Advertisements in this field do not as a rule mention price but strongly sell prospects on the idea that they will receive unusual value for their money. Prospects are then urged to send for a catalog which offers a fine selection with sufficient sales talk to close sales.

Artificial Diamonds

This market, speaking from a mail order standpoint, is far greater than the one just described. It is a growing business; some eight to ten or more firms have been advertising simulated diamonds effectively during recent years. Such stones are claimed to look as brilliant and charming as the real thing, with 58 hand-cut facets, and are guaranteed not to scratch, chip, break or discolor. Most of the ads, following the sales description, merely state the price per carat, without the cost of the setting. The quality of simulated diamonds varies considerbly which affects the selling price per carat. Firms in this field do not as a rule attempt to make sales directly from the ads but depend on the catalog, which offers a choice of settings, to complete the sale. The ads simply quote a price per carat. Such sales are likely to average around $75.00. In any case, the markup is substantial.

Offering credit, either time payments or credit cards, helps induce sales. Some firms in this special field have been running the same ads month after month for years and their business has been thriving. In this case, if the price per carat_is kept low enough, the literature need not be elaborate or expensive. It might consist of as little as eight small pages which a firm can afford to give away —even to "free loaders." Artificial diamonds, in their settings, seem to sell best when the average age of the readers in publications carrying such ads is approximately 35.

Other Jewelry

Surveys show that the volume of sales with respect to the kind of jewelry sold is in the following order:

Earrings—These items lead the market. They come in countless varieties—large and small, gold and silver, with or without precious or semi-precious stones, traditional or contemporary designs—pierced or otherwise, geometrical, floral, animal replicas, and whatnot. In short, in this permissive era in which we live, almost anything goes. There are Oriental, Mexican, South American, Indian, along with other exotic earrings from other areas of the globe—anything that creative designers can conceive to please the fancy of my fair lady.

Pins and brooches—Like earrings, the variety of pins and brooches on the market is endless. Frequently, two sales can be made at the cost of one when a single ad offers a set of earrings and a pin or brooch for less than if one person bought both at their individual regular prices. It seems that almost everyone, including the affluent, seeks to take advantage of a bargain.

Bracelets—Like pins, brooches, and earrings, bracelets come in an infinite number of styles and are worn as the occasion demands. For example, a bracelet worn during the business hours is not likely to be worn at a dance or a wedding. Consequently, the dressers of women contain an array of bracelets for both formal and informal occasions. This, in itself, reflects a vast sales potential for mail order operators.

Rings—Unlike most pieces of jewelry, rings can be for either male or female. There are engagements rings, friendship rings, wedding rings, birthstone rings, fraternal rings, religious rings, astrology rings, all of which widen the market. In most cases, it is wiser to employ class rather than mass publications. In other words, the sales volume will be greater and you will be paying far less waste circulation if rings designed for special affiliated types are advertised in publications read only by those persons within the particular group; for example: engagement and wedding rings would be advertised in bride magazines; religious rings in religious publications; fraternal rings in fraternal magazines.

Charms—These are sold with or without bracelets. The market is tremendous because sentimental as well as generous persons are prone to express their affections with gifts of charms, generally to celebrate certain personal happy events that have taken place in the life of the recipient. Such charms almost invariably are solid gold.

Pendants—Like earrings, pendants come in an infinite variety of designs, some fashioned to express a particular affiliation or personal sentiment; others to complete a dress ensemble or merely to enhance the beauty or vanity of the wearer.

Necklaces—Pearl necklaces, cultured or otherwise, lead the rest in popularity. Necklaces of every description are worn manifestly by all ages from infants to grandmothers. Amusingly enough, in this modern era, they are even seen on the so-called avant garde—as well as on cute little puppies.

Tie tacs, tie clasps, and cuff links—Besides rings, these are among the few jewelry embellishments allotted to the male of the species which can be worn without attracting undue attention. In addition to being ornamental, they serve a utilitarian purpose, keeping ties and cuffs in the proper place. They are probably bought as gifts by both men and women as much as by the men themselves who wear them.

Sales Differ by Regions

Surveys have revealed that charms are in the greatest demand in the West and South Central states and do poorly in the Southeast, while charm sales are average in the North Central and Northeast. Women's reactions to bracelets are different: The response is great in the Northeast and Southeast but not so heavy in the Central and Western regions. Pins sell well in the Northeast but sales are 50% less in the West.

For further details of the jewelry market, write to the author of this book. A survey will be sent to you gratis.

Sell Through Agents

Bear in mind that additional sales can be realized by engaging house-to-house salesmen. Over a dozen firms selling jewelry through this means seem to be doing a thriving business. Month after month their ads appear, some full pages in color. For a list of salesmanship magazines to employ see the chapter "The Specialty Salesman—A Mail Order Prospect."

EYE POPPERS
FOR OUR 25th ANNIVERSARY

A CREATIVITY FOR OUR CUSTOMERS

Realistic colorful Glass Eyes with our own cleverly designed Rings. Pendants. Keyrings. Cufflinks. 14 Kt Gold Pierced Earrings. Shipped on beautiful display stand.

RACK JOBBERS STORE TO STORE SALESMEN—This will open their eyes!

In our jeweled department we make a variety of styles of Rings. including Poison Ring. Combined Bracelet Ring. newly designed Earrings in drops and buttons. stunning manipulated handmade Jeweled Pins. also various Christmas Pins in exciting colors. beautifully styled.
A sure-fire idea for the teen crowd and matured females. Prices as low as $5.75 to $18.00 per doz. for quick easy sales with more than 100% profit mark-up direct from manufacturer.
Send for catalog sheet and price list.

DOLGIN NOVELTY CO., Dept. SS
5 West 31st St., New York, N.Y. 10001

This ad virtually pops out of the page for two reasons: first it represents the most modern of modern jewelry; and secondly, those hypnotic eyes in the picture transfix the reader like red traffic lights. The appeal here is not to consumers but to specialty salesmen and rack jobbers. The ad appeared in both *Specialty Salesman* and *Salesman's Opportunity* magazines.

The old saying, "a picture is worth a thousand words," is vividly expressed here even though the illustration carries only a half dozen words, more or less. Obviously, the petal shaped earrings are almost ample to complete the sales message. All that was needed was to state what they were made of and the price. Enough said! . . . At least in this kind of ad.

Petal Earrings
pierced

Sterling $20.00
14K Gold $95.00

VISA MC Post Pd

Becky Thatcher
Designer/Craftsman

Box 111
Glen Arbor, MI 49636
(616) 334-3826

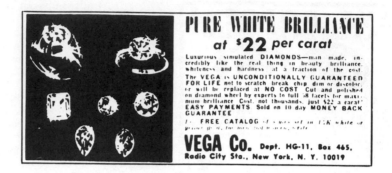

When an ad like the above runs in a dozen or more national publications, month after month for years, you do not ask: Is it profitable? Each ad is keyed, so that every dollar of the thousands spent is accounted for. This is a sound investment. If diamonds are a woman's best friend, artifical diamonds can be a mail order man's friend as well.

ADVERTISING TO "GREEN THUMB" PROSPECTS

Persons who have gardens are natural prospects for mail order items. This is because seed and bulb houses are generally at distant points and are virtually the only sources offering large diversified catalogs in which a variety of plants, seeds, bulbs, trees, and shrubs are presented.

The home gardener is found in rural areas, in suburbs, and even in large cities. Growing plants is an expression of one's love for nature and beauty and it can become a compulsive hobby. For some it involves pride of possession, for others it may mean keeping up with the Joneses, while to still others it is a means of staying active and fit as well as a pleasant diversion. Many successful home gardeners act as consultants to their neighbors, influencing them in their purchase of fertilizers, seed, plants, bulbs, hose, and gardening implements.

The home gardener is generally engaged in home maintenance as well, which induces him to purchase countless products, such as paint, tools, plumbing tools, cement, shingles, to avoid the cost of carpenters, contractors, painters, roofers, and plumbers.

The mail order operator who tackles this lucrative field should take time to study its peculiarities if he is not already acquainted with the needs of gardeners. This does not mean one must make a profound study of botany to succeed; however, one must analyze the seasonal conditions. It is not too important to know the difference between an ajuka and a pachysandra plant, but you should know that there is a time to plant certain seeds, a time to sow lawns, a time for ground cover plants and to plant bulbs, shrubs, and trees. Certain species of the same genus may require early or late planting. Most of this information is available in seed catalogs and in various books on the subject. It is also covered in garden magazines and on the garden pages of newspapers.

In general, it is advisable to advertise outdoor plants during the warm, growing season; and indoor, potted plants during the fall and winter. The more exotic plants usually sell better by mail than the common variety unless one is in a position to offer bargains.

The home gardener can be reached both through newspapers and magazines. He is prone to study the gardening section of the big city newspapers, especially the Sunday editions. They keep him posted by providing gardening hints in keeping with seasonal conditions. As for magazines, some of his favorites are:

Publication	Circulation
Horticulture	102,803
Organic Gardening & Farming	1,310,948
Flower & Garden Magazine	570,309
American Rose Garden	18,196
The Family Food Garden	333,045
The Gardener	9,000

The home gardener is also inclined to read the Shelter Group magazines listed in a previous chapter, "My Fair Lady: A Major Market." You will notice that such publishers realize that the home owner is also an enthusiastic garden owner. That is why this type of magazine combines both home and garden in their titles, for example *House & Garden* and *Better Homes & Gardens.*

Thus, your market for gardeners takes in a vast number of suburbanites, small town dwellers, and urbanites who raise potted plants on window sills. And don't forget the other extreme—those who live in rural areas and possess considerable acreage. With careful planning and judicious selection of items to advertise, you can soon gain a foothold in this fertile field—selling beauty to nature lovers. It is likely to provide a mental lift while adding to your bank account.

... *brand new concept in lighting!*
SPECTACULAR NEW
"Fountain of Light"
provides thrilling decorative drama in all colors of your choice **$19⁹⁸**

LOW INTRODUCTORY PRICE: ONLY

Now turn your living room . . . your buffet table . . . your bar . . . your patio into an exquisite moonlit fairy-land with 200 tiny lights cascading from three graceful tiers. If your guests don't gasp in awe, your money refunded! Actually an exciting application of cold light "Fiber Optics," developed through space-age science.
All light comes from one concealed source in stem. The sprays themselves contain no heat, no electricity, are so safe, they may actually be placed in water.
Change the color of fountain to match your table linens or mood: Almost 2 ft. tall, smokey amber tower, walnut-grained base lovely with all decor. UL-approved. By Poly Optics, Inc. 19.98 plus $1.00 postage and handling charges.

Prompt shipment. Satisfaction guaranteed.
Send check or money order—sorry no C.O.D.'s
FREE: color catalog of unique gifts with order.

HOBI ᴵⁿᶜ   Dept. O-89
7 Delaware Drive · Lake Success, N.Y. 11040

An item as arresting as this is a first rate attention getter. Notice the choice of words in the headings: *new concept, spectacular, thrilling decorative drama.* The ad writer created a theatrical setting for the prospect to gaze at with admiration.

CHARMING

HOLIDAY

CONE

TREE

Make this easily for your own front door or wall, or for gifts or profit. Kit includes exotic cones & pods from around the world, red velvet bow, adhesive, everything. Rounded tree is 22 x 10" assembled. A gorgeous showpiece!
TK, $7.75 + 75¢ postage.
write for Krafty Kits brochure
Z A M B O N I ' S
Longview 7, Wash. 98632

Picture a woman reading *House & Garden* magazine about a month before Christmas when she is already in the grip of the Yuletide spirit. As she turns to a page in which this Cone Tree is advertised, her eyes are bound to fix on this gorgeous holiday symbol. No wonder it sells well!

SELL COURSES PROFITABLY

Mail order courses, better known as "Correspondence Schools," have been in existence since long before the turn of the century and will no doubt continue beyond the turn of the next century. The International Business School is probably the oldest and most successful. The La Salle Institute is also a long established correspondence school doing a big business. Both offer an extremely diversified list of vocations and professions all of which are covered in their courses.

Numerous other concerns operating in this field concentrate on single courses. Thus, the person who aims to improve his station in life by acquiring knowledge of a subject which leads to a profession, a vocation, or specifically to a good paying job has a wide variety of courses to choose from. There are courses in law, journalism, radio and TV repairing, watch repairing, interior decorating, barbering, rug weaving, hotel management, nursing, cooking, operating heavy equipment, and a host of other subjects, including courses in mail order advertising. The advent of computers has opened a new field for courses in computer programming.

Some, particularly the one-volume affairs, are sold as a complete course at a specific price, paid in advance; others, especially those issued in a series of lessons, usually sell on an installment plan basis, with a special discount if the cost of the entire course is paid in advance. A number of firms sell inexpensive one-volume courses to mail order operators for resale to consumers. As in the case of the one-volume how-to books or manuals, discussed in an earlier chapter, such courses are modest affairs, consiting of mimeographed or offset sheets bound in a loose-leaf binder. Courses of this kind might sell for as little as a few dollars up to several hundred dollars, depending on the subject, the number of pages and illustrations.

The object of the cautious operator is to select a course to sell by mail that is not too competitive, yet fills a need. Courses are promoted with ads of all sizes: from full pages, even double-spreads, down to one inch, and with classified ads. When large ads are used, the full story can be told so that follow-up literature is not always necessary. Even here, however, the costly courses, selling for over a hundred dollars, do not mention price but instead invite requests for further information. Some of the large concerns follow up such requests with literature and with a local sales representative. Naturally, the larger the ad, the greater is the impact on prospects. A small ad, display or classified, that cannot give a complete sales pitch generally invites inquiries and depends on the follow-up to land the order. The exception is the low price course that sells for a few dollars. Here the feeling is that a person is willing to risk a small cash advance to buy a course he desires although he knows little about its content or value.

Courses appealing to the general public are advertised effectively in Sunday newspaper magazine supplements as well as in large circulation tabloids, such as *National Enquirer*. Display ads appealing to the more literate prospects are likely to get good results in the book review section of Sunday papers or in magazines such as *Saturday Review, New Republic, The Nation, Harpers, The Atlantic,* and the like. Display ads offering specialized courses are placed in special interest publications. For example, courses in mechanics would be advertised in magazines such as *Popular Mechanics, Popular Science Monthly,* and *Mechanix Illustrated*. General courses advertised in these magazines often appeal to those readers who are interested in changing their field of work. In general, however, law courses are advertised most effectively in legal publications; radio and TV courses in magazines read by radio-TV repairmen and experimenters; engineering courses in professional magazines read by aspiring engineers.

Classified ads featuring courses of a general nature should be placed in large circulation magazines; for example, the Quality Men's Group for courses appealing to men and the Quality Women's Group for courses appealing to women. A list of national magazines that carry classified advertising is found in a previous chapter, "Classified Versus Display Ads."

The market for selling courses is about as large as any other. Millions of ambitious people are ready to take self-improvement courses; especially those who lack a college education or are dissatisfied with the kind of work they do or the pay they receive. They are reaching out for a better future. Let your ads kindle the desire of such people to get ahead in this competitive world.

APPEAL TO BOOKISH PROSPECTS

Among the thousands of titles published, there are only certain types of books suitable for mail order advertising. Fiction and general nonfiction reading are usually sold best through book clubs—to be discussed later.

How-to books are in greatest demand. Evidently, many people

are eager to learn something new for practical purposes or purely for their own enjoyment. Some of these books help people to get a job or prepare them for a new occupation. Others appeal to those interested in changing aspects of their personality or improving their physical appearance. There are titles intended to supplement academic education and those which teach people how to make home repairs; others can train people in the fundamentals of acquiring a new hobby or in improving their mastery of an old one.

Other books that can be sold successfully are of an informative nature either because they are topical (such as books about landing on the moon) or because they appeal to persons with special interests (such as books on electronics, theology, the occult).

Books can be promoted through classified as well as display advertising because the ads do not necessarily require illustrations. An adequate description of its contents, in terms of the readers' benefits, will get results. A classified ad that simply offers a catalog of books, free or otherwise, is rarely successful. It is too commonplace for the average reader to notice or to act on. If you possess a catalog of many titles, it is better to select one, two, or more to be advertised as leaders, and then use your catalog as a stuffer to induce additional sales.

When you select a title for a leader, be sure it is one with a specific down-to-earth appeal rather than of a general nature. For example, a title such as *Learn Stock Market Tricks* might be better than *Learn Business Finance* or *Hypnosis—Self-taught* is better than *The Facts About Occult Science*. Similarly, *How to Win a Husband* is better than *Develop Your Personality*.

In the case of display ads, size is a determining factor in whether to include an illustration of the book. Smaller ads can command attention by playing up the title in large type. For example, a heading *Wild Game Cookbook* will serve as a stopper because it is an unusual type of cookbook. Therefore, if advertised in an appropriate outdoor magazine read by hunters, it should sell well, even without a picture of the book.

Ads, whether large or small, that merely list titles can be effective if—1) the overall heading is potent and carries sufficient punch to catch the eye of the reader, such as MUST BOOKS FOR EVERY ENGINEER and 2) the titles are well known, such as *Random House Dictionary* and 3) the titles are so descriptive as to require little or no explantion, such as *How to Reduce Without Dieting*.

Large display ads in this field win attention if a single book is dramatized with a dynamic heading or if a single book dominates the page while the rest of the space is devoted to less important books.

Book clubs, such as The Book of the Month Club and the Literary Guild have long been successful. They have encouraged many imitators. Book lovers can now join The Book Find Club, The Nostalgia Book Club. The History Book Club, The Scientific Book Club, The Jewish Book Club, The Catholic Book Club, and many others. Most of these clubs offer an inducement to new members. The come-on appeal is usually an offer of one or more books, at a greatly reduced price to encourage joining. The list price of books offered, sometimes for as little as $1 might be worth as much as $50. However, the catch is that a new member is obligated to buy a minimum of three or four books at regular prices (plus postage and handling charges) during the first year. Book clubs are growing by leaps and bounds; much of it is due to their frequent use of provocative dynamic promotional literature. Yet there is still room for more book clubs. It just takes a bit of imagination and managerial ability to organize one.

Another angle, which is often employed by the smaller mail order firms, is to offer to supply books of any title published at attractive discounts. Some companies charge no fee for the service, others charge approximately $5 for membership.

Individual books of a general nature as well as book clubs are advertised effectively in the book review section of Sunday newspapers of which the New York Times Book Review is the leader. Other media recommended are Saturday Review, New York Review of Books, Writer's Digest, Harpers, The Atlantic, The New Republic, and The Nation. Books of a specialized type would manifestly be advertised in their special fields; that is, a law book in legal publications, an engineering book in a magazine read by a specific type of engineer; a Catholic book in Catholic publications, etc.

Classified book ads have a wide range of publications to draw on including those read by the general public as well as those in specific areas restricted to certain types of readers.

The paperback market has grown dramatically in recent years. There is also a field for selling books wholesale by mail. Of course, one must have access to the right source of supply since the price offered must allow for resale profit. Publications in this field include the following:

Publication	Circulation
Christian Bookseller Librarian	9,755
Magazine & Bookseller	29,003
The Booklist	34,738
Catholic Library World	37,723

Publication	Circulation
American Bookseller	7,834
Publisher's Weekly	37,775
School Library Media Quarterly	12,408

Many small mail order concerns do a good business selling so-called books which are actually mimeographed or offset sheets bound in loose-leaf fashion. Some firms refer to such offerings as "manuscripts;" this is itself a misnomer because a manuscript is a typewritten script which an author offers to a publisher in the hope that he will print it. Better refer to it as a manual, particularly if it is not large enough to warrant the name "book."

A list of publishers who specialize in supplying books to sell by mail will be found in a previous chapter covering sources of mail order products.

This ad makes a special appeal to librarians and colleges. It has been so instrumental in selling books that the advertisers keep repeating it. It shows that where there is an opportunity to unload an item in quantity, why confine yourself to single sales?

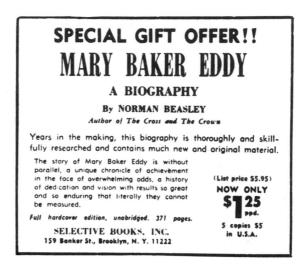

World-famous personalities advertise themselves, but when biographies are written about them and offered at drastic price reductions, as in this instance, the ads have double impact. This advertisement appeared in the most appropriate medium conceivable, the *Christian Science Monitor*, the paper and the cause which Mrs. Eddy created. This ad pulled orders for over 500 books.

With the poster craze at its peak, this advertiser found a ready market for his collection of over 1,000 different subjects. The listing includes posters depicting many important historical and social events, dating from pre-colonial days to 1900. The ads were run in a score of publications. This full page has been repeated a number of times in the *New Republic*.

SELL RUBBER STAMPS AND LABELS

There are numerous concerns selling rubber stamps and labels. Repeatedly these firms run ads side by side in the same publications, indicating that they are all making some profit out of their advertising investment. The market is so vast, covering both regular consumers as well as businessmen, that despite competition there is always room for another firm to enter the business.

Even if the profit on a single ad is small, the same ad in a number of publications adds up to substantial earnings. Suppose, for the sake of argument, a firm ran an ad that cost $100 on which a profit of only $10 was made. In the first place, the firm earned 10 percent on the investment which is better than they could earn from a savings account. Secondly, if funds are available, the company could palce the same ad in 100 publications simultaneously which, on the basis of the same percentage of earnings, would net them $1,000 every time the ad was inserted. This is not mere theory or a pipe dream, but is apparently being practiced by many mail order concerns.

The Rubber Stamp Business

This type of operation draws many newcomers to the mail order field because it requires little initial investment. It can be conducted at home, full time or spare time. Little space is required for equipment and supplies—perhaps a spare room, garage, or basement. Your classified telephone directory may list the firms which sell rubber stamp presses and accessories. If not, consult *Thomas' Register of Manufacturers*, which is carried by most libraries and banks.

You might consider the following three ways to develop business:

1. Sell through door-to-door agents and specialty salesmen, as described in the chapter on this kind of outlet. While it is necessary to sell at a price low enough to allow them to resell at a profit, they are likely to send you quantity orders which, in the aggregate, will net you more than single sale orders to consumers and businessmen.

2. Sell to consumers and business firms by means of mail order advertising. The mail order section of large newspapers is one good area. Magazines such as *Popular Mechanics*, *Popular Sci-*

ence *Monthly, Mechanix Illustrated,* and *Science and Mechanics* are also good media. Besides, there are numerous other business publications that can be employed effectively. The ads need not be large.

3. Send mailing pieces to business firms, preferably the more substantial ones which are likely to use many different kinds of stamps and which employ numerous persons who could use them. Such lists are readily available from list brokers.

The profits in rubber stamps are excellent, especially if you manufacture the stamps yourself. Many firms in the field sell at a price five times their cost which gives them a far greater margin of profit than the average mail order man realizes selling other lines.

You need not confine yourself to the conventional rectangular rubber stamps that carry a name and address. You can offer a variety of types. There are hand stamps, date stamps, numbering stamps, and others of all sizes for all purposes. Once you get your feet wet in this field, you will dive deeper and uncover new ways to make sales.

Printed Labels

This field is closely allied to the rubber stamp business; as a matter of fact some rubber stamp companies sell both or offer labels free as a leader for inducing stamp orders.

The market for name and address labels is just as vast, and the price competition is as keen as in the rubber stamp business. If the mail order man is a printer as well, he can more readily cut in on price competition, otherwise he must find a printer who will sharpen his pencil and work closely with him on prices to build a volume business. Such operations are usually profitable if the printer can "gang up" a large number of individual orders; that is, print them all side by side and one under the other, on the same large sheet in one operation and then cut them apart.

Printed labels come plain and fancy. The fancier type are printed in gold or gold stripes or display a photo. The selling price is commensurate with the embellishments.

The firm that does a business in name-and-address labels can easily spread to other common printed items, such as business cards in ordinary or raised letters, letterheads, personal stationery, billheads, brochures, booklets. This business has another advantage in that it leads to steady repeat sales.

To sum up the rubber stamp and printed label business potential, there are three salient advantages: 1) vast market; 2) wide profit margin; 3) repeat sales. On the other side of the coin, there is also one disadvantage; namely, keen competition. Here is where your ingenuity enters. Either your offering must be novel or your price must be irresistibly low, or your ads must be so cleverly prepared that they stand head and shoulders above competitive ads. This is quite a challenge, but a man with courage, the strength of his convictions and stick-to-itiveness can surely make the hurdles.

GOOD HEALTH IS ALSO
A COMMODITY

Although physiologists tell us that the human body consists of 90 percent water, the average person is concerned with what goes on in the remaining 10 percent.

Children and adolescents generally take good health for granted, except for the small number who are disabled. A healthy adult is inclined to feel the same way, but as he matures he becomes increasingly aware of his physical condition. Assuming that he does not suffer from a particular illness, he must do something to stay fit. He may feel that he should eat certain foods, exercise to keep trim or reduce. And, of course, there are the hypochondriacs who imagine all sorts of bodily ills.

All this opens up a vast field for mail order concerns. There are vitamins to sell and all manner of dietary health foods.

For those who think they require special exercise, the market offers a host of equipment, including home style bicycles, exercisers, dumbells, barbells, gym bars, exercise cushions, or vibrators.

For those who want to reduce, if not for medical reasons but merely for appearance, and this applies to women more than men— there are exercises, appetite depressants, pills, massages, reducing courses, and a variety of other means. This is where the mail order advertiser must watch his step and make no positive claims that this or that will reduce weight. He can safely state that it will help someone to reduce or that the method advertised, plus a specific diet, might help a person achieve weight loss or he can quote a testimonial by a user who speaks of the weight she had lost as a result of the remedy offered.

Every word in this kind of advertising, as well as any other item of a medicinal nature advertised, should be examined thoroughly to avoid unpleasant governmental interference. Such authorities as the Federal Trade Commission, the Food and Drug Administration, the Post Office, perhaps the district attorney and the Better Business Bureau are on the alert for false advertising. This should not alarm one to the point that he refrains from advertising a reducing product. It just means that one must be more on guard to avoid trouble. If a mail order man has any misgivings on the subject, he can relieve his anxiety by consulting an attorney who specializes in governmental regulations, or submit his ads to the proper authorities before running them. In any case, if ordered to modify an ad, do so rather than fight the order. It's a case of discretion being the better part of valor. The advertising of reducing products and any substance to be taken internally, such as tablets, pills, and liquids, is more likely to be scrutinized by the authorities than other remedial devices of an external nature. Yet the author is familiar with accounts in this field which operate successfully year after year and earn as much as $50,000 annually doing just that. There are numerous mail order remedies for those with ailments. In the early days of advertising all sorts of nostrums and quack medicines were offered to the credulous public. Cure-alls for multiple ailments were common. Most advertising of this kind has since been suppressed by government agencies and by a wiser public and is therefore refused by reputable publications. However, some products that offer relief for various ailments are still accepted.

Among the fast-selling health products are braces, hernia supports, exercisers, and pain relievers of many kinds. The market for these products is extremely large and notwithstanding considerable competition, all the mail order concerns handling them seem to prosper. On a single page of a magazine circulated in small towns, three competitive hernia and rupture truss advertisers were recently spotted. All these companies seem to be doing well, as evidenced by their continuing to advertise year after year.

The denture field is a burgeoning one. With the tremendous increase in the number of older people in the population, there are more denture wearers than ever. This means that millions seek relief from loose and stained false teeth.

Aging also affects hearing and seeing so that hearing aid batteries and battery rechargers to keep the batteries working at full strength are selling well. Consequently, eyeglasses, eye washes, eyeglass cleaners, and related products are excellent mail order items.

In the woman's field, merchandise that might be regarded as cosmetics because of the bearing on feminine beauty are actually health products and might be considered at this point. Women deeply concerned over facial blemishes, wrinkles. Countless products are on the market to take advantage of the urge to be rid of any blemish which deprives my fair lady of her feminine appeal. Notwithstanding considerable competition, there is always room for more products of this sort. In order to get a foothold in this field one must find a new angle and then dramatize it to the fullest degree.

Medicinal preparations are best advertised in small town and farm publications and almanacs such as *Grit* and *Capper's Weekly*. The chapter, "The Farmer—A Natural Mail Order Buyer," provides a partial list of such publications.

Thus, the health market as a whole is worth pursuing because mankind is obsessed with his own well-being. There are psychological factors involved which offer a real challenge for an enterprising mail order man.

A List of Remedies Advertised in One Magazine

Tranquillizers
Diaper Rash Relief
Athletic's Foot Relief
Relief from Burning
Hearing Aids
Rupture Truss
Prostate Wetting Protection
Eyeglasses
Hearing Aid Batteries
Asthma Relief
Denture Tightener
Hemorrhoid Shrinker
Drinking Cure
Ear Wax Remover
Itching Relief
Headache Remover
Pile Relief
Aching Back Relief
Eye Strain Relief
Corn Remover
Denture Cleaner
Sore Lip Relief
Hay Fever Relief
Energy Booster
Breath Deodorant
Pimple Relief
Eczema Relief

Acne Relief
Anti-Perspirant
Finger Fungicide
Varicose Ulcer Relief
Oily Skin Blemishes
Laxatives
Salvo for Boils
Health Books
Anti-Gas Tablets
Tooth Ache Relief
Bladder Irritation Relief
Rheumatism Relief
Weight Gainer
Cold Poltice
Weight Reducer
Vitamins
Pregnancy Lubricant
Pain Remover
Pregnancy Tablets
Menstruation Relief
Blood Enricher
Ingrown Nail Cutter
Hair and Scalp Conditioner
Dandruff Remover
Cough Relief
Infection Antiseptic
Kidney Acid Remover

Eye Wash	Neuralgia Relief
Abdomen Flattener	Sore Gums Relief
Aspirin	Groin Itch Relief
Germicide	Denture Repairer
Insect Bite Liniment	Sunburn Relief
Stomach Pain Remover	Pin Worm Itch Relief

Everybody, especially the female of the species, wants to look trim. That is why most of the many types of exercisers sell so well. What is a better eye catcher than the shapely limbs of the beautiful model shown above. The ad appeared in the *New York Times* Magazine.

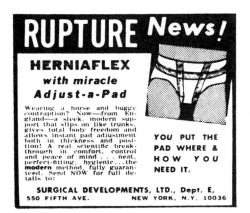
The market for rupture trusses must be considerable, judging by the steady advertising of several firms producing them. Turn to any issue of such publications as *Grit, Elks, Philadelphia Inquirer's Today Magazine, Capper's Weekly,* and you will probably see similar ads. Oftentimes two or three competitive products appear side-by-side.

PET FIELD CAN BE
YOUR BEST FRIEND

When one speaks of pets, the first ones that come to mind are dogs and cats. There are millions of them throughout the United States and a multitude of products that their owners buy for them!

But dogs and cats, while the most common pets, do not constitute the entire market. Other familiar pets sold by mail are birds, fish, turtles, alligators, and rabbits. Less common but widely sold are guinea pigs, chameleons, seahorses, hamsters, ant farms, snakes, mice, raccoons skunks, monkeys, and even ponies.

If you plan to sell pets by mail it is wise to follow the old cliché: "Sell the sizzle and not the steak." In short, promote a pleasant mental picture of the enjoyment to be derived from owning a pet, just like the ads selling vacation houses which do not stress land and houses but "sunshine," "joy," "a heavenly haven of leisure," "a place to raise children," and "to lengthen one's life." In the case of a bird you might speak of "bringing cheery song into your home" or "consider the pleasure you will derive from teaching the parrot to talk." In the case of a small animal, "think of the joy you will get romping around the lawn with this little rascal."

One mail order man has been selling chameleons successfully to boys for years. A single ad in *Boy's Life* brought him $2,000 worth of business. Oddly enough, the chameleons have been sold primarily to create sales of meal worms to feed the chameleons. Thus, there was more profit in the meal-worm repeat business than in the original sale of chameleons.

Therefore, if you enter the pet business, bear in mind that the food and accessories used in connection with pets might constitute a larger market than the sale of the pets themselves.

One trade mgazine in the pet field reported that in a recent year 474 new products were introduced. The publication also indicated a steady annual increase in new products entering the market. Below are 65 pet products advertised in a recent single issue of a pet publication.

Pet Products

Dog diner	Dog clippers
Pet toys	Dog mattresses
Itching relief	Grooming dryers
Fungus infection relief	Dog and cat foods
Food supplements	Aquarium pumps

Kennels
Meal worms
Aquarium foods
Pet stain removers
Dog pillows
Animal cages
Pain removers
Dog combs
Ear clamps
Pet crates
Dog pajamas
Breeders
Aquarium heaters
Gravel filters
Fish tank filters
Deodorants
Fish bags
Fish tanks
Cat litter
Snail killers
Bird cage covers
Dog carts
Bird nests
Bird houses
Dog and cat beds
Shrimp eggs
Litter scoops

Grooming shears
Dog ear bows
Dog pants
Dog tights
Bird foods
Pet books
Aquarium coral
Aquarium decorations
Fish foods
Aquarium tubing
Dog leads
Dog collars
Pet carriers
Skin and coat conditioners
Dog brushes
Nail trimmers
Grooming gloves
Pet shampoo
Dry cleaning lotions
Musical bird perch
Appetite stimulant
Foot toughener
Pet bedding
Hair shedding relief
Flea collars
Fish flakes
Catnip
Aquatic plants

There are hundreds of other products which pet owners buy. Countless success stories can be told in this connection. One that comes to mind is a case where a mail order man had a furniture manufacturer make special cat beds, which were beautiful miniatures of beds people sleep in. For a single cat there was a lovely canopied bed and, for more than one cat, a double-bunk bed with ladder, a miniature of the type boys use. Cute pictures of the cats, either lying in bed or climbing the ladder to the upper bunk, were placed in a cat magazine. The advertising was successful. No wonder! Think of the thrill which a cat lover gets seeing the photos of the cats asleep and pictures her own kitties nestled in such snug, adorable beds. Instead of placing her kittens in a kitchen or basement box, now she can lead them to her own bedroom to the miniature bed which also serves as a piece of artistic furniture. Incidentally, the cats love such royal treatment.

This is an obvious example of a mail order man who used his imagination to establish a unique place in the mail order pet market. Of course, run-of-the-mill merchandise can also be sold; however, one can more readily win an edge on competition when the product is distinctly novel. This is a point worth pondering.

Among the consumer magazines in the pet field are the following:

Publication	Circulation
Cat Fancy	98,543
Cats Magazine	66,070
Dog Fancy	76,322
Dog World	60,538
Hounds and Hunting	10,670
Pure Breed Dogs	44,281
American Field	13,707
Today's Animal News	27,528

In addition to the above, pets and their accessories can be sold effectively when advertised in outdoor magazines such as *Field and Stream*, *Sports Afield*, and *Outdoor Life* because most sportsmen own dogs. Such publications carry special Dog Kennel and Pet Sections with unusually low rates—about 25 percent of the rates covering ads in the body of the magazines. Their large circulations—over a million—make it possible to acquire a considerable amount of orders.

Most newspapers feature Pet Sections, especially on Sundays. The *New York Times* devotes the greater part of a page to pet advertising, both classified and display, therefore, it is a good place to run pet ads.

A manufacturer or distributor who is in a position to offer pet merchandise by mail to the pet trade for resale should consider the following trade magazines:

Publication	Circulation
Pet Age	17,060
Pet Dealer	11,747
Pets/Supplies/Marketing	13,168

Thus, the pet and pet product market whether considered in terms of selling to consumers or to wholesalers, is so extensive that the mail order neophyte, seeking products to promote, should weigh the merits of this field against others under consideration. After all, huge industries have been created based on the pet market potentials.

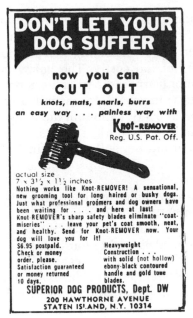

Dog lovers at last found a tool for a pet's "knotty" problems. The heading of the above ad appealed to the owner's sympathy. The advertiser was tempted to show a picture of a dog, but decided it would be superfluous because the ad was placed in *Dog World Magazine.*

What has a more universal appeal than a cute, playful kitten? Very few will pass by this ad without first stopping to see what puss is up to. The ad, which appeared in the *New York Times Magazine Supplement,* makes good use of the relatively small space.

STAMPS AND COINS PRODUCE DOLLARS TOO!

Among the oldest hobbies are stamp and coin collecting. It is indulged in by persons of all ages—from six-year-old youngsters to retired people. There is a fascination about collecting items from foreign lands, especially if they are not too costly. The hobby is educational as well. The stamp collector learns more from his hobby about foreign countries than he acquires in school. He assimilates a knowledge of geography which takes in every nation on the globe. He learns about their flora and fauna, their historical events, their heroes and prominent persons. Apart from the collector of foreign stamps is the person who specializes in U.S. stamps, who learns much about events in his own country.

The coin collector also acquires a knowledge of history. In addition, he learns about monetary denominations used in foreign lands and their exchange value. If he collects U.S. coins, he becomes familiar with the famous people who have contributed to our history.

To most persons, stamp and coin collecting is regarded as a pleasant pastime. Others consider the effort as an act of business and indulge in buying and selling with a view to realizing a profit. Such persons at times spend a fortune acquiring rare stamps and coins.

Starting a Stamp Business

It is not difficult to start a business in this field, yet it takes considerable patience as well as good judgment to pursue it and establish it on a profitable basis. You can begin by purchasing stamps in wholesale lots. The stamp pages of newspapers carry many offerings. Once you acquire a stock—even a modest one—of miscellaneous stamps (or coins), assort them by countries and study the standard catalogs to determine the value of each. (A leading stamp catalog is published by Minkus which recently took over the well-known Scott Stamp Co.)

You are now ready to sell on an "approval" basis, as follows: You advertise either bargain stamps or various sensational stamps representing topical events. These act as your leaders or "come-ons," as some people call them. Even if you do not realize a profit on the stamps sold through the ad itself, you gain by acquiring names of stamp collectors for subsequent mailings. At this point you will be ready to send your customers stamps on approval; that is, you will send them a small group of stamps, neatly mounted in a little packet envelope for the customer to examine and select what appeals to him. Each stamp will carry a price, generally below catalog price. The customer pays for what he selects and returns the rest to you. It has been found that few stamp collectors can resist the temptation of buying stamps that come to their homes. Under the circumstances, a person is prone to purchase stamps which he would not think of buying if he had to go to a store to pick them out.

There is a little risk to such an "approval" operation because some customers neglect to send you money or return unwanted stamps. Of course, there is always a very small percentage who are downright dishonest. However, the percentage of losses is so low that one can afford the risk. By the law of averages, the profits from normal business will far outweigh the losses.

Selling Coins

A coin business is operated in similar fashion, except that coins are generally not sold on an "approval" basis. Some firms advertise a leader in the form of a spectacular bargain as a means of building a list of prospects. Such names are then followed up periodically with forceful literature featuring various kind of coins.

Whether selling stamps or coins, the real profits come in the repeat business resulting from constant new offerings which are sent to prospects. Thus, sales and profits are gradually pyramided over a period of time and you find yourself in a volume business in which every mail brings in a stack of orders. It means that the patient mail order man must keep many irons in the fire so that the law of averages will operate in his favor. Naturally, the more funds you can put into the business—the more publications you use, and the larger the ads—the quicker will you establish your business on a volume basis.

Both newspapers and magazines can be employed effectively to develop business. Most of the large circulation papers carry active stamp pages. The more conservative papers like the New York Times are better for reaching the experienced, sophisticated collector. Magazines used to attract the younger element are Boy's Life and comic magazines. Publications such as Redbook and those in the Shelter Group would be employed in selling to adult women; while advertising in publications like Popular Mechanics and the fraternal magazines would be effective in selling stamps and coins to men.

There is no doubt that money can be made in this field if it is tackled in the right manner. Just check the ads of stamp and coin mail order firms. You will see for yourself that the same firms hammer away month after month, indicating that a profitable business in each case is going on; otherwise they would soon quit. Are you ready for a long, steady growing pull, with potential profits always in sight? Then this is a business to consider!

FIRST COINS MINTED SINCE 1955 at fabulous SAN FRANCISCO mint. Collectors prized set of 10 bright uncirculated coins as illust. 3.95   25¢ p.p. FREE $1 luxurious velvet lined presentation case embossed in 24 KT. gold. SAVE 10 double sets 37.50 $1 p.p. 20 sets $70 p.p.d. 50 sets $165 p.p.d. COLLECTORS SPECIAL—Last silver coins minted. Five coins bright uncirculated 1964 sets from Phila. or Denver mint. Cent to scarce J.F.K. all silver ½ dollar 2.95   25¢ p.p. FREE 50¢ gift case. Double set both mints 10 coins 5.50   . 25¢ p.p. FREE $1 presentation case. SAVE—10 double sets $49.50 p.p.d. Twenty sets $95 p.p.d. 50 sets $225 p.p.d. Money back guarantee. Write for FREE catalog. Member Retail Coin Dealers Assn.—Amer. Numis'. Assn. Est. 1947. Novel Numismatics Dept. 1A 31-2nd Ave., N.Y.C., N.Y. 10003

The advertiser in this case knew that it was necessary to provide essential facts about his coins if he wished to make sales. He managed to cover the subject fully in his lengthy copy within a small space. The ad ran in *Popular Science.*

This one-half inch display ad exemplifies effective utilization of minimal space: the attention-getting headline, set in reverse type, and the maximum amount of copy. Most publications refuse to accept display ads of less than one inch in depth. *Boys Life,* in which this ad appeared, is an exception, and the advertiser has made the most of the opportunity.

FOOD FOR THOUGHTFUL EARNINGS

The mail order market in foods has a high potential, notwithstanding the great number of grocery stores, supermarkets, and delicatessans available to the public. The foods sold by mail are not usually staples but more often are exotic foods appealing to gourmets or special diet foods for food faddists, health-conscious individuals, and hypochondriacs.

Gourmet Foods

The gourmet generally has a passion for good food and he will travel far and wide to find restaurants that will appease his epicurian palate. Moreover, he does not mind paying a good price for out-of-the-ordinary food advertised by mail order concerns. A well-prepared mail order ad will describe delicious, luscious food so eloquently that the gourmet is likely to drool at the mouth just reading about it. Gourmet-appealing foods might come from specific geographic regions in the United States and abroad, noted for their excellence in preparing certain kinds of food.

For example, there are Swiss and Danish cheeses, Texas fruit cake, French and California wines, Hawaiian dishes, Chinese moon cakes, and Louisiana pepper sauce, etc. On this page is a list of some gourmet foods advertised recently. This list indicates the wide range of appetizing foods available in this country. In another land the gourmet is tempted by fried grasshoppers, canned rattlesnake meat, chocolate covered ants, and canned hippopotamus—all of which shows that food is only a matter of taste.

The specific magazines read by the gourmet are:

Publication	Circulation
Bon Appetit	1,073,280
Gourmet	618,026
Cuisine	701,282

Other publications that carry much mail order advertising pertaining to exotic foods are Sunset Magazines and the rest of the Shelter Group magazines listed in the chapter,"My Fair Lady: A Major Market." The Sunday magazine sections of large city papers, which circulate nationally as well as locally, are also recommended for this type of advertising. A partial list of gourmet products advertised are:

Italian cheese	Italian tomale loaf
Smithfield hams	Danish butter cookies
Prime steaks	Shelled pecans
Chinese tea	Hearts of artichoke
California almonds	Louisiana pepper sauce
Swiss cheese fondue	London dry gin
Italian olive oil	Porcelain cooking dishes
Gourmet seasoned red wine	Wild rice

California fruits and nuts
Bitters
Smoked turkey
Liver sausage
Swiss non-alcoholic beverages
Hawaiian Luau party dishes
Salted imported nuts
French Abbey imported cheese
Havarth Danish cheese
California avocado
Cocktail lemons
Cooking pans
Rumnog
Artichoke party dip
South African lobster tails
Atlantic she-crab soup
Rare coffees
Calimmyrne figs
Chianti
Scotch
Japanese steaks
Vodka
Monk's bread
Danish cheese
Champagne
Orange marmalade
Mexican drinks
Jamaica liqueur
French Camenbert cheese
Filet mignon
Chinese moon cakes

Scotch cheese
Coffee grinder
French wines
Hungarian tokaji
Aszer Spanish brandy
Jamaica rum
Soups
Rhine wine
Cocktails
Maine jams and jellies
Hollandaise sauce
Green beans
New Orleans coffee
Whiskey Sour cakes
Florida citrus
Chocolate shells
Corn spears
Grecian water server
Port
Benedictine
Italian wines
Lamb
Canadian whiskies
Gelatin
Pecans
Vermouth
Cognac
Sherry
Burgundy wine
Texas fruit cake
Mushroom gift package

Health Foods

Health food shops are found in most cities, indicating that there is sufficient demand to keep them in business; however, the smaller towns and rural areas cannot as a rule support this kind of specialty store. The inhabitants of such sparsely populated areas must depend on mail order to fill their needs. Thus, the mail order man can be sure of a market if he finds the right foods to advertise. He must bear in mind that his prospects are health oriented people—those who eat special kinds of foods for definite purposes. Perhaps they want to

Here is an ad that appeals to the gourmet and to people intrigued by exotic dishes. The hand gives the picture dramatic action; the close-up of the food whets the appetite; and the type panel, superimposed on the photo, is in position to be read quickly.

This mail order advertiser, who is an Oriental, emphasizes that the tea which people enjoy in Chinese restaurants can now be savored at home. It is a strong point. The ad appeared in the Magazine Supplement of the *New York Times*.

Wild Game Cook Book

It has all the answers of how to change wild game and fowl into tempting delights. Plus interesting lore. This is a book sportsmen have been waiting for. Besides the recipes, it has information on cooking, cooking terms, weights and measures, temperatures, stuffings, stuffing secrets, gravy secrets, sauces and sauce secrets, campfires, barbeque grills, dressing wild game, safety and allied subjects.
Here's a nice bit of information and humor: "Left side of hams (take with a grain of salt) . . . left hams are better because when a hog scratches his right side, he does a Charleston with his right foot and that develops muscles. When he scratches his left flank, he does a gentle shimmy against tree or post. Therefore the right side ham is far more muscular and less tender than that from the left side of the same hog." Now to the game. Do you know what a brant is? It's a species of wild duck. One is told how to cook it. There are four recipes for coot. There's one for crow. Here are more than 20 recipes for a variety of wild ducks. We also find rail, snipe, wild turkey, woodcock, and then comes the big game section. The longest list of recipes falls under venison, but we also find antelope, wild boar, reindeer, elephant, bear. In the small game class is the armadillo, then the beaver, hare, muskrat, opossum porcupine (it can be boiled or sauteed and is said to be good), rabbit, raccoon (we're told how to smoke a raccoon, too!), squirrel—and Martin Rywell, the author, believes that roast or broiled skunk is good . . . for here it is! Then comes the woodchuck.
The sauce secrets are interesting. We're told of a double boiler method and then comes the sauce recipes. Under "miscellaneous" we find directions for making campfire bread. Also, that unique explanation, mentioned earlier, explaining why the left side of a ham is better than the right. There is much down-to-earth information here. *"Martin Rywell has combed the nation for recipes and written an informative cook book."*—San Francisco News   **$1.95**
plus 15¢ for mailing.

PIONEER PRESS, Dept. AR, Harriman, Tenn. 37748

The gourmet and his cook who are constantly in search of exotic delicacies welcome a book of this sort as well as the way it is described. The words, both humorous and serious, are redolent with campfire smells. They envelop the reader in the great outdoors where game is the topic of conversation. The book has been advertised for years. This ad from *American Rifleman* is typical.

PRIME FILET MIGNON

not for sale
(in any market, that is)

These primest of filet mignon are not sold in any market. Yet, you've probably enjoyed them in luxury restaurants. They're Prime Pfaelzer steaks—tender, flavorful, aged. Enjoy them at home, or have them sent as gifts with personalized card. Quick-frozen, packed in dry ice for guaranteed perfect arrival.

Box of 16—
6 oz. each, 1¼" thick.   #30405   **$36**
Now available in Canada.   Shipped Prepaid

Write for free catalog listing more than 200 gift items

pfaelzer *(pronounced FELZER)* **BROTHERS**

Dept. NM • Chicago, Ill. 60632 • YARDS 7-7100
© P.B. 1968

While the clever heading in this ad excites interest, the illustration is designed to stir the appetite of the gourmet. The text, also, is colorful as well as convincing. Whenever picture, heading, and copy are so closely knit that a unified sales pitch strikes prospects forcefully, an abundance of sales generally follows.

diet because they are too stout or too thin, or their doctor advised them to eat specific foods, or they are always concerned about their health. They talk about vitamins A, B, C, and so on, carbohydrates and proteins with as much enthusiasm as others discussing baseball or TV shows. The calorie counters and weight watchers are wonderful prospects.

Magazines in this field with their circulation figures follow:

Magazines	Circulation
Better Nutrition	557,508
Better Health	107,000
Accent on Living	16,888
Let's Live	141,027
Prevention	2,555,030
Weight Watchers Magazine	740,235
Bestways	219,200
American Health	368,260

The phrase health foods as used in this chapter deals with nutrition and diet.

A list of health food products that are commonly advertised follows:

Fillet Slimmers
Shrimps
Crab Meat
Non-Fat Dry Milk
Blender for Weight Watchers
Seasoning and Broth
Red Clover Tea
Air-Vent Gloves
Food Supplements
Bone Meal
Boof Liver
Garlic Oil
Wheatgerm
Garlic Parsley Tablets
Dolomite Tablets
Protein Tablets
Amino Acid Tablets
Brewers Yeast
Super Kelp
Papaya Peppermint

Broiler
Diet Macaroni
Diet Spaghetti
No-calorie sugars
Vitamins (all types)
Lecithin Tablets
Peppermint Tea
Laurel Leaf Tea
Lavender Flower Tea
Licorice Root Tea
Linden Flower Tea
Mullein Leaf Tea
Pink Hybiscus Tea
Plantain Tea
Rosemary Leaf Tea
Sage Tea
Slippery Elm Tea
St. John's Wort Tea
Strawberry Leaf Tea
Uva Ursi Tea

Alfalfa Tablets
Acerola Cherries
Digestive Starches
Calcium Lactate
Health Food Booklet
Energy Boosters
Althea Root Tea
Anise Seed Tea
Blueberry Leaf Tea
Buck Thorn Tea
Catnip Tea
Celery Seed Tea
Centaury Seed Tea
Corn Silk Tea
Couch Grass Tea
Dandelion Leaf Tea
Dulse Leaf Tea
Elder Flower Tea
Fennel Seed Tea
Gentian Root Tea
Hops Tea
Horehound Herb Tea
Huckleberry Leaf Tea
Irish Moss Tea
Juniper Berry Tea
Knot Grass Tea

Violet Leaf Tea
Watercress Tea
White Oak Bark Tea
Alfalfa Tea
Alfalfa Mint Tea
Chamomile Tea
Comfrey Leaf Tea
Comfrey Root Tea
Fenugreek Tea
Herb Blend Tea
Horse Tail Tea
Oat Straw Tea
Papaya Tea
Rose Hips Tea
Sarsparilla Tea
Sassafras Bark Tea
Shave Grass Tea
Spearmint Tea
Brown Rice Cakes
Low Calorie Yogurt
Liquid Wheat Germ Oil
Iodine Tablets
Organic Iron Tablets
Zohey Tablets
Chlorophyll Tablets
Cod Liver Oil Tablets

The Wonder Wheel has been widely advertised and no doubt sells well; or there would be no point in continuing. The Slimmer Belt, featured in the same ad, benefits by the popularity of the Exerciser. This ad appeared in *House Beautiful* as well as in many other publications.

RECORDS AND CASSETTES MAKE CASH WHIRL AROUND

With the advent of high fidelity, the record business and the equipment that goes with the "platters," experienced an amazing renaissance. When everyone thought that the record field was as extinct as the dodo because of films, radio, and TV, the unexpected rebirth occurred. And the business keeps mushrooming with improvements in equipment—amplifiers, receivers, speakers, tapes, and especially cassettes which in recent years often outsell records.

The record field is divided broadly into two branches—popular and classical, according to taste. As a rule, the younger set prefers popular records while the more mature fancy the classics. A fresh interest has sprung up in "speaking records," most of which are of a literary, classical, dramatic, or educational nature and, consequently, appeal to more serious persons.

Records and tapes can be advertised singly or in albums, or they can be sold as groups of a specific type, such as folk songs, sacred music, or hillbilly selections. They can also be advertised as listings of diversified popular or classical numbers.

Record clubs have sprung up just like book clubs. Most of them offer a choice of popular and classical in records, tapes, or cassettes. But, like the book clubs, as a lure they usually offer a number of records at a ridiculously low price as a subscription starter, contingent on the purchase of a number of records during the year, at list or near-list prices. Some record clubs ask from $3 to $5 as a fee for joining, which entitles the subscriber to purchase any records at a drastic discount.

The youth market—buyers of pop, rock and roll, and the like—has grown tremendously, almost overshadowing the serious classical field. The market for children's records is also widespread and active.

The firm that sells records, tapes, and cassettes by mail has the opportunity of selling sound equipment, speakers, microphones, earphones, and other accessories, as well as record holders, files, tables, shelving, cleaners, and envelopes. These items can be offered not only to the regular consumers but also to radio, TV, and high fidelity servicemen and experimenters. Whenever a record album is sold, it is smart to insert an accessory stuffer.

If you enter this field, remember that the *label*, in other words the reputation of the record producer—RCA, Columbia, Westminster, Mercury, Deutsche Grammophon, and the like—often carries as much weight as the selection. Many consumers are partial to certain labels because of their confidence in their quality and they will pay list prices for their favorite label rather than purchase the same selection on another label at a discount.

The record business hums with current activity. It reflects week-to-week happenings in the theatre, opera, concert, movies, and TV. There is money in this field for the mail order man who knows what goes on and how to take advantage of the situation.

Remember the good old days of the player piano? This ad stirs up those nostalgic emotions and satisfies the longing for folk music. It has warmth, humor, attractiveness, and price appeal—a combination that sells. The ad appeared in *Better Homes and Gardens,* a magazine of over 8,000,000 circulation.

THE FARMER—A NATURAL
MAIL ORDER BUYER

From its very inception, mail order businessmen started to sell to hardy Americans who lived on farms. This was natural because roads were poor and village stores were inadequate for even everyday needs. Farmers who had to take time out to travel up to twenty miles on horseback or by cart or carriage, over rough dirt roads found it easier to order by mail. The mail order houses that sprang up in the early days knew that they were in the saddle of a galloping market. Sears-Roebuck, Montgomery Ward, and other early operators mushroomed into the big firms that exist today.

In virtually every farmhouse, women study the catalogs to find out what wearing apparel is fashionable, while the men look through them for tools, garden implements, fencing, paint, seeds, and almost everything that makes up a farm—farmhouse and barn.

Farmers have always been economy-minded because of the difficulty of making a living from the soil in the face of unpredictable weather conditions, fluctuating market prices, mortgages, and rising taxes. Even in today's more prosperous economy, the farmer tends to be thrifty. Therefore, when you try to sell him merchandise through advertising, be sure to convince him of your sincerity and your desire to provide honest value. Once you have his confidence, especially after his first purchase, you have made a friend and a steady customer. Never betray that confidence if you wish to develop a solid following among farmers. Taking every factor into consideration, your job of selling the farmer is easier than selling to urbanites. He has already been educated to buy by mail and he still continues this practice despite modern paved roads, fast cars, and shopping centers.

During the growing season the farmer is likely to purchase whatever helps to make crops and livestock thrive. After the harvest season, the farmer is inclined to "mend his fences," so in the fall and winter he fixes whatever needs repair. When spring comes around, he can spend all of his time outdoors again without worrying about leaky roofs, loose shingles, or broken fences. Of course, during the months when all the repairs are made, he orders many items by mail—ladders, tools, paint, farm implements, plumbing supplies, roofing material, and a host of other items. This offers a tremendous opportunity to the alert mail order operator.

Bear in mind that seasonal conditions in various parts of the country differ. For example, the farther south you go, the earlier and longer the growing season will be, while the reverse is true as you travel north. Study the farm papers to gain insight into what concerns a farmer during a given period, examine the ads to get an idea of what he is most likely to buy.

As in any other business venture, the more intensely you study the field the more you analyze the thinking of those who till the soil, the better are your chances of success. It is a highly interesting field and well worth cultivating as a sales objective.

What Is Read Down on the Farm

Farmers' main concern is the crops and livestock and so they read specific farm magazines that show them how to improve their output and make more money. They are also concerned with market conditions, government subsidies and news in general.

The farm publications can be divided into four broad categories: 1) national publications; 2) regional publications; 3) state publications; 4) crops and livestock publications. Space does not permit listing all of the more than 300 magazines. Only those with the largest circulations are supplied here:

A. National Farm Magazines	Circulation
Progressive Farmer	685,977
Successful Farmering	606,088
American Agriculturist	70,198
Farm Journal	1,012,930
Prairie Farmer	197,031
The Farmer	152,270

B. Regional Farm Magazines	Circulation
Midwest Farm Paper Unit	618,141
Northwest Farm Paper Unit	117,359
South West Farm Press	81,843
Western Farm Paper Unit	153,801
Capper's Weekly	413,707

C. State Farm Papers

	Circulation
California Farmer	58,177
Ohio Farmer	103,028
Harvest State Farm Paper Unit	393,996
Kansas Farmer	69,846
Michigan Farmer	74,489
Wallaces Farmer (Iowa)	113,802
Nebraska Farmer	16,960
Pennsylvania Farmer	75,092

D. Crop & Livestock Publications

	Circulation
Hoard's Dairyman	202,852
The Drover's Journal	54,305
Beef	121,512
The Crower	19,882
American Fruit Grower	50,613
Cotton Farming	45,141
The Peanut Farmer	12,817
Rice Farming	11,778
Soybean Digest	150,942

The above indicates that a special farm paper is available for almost every type of crop or livestock.

Other farm groups include rural electrification associations, farm organizations, cooperatives, and educational clubs, each of which has its own publication. Typical ones follow:

Other Farm Publications

	Circulation
Farm Weekly	59,083
National 4-H News	65,780
Cooperative Farmer	202,362
Pacific Grange Farm Group	97,042
Tennessee Farm Bureau News	224,139

Farm Almanacs

The almanacs date back over a hundred years. Farmers still read them avidly as indicated by the large circulation. Since most of them are annuals, the advertisements placed in them have a long pull. Generally, a volume of orders follows several weeks after the almanacs come off press. Then a steady flow of sales follows throughout the year and sometimes even longer. Ads featuring appropriate items are highly productive.

The names and circulation figures for the major almanacs follow:

Magazine	Circulation
Grier's Almanac	3,000,100
Old Farmers Almanac	2,685,156
Blum's Farmer & Planter's Almanac	400,000
J. Gruber's Almanac	214,028
Old Moores Almanac	350,000

LEAKY ROOF? Tough "SUPER STURDY" sticks even to wet roofs. Covers any flat roof. Waterproof. Lasts for years. Better than tar. Can't crack, shrink, melt. Ideal for total re-roofing or emergency patching. Just brush on! Save up to 75% eliminating skilled labor. Write for details. THE ROBERTSON CO., Dept. GC 3119½ Court U. Ensley, Birmingham, Ala. 35208

This little ad has been running for years in *Progressive Farmer* and has never stopped pulling. It is proof that even a tiny ad in a big magazine is seen, read and acted upon if it offers a sound remedy to a common problem.

PREMIUMS LEAD TO BIG BUSINESS

The mail order man who is also a manufacturer or a distributor, with sales rights, which permit him to buy at a low price and sell wholesale at drastic discounts, can acquire substantial earnings selling premium merchandise.

At the outset it might be well to bear in mind that there are three major types of premiums:

1. The Self-Liquidating Premium

This is the kind that one sees featured on packages and cans of grocery items, especially cereals. The food company buys the premiums at wholesale prices and offers it to the consumer at the same unit cost, contingent on sending in a certain number of box tops. For example, the premium mail order man sells an item in quantity to a cereal manufacturer at 50 percent off the list price of $2. Since it costs the cereal manufacturer $1, he in turn offers it to the consumer for $1. The consumer is expected to send in his box tops at the same time. Thus, everyone benefits—the premium mail order man makes a substantial sale, the cereal concern buys a premium that costs him virtually nothing because of the "self-liquidating" price which serves as an inducement for consumers to buy more of his products, and the consumer gains by being able to purchase a premium at a wholesale price.

Other large users of premiums are gas stations and movie houses. Considering the volume of business generated by premium offers, advertising self-liquidating premiums can lead to a huge source of profits for an enterprising mail order man.

2. The Goodwill Premium

This is the type of premium that is more in the nature of a gift. It is used by industrial concerns, magazine publishers, advertising agencies, and various other kinds of businesses to win the goodwill of customers and prospects. Some are given away throughout the year, such as pens, pencils, rulers, calendars, as well as other small objects. These are generally inexpensive items. However, goodwill items receive their highest distribution at Christmas, when the spirit of giving is at its apogee. Some premiums or gift items are costly, especially those given to executives and other VIP's. One firm advertised an imported Italian leather hand-carved trash basket at $45 and received an order from a bank for 50 baskets which they gave to executives. The small goodwill items which house-to-house salesmen use as "door-openers" were discussed in an earlier chapter.

3. The Free Offer Premium

This type of premium, used commonly by mail order advertisers to promote sales, plays on the emotions of consumers who want something for nothing. Human nature is such that most people, regardless of income, jump at a free offer. The premium-selling firm can "sell" a host of mail order operators if the item carries a low list price.

Other users of free gift premiums are retailers—especially when opening a new store—and banks which offer them to new depositors. It does not take much research to discover more outlets for premium merchandise. A person with imagination as well as sales ability can create new uses for premiums in the minds of prospects. This field is a challenge to go-getters, the opportunity-seekers and other money makers in the field of mail order.

Mailing lists of premium buyers are available. However, premium magazines may bring better results. The leading ones follow:

Publication	Circulation
Incentive Marketing	34,823
Advertising Age	79,417
Premium/Incentive Business	30,233
Potentials in Marketing	67,116

The preceding publications are read largely by the regular premium users, usually big concerns. If you aim to reach special prospects, such as banks, you would advertise in banking magazines. In the case of others, such as gas stations, groceries, motion picture theatres, you would advertise in the special trade publications read by and geared to the readers of those magazines.

The contrast between large and small ads on the same page can be severe. The small is overshadowed by the greater impact and superior position of its larger neighbor. Yet there are times when it is wiser to use small ads in many publications than large ads in few. This ad, appealing to premium users by means of a popular cook book, makes the most of one inch of space.

BUILD VOLUME BY "SELLING" DEALERS

The dealer market can be considered from two aspects: 1) If you have a product which the dealer can use in his store, such as a fixture, equipment or a display piece; 2) if you offer a product which he, in turn, can sell to his customers. In the latter case, you would either be the manufacturer or be in position to buy the article at a low enough cost to allow you to offer it to a dealer so he profits on his resales. So here you have an opportunity to build a volume business by selling in dozen and gross lots.

The advertisements aimed at dealers should be written in simple, straightforward language that is practical in tone and devoid of the kind of emotional rhetoric used in consumer ads. The dealer wants to know primarily what the product is good for, the type of people who buy it, the suggested retail price, his discount, and perhaps the support he will receive from the manufacturers or suppliers in the way of counter and window-display cards, window streamers, cooperative advertising, etc. If you can add a special deal, for example, a free offer if he buys a certain quantity or some other inducement, you will increase your chances of making a sale.

You can reach the dealer either through mailing pieces or publication advertising. Lists of dealers, classified according to the type of stores, are readily available through list houses and list brokers. Such lists are more reliable than consumer lists because the names come from business directories, the *Dun & Bradstreet Directory* or from the classified telephone directories. If you wish to save the expense of buying such lists, and if you have the time as well as the patience to compile them yourself, you can cut down your mailing costs considerably.

The dealer can also be reached through publications in two ways:

1. If you plan to advertise your offering to one or just a few types of dealers, you can keep costs low by selecting the leading publication in each field for your test advertising. If the initial test is successful, you can then use additional magazines in that trade.

2. Should your product be of such a nature that it is necessary to advertise it to a great variety of trades, your costs might be prohibitive, especially if it entails using many publications. The way to get around this situation is to cut horizontally across all trades by employing publications read by all types of businessmen. For example, you might use the *New York Times* (Business Section), and the *Wall Street Journal*.

Ads placed in trade magazines are most effective if they run for a period of time, generally from six months to a year. This is different from consumer advertising where each ad more or less stands on its own feet; that is, a single ad can serve as a fair test of public response to a given item.

Often an ad that ostensibly is aimed at consumers can produce dealer sales as well, just by introducing a line to the effect, "Dealer Inquiries Invited." Alert dealers watch consumer publications to keep in touch with new products being advertised. Many a mail order man who though his major business would come from consumers has been surprised by the big dealer orders resulting from his consumer advertising. In many cases, a single dealer's orders more than paid for a year's advertising.

A case in point is a mail order ad that was placed in a New York newspaper in November for Christmas gift business. The ad was spotted by a department store buyer who liked the article and thought that it would sell well in his store. Since he did not know of any other source from which to obtain the item, he contacted the relatively small mail order firm and placed a substantial order with it.

Generally, the department store buyer is more difficult to sell through advertising than the specialty store man, because he expects salesmen to visit him at the store, and he lacks the time and patience to examine the flood of mailing pieces sent to him, or even to study trade publication ads.

Dealers as a rule have their fingers on the pulse of the buying public in their fields. They watch fashion and economic trends and sense what sells and what is not likely to sell. Because of the vicissitudes of retail selling, they observe conditions from week to week, and even from day to day, to guard against loading themselves up with "shelf warmers." In short, they seek quick turnover profits. Mail order ads should be prepared with this in mind if they are to pull.

A similar approach can be followed if you sell to jobbers, distributors, or wholesalers. Here, of course, it is necessary for you to allow for two profits: one for the wholesaler, another for the retailer.

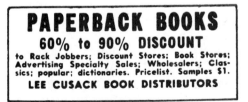

The revival of paperback books has caused phenomenal sales. Paperbacks now outsell hard cover books. This advertiser accepted the theory that a small ad with a big discount offering would outpull a large ad with a smaller discount. It appeals to dealers and wholesalers who are extremely discount-minded.

ADVERTISING OFF-BEAT ITEMS

A host of unconventional products are available for mail order advertising. Such items might include books on hypnotism, yoga, mysticism, occultism, and eroticism. Astrological ornaments, jewelry, and books are also popular in this field.

Products of this type generally sell well in what might be termed sensational weekly tabloids as well as in magazines which appeal to the same class of readers who are prone to seek out-of-the-ordinary stimulation of body and mind. Some of these publications have a preponderance of women readers while with others the reverse is true. As a matter of fact, such publications appeal to a varied and mixed readership, which makes it difficult to define the character of the circulation. In addition to the off-beat items listed above, strange to say, the publications are effective for advertising of more common items which are found in standard publications. A partial listing culled from recent tabloid issues follows:

Body building products	Hair and scalp treatments
Insurance	Loan companies
Reducing tablets	Rupture relief
Corn removers	Treasure hunters
Wigs	Face lifting
Cut price products	Trick party cards
Artifical diamonds	Money-making offers
Binoculars	Exercisers
Chronographs	Insect killers
Magnifying glasses	Magnifying glasses
Anti-mugging spray guns	Chin straps
Wrinkle relief	Correspondence courses

It will be observed that the above list consists of diversified products. Included are gimmicks as well as more ordinary products, but all seem to appeal to an unsophisticated mass audience. Since the editorial content of weekly tabloids and the like is of a sensational nature, to be effective the advertisements should be prepared in the same vein.

The leader in the tabloid field and the most conservative of the lot is the *National Enquirer*. It has a circulation of approximately 5,000,000. It does not accept the more blatant sex ads found in some weekly sensational tabloids. Others, with far smaller circulations, offer commensurately lower rates. A partial list of such weeklies and a few monthlies in this field follows:

National Enquirer	The Star
Front Page Men's Group	Gay
Single Swingers	Gent
Monsters	Nugget
Charlton Action Group	True Men's Stories
Midnight/Globe	Gala Group

National Examiner
Victory Sport's Group
National Bulletin
Rostem's Men's Group
Wild World
Hot Line
Limelight
National Mirror
Confidential Flash
Man's Magazine
Confidential
Whisper
Acme Girlie Group

Monsieur
Dapper
Topper & Rogue
Hush-Hush News
Offbeat
Bedmate
Tab Men's Group
Dude
Saga
Valor
Dilo Western Group
Real West
Combination Men's Group

The emblem-conscious sportsmen responded to this advertisement. Its international aspect, as well as the low price, contributed to its appeal. Appropriately, the ad appeared in the *New York Times* "Shopping Guide" of the Sports Section.

The high crime rate provided the ideal situation for promoting this product. Ads, aimed at specialty salesmen, ran constantly in a half dozen publications. The results have been excellent.

FADS AND GAGS CREATE BUYING TRENDS

A certain type of mail order operator is always ready to hop on to a new fad or buying trend. This is good thinking if you act fast and carry out your advertising program before the public's demand for the product wanes.

A case in point is the landing of a man on the moon. This historical and spectacular event stirred manufacturers, who deal in mail order products, to make innumerable mementos to tie in with the moon landing. There have been wall plaques, medallions, jewelry, watches, color slides, and so on, and the sales have been good, judging by the number of times the ads were repeated.

There are other fads of longer duration. An example is the trend in posters, all sorts of which are advertised. One firm has been spending thousands of dollars every month in national magazines, selling historical posters. His ads, some of which run a full page, merely list the posters depicting events and milestones in United States history. The ads are set in small type to permit maximum listings. The business has been thriving, as exemplified by the continuous advertising schedule.

Another example in the poster field is the photo blowup poster. This type of poster is based on a customer's personal photo blown up to a huge size. Many firms have entered this field. One in particular has been spending tens of thousands of dollars advertising his posters successfully.

In addition, there are psychedelic posters, travel posters, pop art posters, and countless others, nonsensical and serious—all of which are apparently hung up in the homes and offices of consumers, while mail order operators go to their banks with the profits.

Lately, electronic flying insect killers plunged into the market as a summer item. They did so well that a half dozen or more dived in after the first adventurer. One firm known to the author spent about $25,000 in advertising the first summer and came out well ahead. This was quite an achievement considering the short season.

In recent years, there has been a demand for heraldic family coats of arms to be displayed on plaques, clothing, and other objects. This requires research into the family tree. Other trends are antique maps and objects featuring astrological zodiacal sign. Personalized articles also sell well.

Thus, the alert mail order man, who builds his business on popular trends, will find many items to promote, some of short duration and others longer, even running for years.

The fad that is brief is best promoted through newspaper advertising because the forms close but a few days in advance of publication. On the other hand, the fad that is sustained over a longer period can generally be advertised more effectively in national magazines which have a longer life than newspapers.

The selection of publications is contingent on the nature of the items to be advertised. Is it something used by youngsters? Then *Boy's Life* or the comics might be employed. Will it be used by adolescents, by men, by women? Each has its special type of prospects and the publications used must possess a readership keyed to the average purchaser of the item. That is age, sex, tastes, buying habits, education, culture, and income, as discussed previously in this book, are some of the determining factors.

This ad is in step with the extensive poster boom. Judging by the heavy sales of all kinds of posters, it would seem that every householder is discarding paintings, etchings, and prints and replacing them with posters—both comic and serious. The poster shown here is recommended for dens and nurseries.

ANTIQUE GUN PRICES

NEW ILLUSTRATED BOOK gives up-to-date prices of over 2,000 American pistols, revolvers. Describes every make, model from Flintlock through Automatics, plus information how to collect old guns, make money, etc. Valuable for Buying, Selling, Collecting. 100 pages, only $1 postpaid. Order Now.
Department A
PIONEER PRESS, Harriman, Tenn.

Collecting guns, especially the antique type, has become a widespread hobby. This mail order operator not only recognized the trend but took action to get this share of the market. The book described in this ad has been selling for years. The ad appeared in *American Rifleman*.

Above: U.S. Training Ship "Eagle," 21" L x 14½" h. Complete kit with carved wood hull, sewn sails, all fittings and mounting board. Complete $19.95 plus 75¢ shipping.

Ship Models

Ships played a part in the family history of most of us. Perhaps that's why a ship model is so warming to have and so lovely to look at.

Our new fully illustrated 128 page catalog shows over 40 Historic Sailing Ships — all available in kit form and some as finished models. Also shown are more than 100 pictures of Ships and Sea — figureheads, Brass Cannons, and decorative marine items by the score. Catalog 25¢. Send check or M.O. to:

PRESTON'S
100-X Main St. Wharf
Greenport, L. I., N. Y. 11944

SATISFACTION OR MONEY BACK

The ship modeling craze preceded miniature airplane construction, dating far back even before F.D.R. made it famous as his hobby. The market for this type of item still runs strong. The ad appeared in *House Beautiful*.

What's in a name

Coat of Arms Plaque can glorify yours as in days of old!

We'll search out your family's authentic Coat of Arms, make a metal casting of it, paint it by hand in true colors and mount it on a solid walnut plaque —ready to hang! Strikingly handsome with its 3-dimensional shield, helmet & mantling.
9"x13" metal & walnut (as shown) $24.00
6"x8" sculptured metal $14.50

ENGRAVED ENGLISH PEWTER TANKARDS
Your Coat Of Arms, or any other devise you send us a simple sketch of, engraved in old English style . . . along with your name or that of club, school, etc. Half Pint—$14.00. Pint—$17.00. A great gift for the college student.

HERALDIC INSTITUTE,
188 Second Ave.
New York, N.Y. 10003
Dept. T-1

There has been a marked trend toward products that carry a family coat of arms. Some firms in this field offer to search a family tree over many generations to uncover a heraldic emblem representative of the family name. The above ad appeared in the *New York Times Shopping Guide*.

History is being created every day and the average person is aware of this. Therefore, he is influenced by the press which compares current accomplishments with the past. Perhaps that is why items such as Civil War newspapers sell. They also appeal to innumerable collectors of historical documents.

Who ever thought that shopping bags would be subject to fashions? Yet that is what has happened! Flashy-looking tote bags became the rage and so this enterprising advertiser jumped on the profitable bandwagon. The ad was placed in many magazines and newspapers.

An ad which appeared in a widely read paper capitalizes on the public interest in a world-shaking event. What might be considered modest, ordinary-looking containers are suddenly thrust into the blazing limelight by their association with men landing on the moon. What a scoop!

USING SPECIAL ANGLES
TO MAKE SALES

Notwithstanding certain physical and pricing characteristics which play a major part in the success of a product, one must bear in mind that ordinary staple merchandise carried by stores can oftentimes produce substantial business if a special or unique "angle" is devised to put it across. A few examples follow:

Shirts, Shoes, Suits, and Dresses have been sold successfully by mail by offering either extra large or small sizes. The appeal is made to the unusually large or small person who finds it difficult to be properly fitted in stores catering to normal sized trade and which lack an adequate stock of odd sizes.

Hosiery can be sold to teachers in particular at attractive prices. The advertising is directed at teachers because they are inclined to wear out stockings faster than most women and must look right at all times.

Musical instruments designed for boys have been sold effectively by directing the advertising to their fathers who are musicians. The reasoning here is that a musician normally would like his son to follow his father's footsteps by developing an appreciation for music and playing a simple instrument to start with.

Cigarette lighters for the desk, shaped like a gun, failed to sell through appropriate magazines catering to gift buyers but went over big when advertised in gun publications because the readers were gun hobbyists who relished such a symbolic item on their desks.

There are countless other examples to indicate that the product itself is not the only thing needed to make sales. Imagination, deep analysis, and smart tactics are equally important.

This advertiser intrigued women with dual interests; namely, "home sewing" and "fabrics made abroad." The average woman visiting a foreign country seems more concerned with what the shops have to offer than with the scenery. This advertiser satisfied such a longing by bringing world-wide fabrics to American homes. A unique club plan was instituted to accomplish this.

USING TRICKS AND GADGETS

The market is full of interesting attention-getting gadgets to include in your mailings. One can safely state that the average person receives such a large quantity of circulars in the mail that anything reasonable you do to make your mailing stand out above the mass of competitive material is worthwhile. There are pop-ups, plastic and metal gimmicks, gadgets that appeal to the sense of smell, and other useful attention-getters. If used sparingly, they frequently accomplish results, but be careful not to "over-gag" your prospect. Your stunt may be so arresting or so funny that the prospect will not take your offer seriously.

Another thing: watch your costs. What you pay for a gimmick may be far out of proportion to what it will produce in sales.

PREPARING ADVERTISEMENTS

The preparation of strong-pulling mail order ads is generally assigned to a professional advertising man specializing in that field. It takes years of training and definite talent to write good ads. Whether or not you prepare your own ads, there are certain essentials about mail order advertising with which you should be familiar.

Broadly speaking, there are two kinds of mail order ads: one makes a complete sale; the other simply arouses a person's curiosity to the point that he writes for more information, in which case the burden of making the complete sale rests on the mailing piece that follows. The advantage of making a complete sale in an ad is fairly obvious. It saves time, effort, and the expense of follow-up. However, the complete sale ad generally requires more space than an inquiry ad, and for the same reason might cost more. The person who would send in his money for a product without seeing it first, to a firm he knows nothing about, must be convinced beyond a doubt that he is getting desirable merchandise and good value.

Unless the nature of the item and its construction are self-evident—you will need space to describe it adequately. On the other hand, if all you seek are inquiries for more information, than an arresting headline or illustration and a few well-chosen words will suffice to stimulate curiosity. However, you must be careful to ward off letters from "free loaders," for what good are a host of inquiries if they cost you a lot of money in circulars and postage, but bring no orders? One way to discourage those who do not mean business is to require a certain amount in advance—20¢, 35¢, or even more as conditions require—for a catalog or for "postage and handling."

The inquiry ad is also employed for higher-priced articles because, unless you buy very large advertising space, it is difficult to cover all the points of such an article within the space of an ad and to convince a person to send a large sum of money through the mail. An article that sells for, say, over $20 is more likely to require a strong-selling follow-up circular of two to four pages to land the sale.

The large-space ad featuring a number of items is frequently used in the mail order field to resemble a catalog page. In this case, a page ad is broken up into smaller units, each devoted to a different item, which is illustrated and set in small type. Thus, the prospect is given a choice of many articles. This kind of advertising is especially effective if all the items are in the same category and you are using a medium read by a specific group interested in that field. For example, you might have a full-page advertisement of tools in a magazine such as *Popular Mechanics*—or various items used by nurses in a magazine like *Nursing World*. One firm advertised 15 to 20 articles which letter carriers used on their mail delivery trips—such as caps, shirts, raincoats, umbrellas, shoulder pads. The firm used a page every month and the ad brought substantial results.

What Constitutes a Good Ad?

Generally speaking, every ad—mail order or otherwise, classified or display—should do the following:

Attract attention with a headline that is a stopper.

Arouse interest by containing information pertinent to the reader's activities.

Convince by presenting logical, plausible facts showing that the prospect will benefit by the purchase.

Close or get the prospect to act—either order the merchandise or send for information or whatever else you want him to do.

These rules apply to sales letters, circulars, and even to post card mailings. When writing a mail order ad, it is especially important that you conserve words—use short crisp sentences and forceful language. Watch your verbs more than adjectives and adverbs. Active verbs have a way of making an ad more exciting. Even when using words sparingly, it is necessary to describe what you are selling, as well as the terms so completely that the prospect understands every phase of your proposition. Do not leave any questions in his mind that would necessitate correspondence to complete the sale.

Take a hint from a Sears-Roebuck catalog. Notice how thoroughly each item is described. Surely, this multimillion dollar corporation knows how to sell by mail after all these years.

It is better to set the ad in fine type and include *all* the facts than to leave out essential information because you wish the type to be more readable. If space permits, use a picture of the article and one of its application as well. Even when you employ illustrations, it is good policy to use word pictures in your copy. It helps the prospect to visualize hmself using the product, and speeds up the sale. You can even use the phrase, "Picture yourself today using this handy dishwasher. Imagine the time and effort you save as you stack your dishes in the washer, close the door and push the electric switch . . . and no more dishwashing hands to worry you."

KEYING THE ADS

Once you start using more than one publication, it will be necessary to key your ads either in the coupon or in your address at the bottom of your ad; otherwise you will have no way of crediting the returns to the proper medium. Naturally, if you know the source of your sales, as indicated by the key, and the returns show that a publication is profitable, you will be inclined to continue using it, at least until results show otherwise. You can employ your own ingenuity in devising keys to identify ads. Here are some common methods:

1. **Use Department Number:**
   Henry Wadsworth Co., Inc., *Dept. A* 711 Main Street, Memphis, TN

2. **Use Name of Ficitious Person in Company:**
   Mr. Philip Jones, Henry Wadsworth Co., Inc., 711 Main Street, Memphis, TN

3. **Use Different Initial in Company Name:**
   Henry *A.* Wadsworth, Inc., 711 Main Street, Memphis, TN

4. **Use Different Street Address, or Building Number:**
   Henry Wadsworth Co., Inc., *713* Main Street, Memphis, TN

5. **Alter Spelling of Company Name:**
Henry *Wadsworth* Co., Inc., 711 Main Street, Memphis, TN

6. **Use "Studio," "Room," "Desk," "Suite," "Section," etc.:**
Henry Wadsworth Co., Inc., *Room 309*, 711 Main Street, Memphis, TN

7. **Use "Booklet," "Circular," "Folder," etc.:**
Write for *Booklet T*, Henry Wadsworth Co., Inc., 711 Main Street, Memphis, TN

8. **Use Building Number:**
Henry Wadsworth Co., Inc., 44 Wadsworth Building, 711 Main Street, Memphis, TN

9. **Use a Code Number in Corner of Coupon:**
DD 14, Henry Wadsworth Co., Inc., 711 Main Street, Memphis, TN

10. **Use a Letter After the Street Address:**
Henry Wadsworth Co., Inc., 711 - *E* Main Street, Memphis, TN

11. **If Small Town Use Fictitious Streets:**
Henry Wadsworth Co., Inc., *711 Woodside Ave.*, Memphis, TN

12. **Use Name of Post Office as Address:**
Henry Wadsworth Co., Inc., *Downtown Post Office*, Memphis, TN

13. **Use the Names of Members of the Staff in Place of Actual Streets:**
Henry Wadsworth Co., Inc., *Wadsworth Ave.* and Main Street, Memphis, TN

14. **Change Company Name in Each Advertisement:**
Wadsworth *Woodworking* Shop, 711 Main Street, Memphis, TN

15. **Change Title of Officer:**
Mr. Henry Wadsworth, *President*, Henry Wadsworth & Co., Inc., 711 Main Street, Memphis, TN

16. **Use Fictitious Box Number:**
Henry Wadsworth & Co., Inc., *Box 342*, 711 Main Street, Memphis, TN

17. **Use a Different Department Name in Each Advertisement:**
Henry Wadsworth & Co., Inc., *Rush Order Dept.*, 711 Main Street, Memphis, TN

18. **Use a Different Color in Each Ad.**

19. Use a Slightly Different Typeface in Ad.

20. Look for Differences in Size of Coupon, when ad is set by the publication.

21. Use the Initials of the Publication, followed, if you wish, by a numeral to identify the month of issue.

Should you overlook keying a coupon or use a wrong symbol, you may find other ways to identify the publication, if you look sharply. For one thing, turn the coupon over to see what appears on the reverse side. One magazine will generally differ considerably in reading matter or ad that appears in another. You will find other differences: variations in the type style, dotted border, quality and texture of paper, shade of ink.

PREPARING DIRECT MAIL LITERATURE

The value of direct mail literature in mail order selling is fairly apparent. It is an efficient, economical medium wherever:

- speed is a calculable factor;

- the sales story calls for detailed explanation beyond the scope of other media, such as ads in publications, radio and television;

- samples or other supplementary material, such as testimonials, order blanks, return envelopes, must be included in the sales effort;

- circumstances call for a personal communication rather than a general message addressed to a large, diversified audience;

- a valuable personal relationship with your customers has already been established and you are endeavoring to capitalize on this good will;

- your potential prospects are restricted or clearly identifiable by such factors as age, sex, economic status, buying habits, special interests or extra susceptibility.

The success of a mailing campaign depends on these five elements:

1. The desirability of the products, assuming that the price is right.

2. The quality of the list.

3. The effectiveness of the sales story.

4. The attractiveness of the mailing piece.

5. The timeliness of the mailing.

The first two preceding items have already been discussed on previous pages. An attempt to clarify the other points will now be made. Taken as a whole all five elements constitute a well-planned program.

HOW TO WRITE ADS THAT SELL

Most mailings consist of these basic components: Letter, circular or catalogs, order form, return envelope, mailing envelope. Some contain additional pieces such as samples, swatches, bonus offers for quick responses, premiums, testimonials. The essential components will be discussed in the following pages.

The formula for direct mail copy is similar to that for preparing ads. It is sometimes referred to as the "AIDA" formula:

A-ttention
I-nterest
D-esire
A-ction

Some copywriters argue that an effective sales letter or mailing piece should not follow a set formula but should read as though it is spontaneous. That may be true in some instances, but in nine cases out of ten the AIDA formula creeps in even though it may not be apparent on the surface. Enthusiasm is contagious and that is why it is so important to inject it into your copy. This along with sincerity helps to make the prospect feel that you have faith in your merchandise and wish others to share its benefits.

When confronted with a new product to write about, the first step is to analyze it and dig up every salient point about its construction, use, and benefit. Jot these points down and number them in the order of their importance. If convenient, collect pertinent magazines and other data in the same general field as the item for background material. For example, if it is a cosmetic, study literature in the beauty field; if an auto accessory, examine automotive magazines. In this way, you will acquire much information to use as source mate-

This is one of a double, or return, postcard; as a matter of fact, it represents one of a series of six human-interest cards sent to roofing prospects. The reverse side is in the form of a coupon on which the prospect checks off the type of roofing ordered. It is a mailing piece that is exciting enough to stop a person, especially if his roof needs repairs.

rial and at the same time become more familiar with the vernacular and jargon of that field. Moreover, what you write will then carry the stamp of authenticity and authority.

Every copywriter has his own method of preparing a mailing piece. One man will tell you that when he is confronted with the problem of writing about a new product, he places himself in a "brown study" in which he concentrates on that kind of item, to the exclusion of everything else in his consciousness. Then he endeavors to recall every example of forceful copy through which a similar product was marketed. He claims that these reveries invariably produce a fresh idea.

Another man who is visually oriented says that when preparing a circular, he starts with a rough layout built around a strong heading or theme. The pictures fortify the heading which embodies or epitomizes the theme. His copy is then directed to the layout and finally when the copy is completed, he modifies the layout to tie in even more closely with the copy. As a result, copy and layout are so closely knit that both pull together—presenting a compelling, forceful argument.

Good copy does not ramble. Any composition, whether an ad, sales letter, circular, novel, play, song, or poem should have a beginning, middle, and end, presented in an orderly way. By organizing your own thoughts so that all component parts of the message are in proper sequence, leading up to a crescendo and finale, you will carry the prospect along with you to the desired end—the order.

If a single sentence does the work of a whole paragraph, by all means cut down the words. However, after you have completed all your planning, don't worry if the letter or circular seems too long. In mail order, it is more important to tell a complete story than to use fewer words. Remember, you are not there to demonstrate the product and answer objections that might arise. So you must present the whole picture in everyday, understandable language and at the same time convince the prospect with a rational, yet emotional appeal. An editor was asked by a cub reporter, "How long should my story be?" To which the editor replied; "Measure the length of a story as you would a woman's skirt. It should be short enough to get attention but long enough to cover everything." The same applies to a sales letter or a circular. Three-page sales letters often outpull half-page letters and vice versa.

The subject of copywriting is inexhaustible. Keep in mind:

1. Use simple clear language, unless writing to the highly intellectual. Avoid extremes of style that draw attention to the words and away from the idea or product you are putting across.

2. Modify your style in accordance with the reader's interests, sex, income level, business, or profession. When writing to a woman, a more personal approach is in order, while an executive expects a dignified businesslike style. A professor expects a scholarly message; a mechanic, a semi-technical he-man style.

3. Do not be afraid to repeat yourself if it is something of vital importance for the prospect to keep in mind. Prospects have short memories, as a rule. Don't expect them to recall what you said in a letter you wrote them the week before.

4. If your copy is long, break it up with heads divided into paragraphs. Reading down the page, the subheads highlight points of the message in sequence, for the man who has little time for reading.

5. Try to keep your message lively and full of human interest even when merely reciting facts.

6. Close on a high key of excitement which directs the reader's attention to the coupon or order form.

WORDS THAT PULL

Certain words in a mail order copy have proven especially effective. The word FREE never fails to attract attention. Most people want something for nothing, even if they possess a lot of wordly goods and a substantial bank account. If you cannot offer a free sample catalog or trial offer—try to dig up some other free angle.

The word NEW also commands attention. Apparently, everyone wants to keep posted on the latest developments in appliances, accessories, and other merchandise and gadgets, and will stop to investigate anything that appears to be an improvement over what he has been using.

The word AMAZING, which is much overused and abused in mail-order advertising, is still a puller because it suggests a revelation just as the word "new" does. Similar words and phrases are JUST ("Just arrived from Paris"), REVOLUTIONARY ("The answer to your sewerage problems"). These are rather trite and if you can create something fresh and original that conveys the same excitement so much the better.

An ad that is as timely as this one is bound to demand attention. The recent flurry in the output of new computer inventions has aroused nationwide excitement. Ordinarily, an ad which starts with a catalog offering is ineffective because catalogs per se, are so common, yet this one is an important exception because the average computer prospect is hungering for the latest information on the subject.

FOR LADIES ONLY

A necessity for every lady who likes things orderly.

Beautiful genuine pigskin secretary holds 24 credit card charge plates or photos in protective plastic windows; has memo pad and gold mechanical pencil, flip-up address book, 2-bill pockets, a change pocket for coins that snaps closed. Has outside snap closure. Fits into purse.

Rich black pigskin with 24 Kt. Gold Monogram 4¼" X 6¼"
Only .... Prepaid .. **$4.95**

Send check or money order to . . .

CLIFF'S SPECIALTY HOUSE
513 YOLANDA LANE
SHREVEPORT, LOUISIANA 71105

The buying motive in this case is "orderliness," which is mentioned in the sub-caption as well as in the text. Of course, all women do not have a craving for neatness. There are both good and bad housekeepers, yet this advertiser believed that the millions of orderly-oriented women alone constituted a rich market.

STATE TERMS PLAINLY

Be sure that you state the terms clearly. If the item is to be sent postpaid, say so. If there are postage charges or if an extra amount is added for C.O.D., be equally explicit: "Add 25¢ for postage and handling," or "For C.O.D., pay postman 25¢ on delivery," or "No C.O.D.'s," or Save 32¢ C.O.D. charges, send $2.25 today." Experience shows that the sale is expedited if the advertiser includes the postage in the quoted price. The average person does not know the cost of parcel post shipments because of the difference in zone rates, and he hesitates about guessing at the amount for fear of overpaying. Experience also shows that offering items on a C.O.D. basis increases sales by as much as 70 percent in some cases. However, it requires more handling for the mail order operator because each package sent C.O.D. must be taken to the post office in addition to the extra paperwork.

It is good policy to tell prospects in your ad that they pay mail charges when ordered C.O.D., and that you absorb the postage otherwise. This encourages buyers to send the money in advance. C.O.D. shipments have another disadvantage; the customer may change his mind and refuse the shipment when the postman delivers it. In this case, the mail order firm pays the return postage. Where higher priced items are involved, it is good practice to ask for a small down payment and the balance C.O.D. This down payment will cover the cost of shipping both ways, on a package that is refused.

PREPARING THE LAYOUT

We have already given some pointers about making the layout tie in with the copy. A catalog is fairly simple to lay out, except for the cover which presents interesting problems of getting attention and inducing prospects to open it. The text pages are generally divided into fairly equal units of product pictures and description— with or without the use of color. If possible, try to avoid combining photos or "wash" illustrations together with line drawings on a single page. The lack of unity is generally not pleasing. However, a page showing products can readily be embellished with interesting sketches of persons using the items.

When laying out a circular which concentrates on a single product, it is well to keep it simple. The strongest circular is generally one that has a few illustrations and only one dominant element (usually vertical or slanted). If you must show many little additional elements, try to group them within a panel of some kind so that all will appear as a single grouping, and not detract from the main element. The layout and artwork should be handled in such a way that the ultimate cost of completion—including printing—is kept within bounds of your budget.

If you lack the experience to do a professional-looking job, utilize the services of a competent printer, or better still, a good artist or an agency. They will design your letterhead, circulars, and catalog with imagination and skill. Let them give you an estimate before starting so you can keep your expenses under control.

A fine example of a small ad making maximum use of its space to get its story across with a bang. It demonstrates that it pays to spend a few extra dollars for artwork and cuts. Just because an ad is small is no reason to be "pennywise and pound foolish" by skimping on production costs.

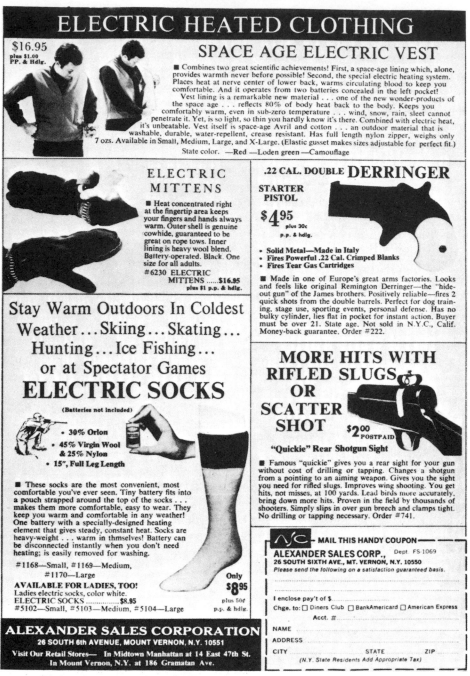

In this layout, the artist made excellent use of black, gray, and white to achieve contrast and to separate elements that would run together in confusion. Notice the reverse type in the heading and in the name and address panel at the bottom. Note also the use of benday backgrounds to separate two of the items from the others. Finally observe that all the illustrations point into the copy to insure reading. The ad appeared in *Field & Stream*.

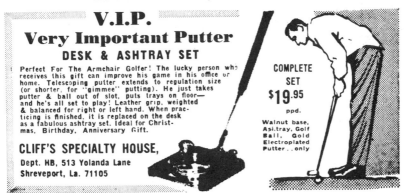

V.I.P.
Very Important Putter
DESK & ASHTRAY SET

Perfect For The Armchair Golfer! The lucky person who receives this gift can improve his game in his office or home. Telescoping putter extends to regulation size (or shorter, for "gimmee" putting). He just takes putter & ball out of slot, puts trays on floor—and he's all set to play! Leather grip, weighted & balanced for right or left hand. When practicing is finished, it is replaced on the desk as a fabulous ashtray set. Ideal for Christmas, Birthday, Anniversary Gift.

CLIFF'S SPECIALTY HOUSE,
Dept. HB, 513 Yolanda Lane
Shreveport, La. 71105

COMPLETE
SET
$19.95
ppd.

Walnut base, Ashtray, Golf Ball, Gold Electroplated Putter . . only

A striking ad for men who strike golf balls! The layout and artwork are top notch. Notice how the figure leans in the direction of the object to be sold which in itself stands out. The putter and the desk set are parallel thus attracting attention. Note how the border breaks into the heading as another innovation.

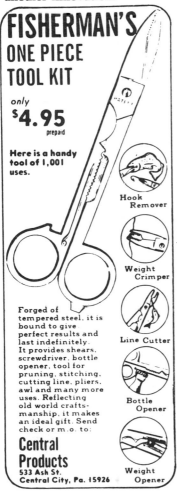

FISHERMAN'S ONE PIECE TOOL KIT

only **$4.95** prepaid

Here is a handy tool of 1,001 uses.

Hook Remover

Weight Crimper

Forged of tempered steel, it is bound to give perfect results and last indefinitely. It provides shears, screwdriver, bottle opener, tool for pruning, stitching, cutting line, pliers, awl and many more uses. Reflecting old world craftsmanship, it makes an ideal gift. Send check or m.o. to:

Line Cutter

Bottle Opener

Central Products
533 Ash St.
Central City, Pa. 15926

Weight Opener

The layout shown is simple and dignified yet eye-catching. It contains one dominating element which is placed on a slant to suggest action as opposed to a straight horizontal or vertical picture which is more static. The six thumbnail pictures are clearly drawn and defined. They are grouped so as not to distract from the main illustration.

PREPARING THE ORDER FORM

The order form is too important to treat lightly. It is your final effort to land the order. Here are some pointers:

1. Since you are not limited by space, as in the case of a coupon, give the prospect plenty of room in which to write.

2. Use a paper stock that will not blur when ink is used.

3. If possible, don't incorporate the order form into the descriptive literature or catalog. Surveys show that a separate order form brings better returns.

4. Make the layout as inviting and attractive as possible, but don't overdo it. Remember the purpose of the form is chiefly functional, and none of the artwork should interfere with that role.

5. A little final selling on the order form will help immensely. But keep the sales talk brief. A recapitulation of the salient sales arguments in vigorous language can be very potent.

6. If there are qualifications in your offer, don't hide them in microscopic type. Prospects resent such tricks. State your offer honestly and boldly. Besides, the Post Office Department does not tolerate deception.

7. Use white paper or pastel colors. Avoid dark colors in a coupon because the type is not legible.

8. In any case make it as simple as possible for the prospect to act. Do nothing to slow up his filling out the coupon, enclosing it with a remittance in your envelope and mailing it at once. In other words, do everything you can to hasten the order.

DESIGNING THE ENVELOPE

The envelope, like all the other mailing pieces should have eye appeal—make a good first impression and stimulate interest. Here are a few thoughts on the subject:

1. Monarch size or baronial, square, is generally more appealing to consumers than the standard 6¾ inch or the No. 10 envelope. In

ORDER FORM

8 IMPORTANT REASONS

WHY YOU SHOULD FILL OUT THIS ORDER FORM

FOR **SUPER STURDY**

AND START ENJOYING THE BENEFITS OF A TOUGH – LEAK-PROOF

ROOF

- Can't Crack
- Can't shrink
- Can't melt
- Can't run

- Better than tar
- Goes over any surface
- Lasts for years
- Requires no skilled labor

7 YEAR GUARANTEE

- -

FILL OUT AND MAIL

The Robertson Co.
3119½ Court U, Ensley
Box 3868, Birmingham, Alabama 35208

I would like to try your extra tough roofing which I understand is guaranteed for 7 years. Please send me the following:

SUPER–STURDY . . . . _____ gal. at _____ per gal.
SILVER BRIGHT . . . . _____ gal. at _____ per gal.
TIFF–A–LUME . . . . _____ gal. at _____ per gal.

Enclosed find my check amounting to $ _____ . I would like to open an account with you, so I am listing 3 references:

NAME	STREET	CITY, STATE, ZIP CODE
_____	_____	_____
_____	_____	_____
_____	_____	_____

My Name __X__ _____

QUANTITY PRICES		Net Cost
	5 GAL. 55 GAL.	5 Gal. $ 12.73
		10 Gal. $ 25.46
SUPER STURDY	$ 2.52 $ 2.32	20 Gal. $ 50.90
	per gal. per gal.	55 Gal. $128.88
SILVER BRIGHT	_____ _____	
	per gal. per gal.	
TIFF–A–LUME	_____ _____	
	per gal. per gal.	

FREIGHT PREPAID ON 20 GALS. OR MORE – WHEN REMITTANCE IS SENT WITH ORDER
FREIGHT ALLOWED ON OPEN ACCOUNT ORDER OF MORE THAN 20 GALS.

The order form recapitulates all the salient points in the circular which accompanied it. This helps to close the sale at the critical point when the prospect is deciding whether he should order. The illustration serves to enliven the form.

large quantities they cost little more than the conventional sizes. Where standard No. 10 envelopes might do in a message to businessmen, women generally respond to an odd size envelope which looks informal.

2. Tinted paper tends to get more attention than plain white.

3. Two-color printing is more striking and restful; it costs a little more.

4. A return address printed on the back flap, instead of in the front upper left corner, tends to add interest; the same is true of a "blind" return address such as: Suite 309, Empire State Building, NY.

5. The envelope might well be a clue to the type of material inside. If it is conservative, such as a bank service, then make your envelope dignified. Is it a bargain offer? Then you are justified in using a louder mor forceful presentation. There are many tones between these two extremes. In any case, the envelope should not only be appropriate to your message but also in good taste.

6. At times it is advantageous to print a teaser message on the address side of the envelope. Naturally, it is done to induce the prospect to open it in high anticipation of what is inside.

TESTIMONIALS—POTENT SALES AMMUNITION

Testimonials have been used since the advent of advertising. Yet they are still potent despite the fact that many persons are skeptical of their authenticity. It is true that some firms have been known to buy testimonials, but fortunately such concerns are in the minority. Notwithstanding some disbelief, most testimonials are honest and are still persuasive in generating sales.

Testimonials can be used effectively in both advertisements and direct mail literature. In the former case, some advertisers find it advantageous to make a heading out of a strong testimonial. Large display type, with or without a picture, is used to create a forceful impact on the prospect. The thought behind this type of approach is that what a consumer says about an item is more believable to a prospect than what a mail order firm says about its own product.

Other mail order ads simply contain testimonials, in whole or in part, which are placed to the side of the main copy as supplementary, supporting data. Still others employ a partial testimonial in the copy. It is put in quotes, as for example: "Mrs. Stewart says: I have been using hand lotions for 20 years but yours is by far the most effective."

Circulars, because they are less limited by space, can profit by using as many testimonals as possible. Their importance is such that it is often considered advisable to prepare a separate testimonial sheet. It can consist of a straight typed listing of testimonials or it can be embellished and dramatized with illustrations.

A good product is like a magnet in that it draws testimonials unsolicited. Although it is not recommended that any firm pay for testimonials, it is considered legitimate to draw them out of silent customers. A letter asking customers how they liked the article could produce many flattering remarks. Another method is to send customers a questionnaire containing inquiries about the product such as: How do you use this article around your home? Space is left for additional remarks which usually produce many flattering comments.

It is advisable to be on the alert when examining incoming orders and other mail from customers to see whether unsolicited testimonials are lurking in their midst. Put such testimonials aside in a separate file for future use. If the testimonial is an integral and inseparable part of a current order or letter, make a photocopy. Your testimonial file will serve a dual purpose: by separating them, you can be sure to lay your hands on them when needed; they will serve as evidence in case a skeptical person questions their authenticity. Whenever you use a testimonial, make some notation on it, stating in what circular, letter or advertisement it was employed.

In order to guard against lawsuits, it is wise to secure permission from a customer before printing his testimonial. For this purpose, a quantity of special release froms can be kept on hand. Some customers object to a printed testimonial that carries their full name. The objection can be met by using only their initials and perhaps the city and state with it. Many mail order firms feel that it is safe to use a testimonial without permission if initials rather than full names are used.

So here is definitely another tool for landing business. Why not make the most of it? Instead of handling it in a perfunctory, run-of-the-mill fashion, study it from the consumer standpoint and decide how you can present your testimonials in the most striking manner.

Encyclopedia Collection of Rich Jewish Humor

LAUGHING WITH TEARS
By Martin Rywell
Pioneer Press, Harriman, Tenn.
Price $3.10

Gathered here is an encyclopedic collection of Jewish humor, parables, proverbs, fables, folk tales, anecdotes, allegories, legends, myths, satires, fairy tales, quotations, riddles and enigmas.

It is a book that cannot be read continuously as one reads a novel. Rather it must be tasted, a sip at a time, to fully enjoy its rich flavor. As you chuckle at the comic capers of the characters and characterizations, the wry wit, the quibbling quips, the stinging satires, the illustrative irony, one sees the many-sided life of the Jewish people. Rich with learning and understanding, this is the finest collection of jesting philosophy. When I started the book I marked the stories that I especially liked and soon found a mark on every page.

Excellently-selected, this superior collection of innumerable good Jewish stories is admirably presented by Martin Rywell in an easy, breezy style. A Tennessee hill-billy, he edits "Listen" and is the author of more than 30 published books on as many subjects.

The world can never get too much genuine humor and this book is worth more than a dozen ponderous Ph.D. theses on the Jews as a human being. It is needed in these days of stress not only by Jews but also by non-Jews.

A commendable achievement, these well-chosen gems of Jewish genius for gaiety and treasure of J e w i s h folklore and tradition should be in every home and is an ideal gift for any occasion.

(B. B. B.)

An ad in the guise of a book review acts as a testimonial. Instead of the advertiser blowing his own horn, he lets someone else do it for him. This takes the reader off his guard. It is more believable because a prospect is more likely to accept the objective opinion of an outsider than that of the firm selling the book.

Here is an excellent example of a mailing piece that dramatizes testimonials. It is but one side of the printed sheet. (The other side is equally dynamic.) A run-of-the-mill list of testimonials is thus enlivened in this way. The prospect is drawn into the subject by the enthusiasm of those who wrote the testimonials. He is soon convinced that the writers benefited from the contest's unusual features.

WHAT MAKES SALES LETTERS CLICK?

A sales letter, like an advertisement, is nothing more than salesmanship on paper. A good salesman, in his opening remarks to a customer, indicates by his attitude a desire to render service. He reflects a sympathetic understanding of the prospect's needs and he tries to convince him that his offerings will bring a satisfactory solution to the customer's problems.

The writer of a sales letter should use the same approach. If his opening remarks to his prospect are about himself, the superiority of his business or the greatness of his product, he makes a great mistake. Should sales fail to come up to expectations, as they generally do in such cases, he is inclined to attribute the lack of orders to factors other than his lack of rapport with the prospect.

Before writing a sales letter it is wise to enter into a "brown study" in which you concentrate deeply on the typical prospect, man or woman, who answers your ads or represents the average name on the lists you are employing in a direct mail operation. Does he or she operate a business or belong to a profession? Is the prospect a housewife or a retired businessman? In each case, the reaction to your letter is likely to be different. So consider all the circumstances—financial, social, and vocational—to determine how such a person would respond to a given product, weighing the factors which most influence his purchases.

An analogy might be a person who arrives late at a railroad platform and tries to board a train which is pulling out of the station. To avoid stumbling, he runs along the platform and when his pace equals that of the train's, he hops aboard without difficulty. Similarly, if you wish to win a sale, you must establish rapport with the prospect's consciousness by putting your thinking in step with his.

Starting the Sales Letter

The letter that starts like this: "In answer to your inquiry, we are sending you our catalog of merchandise which we think contains the finest kits that money can buy . . ." fails to speak to the prospect's own interest. He does not care what the manufacturer thinks of his own product. What is important to him is how the product will benefit him. It is, therefore, essential that your opening statement impels your prospect to become emotionally involved with your merchandise to the point that he yearns to own what you have to offer. This sort of appeal disarms the skeptic who is on guard against being sold something that he does not need.

Always bear in mind that most persons receive loads of what is called "junk mail;" therefore, your approach must be clever enough to penetrate the mental barriers of even the most cynical recipient.

The preceding opening could have been improved many ways. Here is one version: "May this catalog stimulate fresh excitement for your pet hobby. May it also bring you much joy in achievement as the units you assemble so easily work to perfection." This introduction serves to paint a satisfying mental picture which encourages the prospect to read on.

Once you have a prospect's sympathetic attention, he is inclined to be receptive to what you have to say about your product. But even a presentation of facts should not be stated in a stereotyped, lackluster "nuts and bolts" fashion. This, as well as anything else you say, should be sales-slanted, always bringing the prospect closer to your final goal—the order. Here is an example: "Think of converting your plain paper into expensive-looking raised-letterhead! Imagine embossing your name and address into a 3-dimensional, sculptured effect, all in a jiffy! Who wouldn't love to own, or to receive as a gift, this clever device?"

Closing the Sales Letter

Finally, when you come to a close, do not be content to end your letter with the usual cut-and-dried-pitch: "Send us your order today." If possible, endeavor to inject a last minute desire for what you have to offer, plus the feeling that the prospect will regret letting the opportunity slip by. An investment house accomplished their objective this way: "Don't let this carefully thought-out plan pass by as 'just another angle,' but think of the extra income you are sure to earn and how handy this money will be when you face retirement . . . when your normal income is drastically reduced! Surely, this is worth a few minutes of your time to investigate."

If you are worried because your letters seem too long, forget it. Do not pay attention to those who say that people lack the patience to read lengthy letters. After all, a letter is only as long as the interest in it is maintained. So do not let it lag at any point. Keep your prospect keyed up with colorful, stimulating language. Even a hard-headed businessman will relish it, if the language is not insincere. If you have been receiving mail from the big book and record clubs you must have noticed their sales letters run to two and three pages. This does not prevent them from making millions.

Answering Inquiries

A letter answering inquiries that result from publication advertising requires a different type of opening than one sent to a cold list. The inquiry is generally answered by first referring briefly to the ad and then immediately plunging into what is of interest or benefit to the prospect. It might start as follows: "Apparently you answered our ad because you are concerned about your home being burglarized or the possibility of your being attacked under your very roof. Are you wondering what we can do to help ward off this impending danger?"

The letter to a cold list demands a strong, arresting opener. The stopper might be along such lines: "Crime is on the increase! Homes are being looted in your neighborhood! Women are being attacked by intruders in their bedrooms! Headlines like these appear daily in your local newspapers. Surely you want to take drastic measures to prevent these horrible things from happening to you. Let us show you how."

Sample sales letters appear at the end of this chapter.

The Mailing Campaign

Surveys have shown that when a mailing consists of a piece of literature accompanied by a sales letter, the results are better than one in which the mailing piece is sent without a letter. The companion sales letter has the virtue of being man-to-man and warmly personal in tone. Even if the brochure, circular, flyer, catalog, etc. is colorful, dramatic and dynamic, at the same time it seems aloof because, in its printed state, it reflects a less personal appeal.

If your direct mail campaign involves contact with different kinds of prospects, you can use the same circular which gives a general description of your product but with each circular you would attach a special sales letter geared to the specific and unique interests of each kind of prospect. For instance, you might have a circular depicting hi-fi loud speakers to be sent to both consumers and TV repair shops. Each would receive a special letter but with the same circular.

If you are mailing a series of follow-up letters, endeavor to show some continuity as you build up a desire for your merchandise to a crescendo. When a catalog or brochure is sent, your follow-up letter would be more to the point if you ask the prospect what he thought of this or that feature, or if there is something not shown which he wants to discuss with you. Let him feel a closeness between his needs and your ability to satisfy them. This develops confidence.

The foregoing offers only broad principles to bear in mind and need not be followed literally. One should not be inflexible about methods for preparing sales letters. Each should be tailored to fit the product and kind of prospect. To do a first-rate job requires thought and skill. However, if you lack the talent and experience, it will pay you to use the services of a mail order agency specializing in such matters. In the long run, you have much to gain.

Dear Sportsman:

How many angling hours have you wasted without even a single good bite? How many fly patterns have you given up as a waste of time? How many streams and lakes have refused to yield any action despite their reputation?

If the answer is "too many," we think we have the answer. We're enclosing a list of new and old patterns tried by the foremost American and foreign craftsmen—all of them have been tested time and time again in American waters, under local conditions. Thus, regardless of where you fish, we've concentrated on the flies that work in that particular area to save you time and money and insure better catches. No wonder we have probably the largest clientele of satisfied sports fishermen in the country!

Another advantage of buying through V & C is our interest in your preferences and problems (we hate to see grown men cry). We'll be happy to have you consult with us before you plan a fishing trip so you'll have exactly the right lures. Don't be afraid to ask us questions . . . that's why we're here. If you're looking for a particular fly that isn't listed, we can custom-tie it or import if for you.

And remember, if you're dissatisfied with any item you purchase from us, simply send it back for an equivalent product or full refund.

Furthermore, being situated in one of the top trout areas in the U.S.—with pike, bass, crappie, bluegill, and perch as runners-up—we speak your language, no matter which game fish you fancy (incidentally, several of the streamers listed and used on fresh water game fish will also produce in salt water). Coming to Montana? We're ready to help plan your fishing stops and can provide guide service if you wish.

FREE WITH YOUR ORDER—A NEW 3 COLOR MAP OF MONTANA'S TROPHY LAKES! Includes dry-fly, nymph, and streamer techniques for both streams and lakes.

Get acquainted with V & C of Montana. It will bring you more than luck.

Very sincerely,

Vern Field
Manager

VF/sc

Dear Bookstore Owner:

Whether you understand today's younger set or not . . . here's one thing that's really clear: "mod" items are here to stay.

One profitable way to cash in on the trend to bold motifs, pizazzy colors, and groovy sayings is through MOD TOTES. This spectacular line of heavy-duty, long-lasting vinyl tote bags created by Visual Discoveries has caught on with the "now" generation.

Designed for the practical purpose of carrying books, gym and other scholastic paraphernalia, these 50¢ retailers are printed with the most imaginative patterns and slogans, and designed by the top pop artists.

Imprinted differently on each side with snap-lok plastic handles, they'll carry up to 20 pounds through all kinds of weather. The new register-ringers for bookstores everywhere! Place them near the check-outcounter and just watch the action. And remind customers that MOD TOTES make great gifts for Mom. Each measures a roomy 15 × 20 inches.

AND NOW THE BIG DEAL: 40% OFF ON A 100-BAG ASSORTMENT (minimum order) SHIPPED PARCEL POST. A MARK-UP YOU CAN'T AFFORD TO MISS . . . on a timely item that's priced to move and move with the crowds. Note these attractive costs to you: 100 bags, $30; 250 bags, $100; 500 bags, $300.

Narrow the generation gap while you fatten your earnings. MOD TOTES are the medium with the message . . . and the message is SALES! Examine the enclosed brochure, then send your order in now for GUARANTEED 1 WEEK DELIVERY.

Sincerely,

VISUAL DISCOVERIES, INC.

SS/bc   Sam Schwartz
Encl.   Sales Manager

PREPARING THE LETTERHEAD

It has already been stated that the letterhead is important enough to warrant using outside expert assistance to give it that extra touch of distinction. There are printers and artists who specialize in letterheads. Your regular artist, printer, or advertising agency may turn out a creditable job.

To begin with, the stock and style of printing should be the same for letterhead and envelope. But it should be remembered that once the envelope is tossed away, the letterhead stays before the recipient for hours, days, weeks, or even longer. Therefore, it should leave a pleasing impression, truly representative of the kind of business you proudly operate. It's your hallmark or image which, like the clothes you wear, helps to attract the kind of friends and customers you seek in the world of business. Whether you print it in one, two, or three colors—whether engraved or printed by letterpress or offset—on ordinary bond or expensive rag stock these factors will greatly affect the cost.

But more important is the reaction of those who receive the letter. The nature of the message that goes on your letterhead is covered in an earlier chapter entitled "What Makes Sales Letters Click."

WHEN TO USE COUPONS

If the advertising budget permits the cost of the extra space, add a coupon to the bottom of your advertisement. This coupon should be a minimum of one inch in depth in a single column ad; otherwise there is insufficient space for the customer to write his name and address legibly. In any case you will save your eyesight and time, and will also insure correct delivery by stating, "Please print plainly," on the coupon. The importance of a coupon is obvious. Many people are fairly well sold on an item after reading an ad, but their enthusiasm diminishes when they must hunt up pen, stationery, and envelopes to write a letter. It is far easier to whip out a pencil and scratch in the name and address on a ready-made coupon. One of the basic principles of selling is to make it easy for the customer to order.

The coupon can also be made a potent sales tool. If space permits, you can well include in the coupon a recapitulation of the sales arguments, terms, and guarantee, in enthusiastic language, written in the first person: "Kindly send me your unique (device) . . . which will save me hours of time and trouble, at your special low price of $00.00. I understand that if I am not thoroughly delighted with the purchase, I may return it for full refund—no questions asked." Picture your prospect reading down to the bottom of the ad, with pencil poised in hand, hesitating. At this juncture he reads the stimulating words which you pack into your coupon. The chances are he will get busy and fill out the order.

When the advertisement is of such a nature that the prospect is invited to select one or more items out of many offered, the coupon simplifies matters. The prospect then merely orders by number or checks off the boxes adjacent to the listed items being ordered.

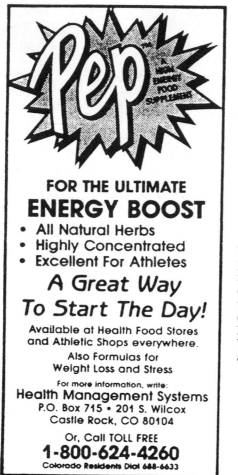

FOR THE ULTIMATE
ENERGY BOOST
- All Natural Herbs
- Highly Concentrated
- Excellent For Athletes

A Great Way
To Start The Day!

Available at Health Food Stores
and Athletic Shops everywhere.
Also Formulas for
Weight Loss and Stress

For more information, write:
Health Management Systems
P.O. Box 715 • 201 S. Wilcox
Castle Rock, CO 80104

Or, Call TOLL FREE
1-800-624-4260
Colorado Residents Dial 688-6633

The word "Pep" pops out of the page in this ad so that it is difficult for even the hurried reader of a publication to pass the ad by unnoticed. The two secondary captions, "For the ultimate ENERGY BOOST" and "A Great Way to Start the Day!" also carry a lot of clout.

BUILDING A MAILING LIST

The "do-it-yourself" type of person will want to build his own list. All you need are some 3 inch x 5 inch cards and a good directory. If you are selling to a special trade or profession, the task is not too difficult because there are trade and professional directories available. They can be consulted in libraries or purchased outright. Moreover, the classified telephone directories carry such listings. But in the matter of consumer names the task is more difficult. About the only lists available are in telephone and city directories. These are not of much value because you have no way of knowing whether they contain good mail order prospects, although you can guess at their income from the kind of neighborhood.

A simpler and more reliable way is to contact mailing list brokers who possess ready-made lists available for purchase. The lists are broken down into various categories to suit your particular purpose. In addition to selling names, letter brokerage houses will rent you the actual letters received from customers for similar merchandise. For example, suppose you are selling an automotive device, you might find it advantageous to rent letters which served as orders for another type of automotive device. Incidentally, these same brokers who rent letters to you, might very well purchase letters from you which you had received from customers, as a result of your advertising, and which are of no value to you any longer—perhaps because you had decided to give up that class of product. Ultimately, selling your names might prove a good source of extra income.

Look into your classified directory for the names of list and letter brokers. All kinds of names are on hand. You can obtain the names of owners of cars of all makes, the names of mothers of newborn babies, of persons engaged to marry, of persons who invest in stocks, and countless other categories. And, if you are using the services of a mail order advertising agency that knows its business, it will be of big help to you in this direction.

WATCH YOUR TIMING

An advertising man I know once stated: "I would rather have a lousy-looking piece that gets there at the right moment, than the most beautiful piece in the world that is a "Johnny-come-lately." This may be overstating the case, but it contains a seed of truth. It does not pay to be a perfectionist, if by so doing you kill the campaign with time-wasting improvements. No mailing piece is really perfect and many of the little imperfections that bother those who work on the mailing pieces will be overlooked by the prospect whose mind is oriented to the product—not on misplaced commas or marring flyspecks. No one is trying to encourage sloppy work. If there is time, by all means perfect the mailing piece to the best of your ability, but always keep one eye on the time schedule.

The answer to all this is "Plan Ahead." Either your own experience or the experience of those whom you hire will tell you how much time to allow for production of the necessary elements within a given time. Figure the time needed for layout, artwork, copy, printing, processing letters, addressing envelopes, collating, enclosing material, and delivering to the post office. Make a chart of each operation and adhere to it as closely as possible. Better allow extra time for the suppliers who drag their feet or fall down on the job. Some of the operations can be worked simultaneously. For instance, while the envelopes are being addressed, your printer can be completing his assignment. This can all be planned ahead.

SHIPPING AND RECORD KEEPING SYSTEMS

The small mail order business should not burden itself with intricate and time-consuming operations. You are chiefly concerned with getting the shipment off within a reasonable time, at the lowest cost and effort. Mail order buyers—especially those who send money in advance—tend to become impatient if a shipment is late in arriving. Surveys show that the average person will not remain patient beyond ten days waiting for merchandise. After that, he is liable to make a fuss. You are lucky if he merely complains about the delay. He is apt to go further, contacting postal authorities, the district attorney, the Federal Trade Commission, the Better Business Bureau, or the publication in which your ad appeared. So try to get your mail orders filled within a few days. Should an unavoidable delay arise, it is wise to drop him a card, stating the reasons and approximate time of the expected delivery. This tends to pacify the customer and restrains him from taking unpleasant actions.

Here are the primary steps for the beginner to take when handling incoming mail:

1. Separate the mail according to the key symbol so that you can trace each order to its source.

2. Using these keys, credit the orders to the publication or mailing list that was the source of the business.

3. Take three sheets or labels, with carbons between, and type out the names and addresses. On the bottom of each label you can type a code symbol which provides a history of the purchase. For example: 1.39 pd 6/3/73-EL is your record that the customer had paid $1.39 in advance for a bottle of English Lavender on June 3, 1973. The duplicate labels can be used for follow-up to the same customers.

4. Your regular parcel post blank label is then pasted on the package and the smaller addressed label (described in No. 3 above) is pasted above the parcel post label. If you do not carry your own merchandise but operate on a drop-ship arrangement with your supplier, simply send the addressed labels to the manufacturer or distributor along with your remittance, covering selling price less your discount.

Easy Record Keeping

This is about the simplest system you can devise. The only addition recommended at this point is possibly starting a 3 inch × 5 inch card system of customers. Each customer's name is entered on a card. At the bottom, record all pertinent data such as item purchased, date, amount, publication or list, or type of mailing which brought the order. Thus, your card becomes a customer's ledger on the smallest scale. As your business grows larger, your system should expand progressively. You can keep all sorts of card files, recording sources of lists, publications, costs, and analyses of returns. Broadly speaking, the more you know what goes on in connection with your business, and the better you control its operation, the greater will be your chances of success.

However, there is always the possibility that you will become so tied up with paperwork and red tape as to slow down the movement of goods to the customer or else you might increase your handling costs beyond reason. So it is wise to be cautious.

Expand Your System Slowly

The big mail order business houses naturally are in position to use the latest business machines and computers: mail is opened mechanically; money is counted automatically; conveyor belts carry products from stock bins to shipping department where merchandise is wrapped and labeled by machine. The billing is also performed by machine.

After the small operator has outgrown his swaddling clothes, he has a choice of hiring help to supplement his own efforts, or sending his material to a letter shop or similar organization to take care of mailing and orders. Many such firms are equipped to take care of every detail as well (or better) than you could do it yourself. Addressing, packaging, shipping, and all operations of circularizing can be performed outside. Even if you must give up a small amount of your profits on each order, it may pay you to have this work done for you.

All this leads to one conclusion. You are in business to make a profit. To do so you must turn over merchandise with the greatest speed, consistent with economy and profits. So check your controls every step of the way: the salability of the merchandise; the pulling power of ads and mailing lists; the effectiveness of mailing pieces, your facilities; the cost of keeping records and forwarding shipments. This is a tall order for anyone. You may not succeed in doing everything with 100 percent efficiency—no one can. But by striving for a high level of attainment, you will most likely MAKE MONEY IN THE MAIL ORDER BUSINESS.

RADIO AND TELEVISION ADVERTISING

Success in selling mail order items through the medium of radio or television is the exception rather than the rule. The cost of time on big city stations and networks is prohibitive in most cases. Even the cost of a single minute runs into an enormous sum, and it is difficult to put across your full story and to mention your name and address a couple of times, so they will be remembered, in so short a time. This is especially true of radio. The person who listens to his car radio had neither the time nor the opportunity to jot down your name and address and he is not likely to stop his car for that purpose. Similarly, the housewife, who listens while cleaning, cooking or washing dishes, is disinclined to stop everything so she can scribble down your name and location. After all, a minute's talk amounts to only 125 to 140 words, and at least three to five minutes are ordinarily needed to deliver a convincing sales talk.

However, it is possible to achieve your objective and keep costs at a reasonable figure by localizing your efforts. Purchase spot commercials on a small radio station and, over a period of time, saturate the surrounding area with your sales message. Then move on to another region and blanket that area through the facilities of the local radio station. In this way, the cost of radio advertising need not be prohibitive.

Another method of advertising is on P.I., or "Per Inquiry," stations. Under this system instead of charging you for the time, the station makes a commission on each order received. The orders with remittance come directly to the station which deducts its commission and sends the balance, with the names and addresses of the customers to the advertiser.

Most mail order houses will eagerly make such an arrangement because it entails little or no risk. However, no one knows in advance which stations have free time available. Generally, stations offer a "per inquiry" deal on unsponsored time left after all their efforts to sell it have failed. It would be necessary to contact about 3,000 radio stations and 500 TV channels at frequent intervals to ascertain which of them has free time for a "per inquiry" deal.

In addition, numerous stations will not make such an arrangement unless they are convinced that the product is salable. Many require proof that the item has been advertised and sold profitably through other channels; others demand a substantial advance against future commission.

CATALOG
SELLING HOUSES

Are you interested in distributing an attractive catalog without incurring the expense of having to print it yourself? This is made possible by the catalog houses listed at the end of this chapter. Their purpose is to sell printing in the form of catalogs, rather than to earn a profit selling merchandise. The catalogs, with your firm name imprinted on the cover, would be offered to you at so much per thousand copies. The cost would depend on such factors as the number of pages, number of colors, quality of the paper used, general artistic appearance, as well as the size of the catalog. The price range would be between $50 and $100 per thousand, or perhaps more.

Most of these catalog houses will invite you to select items from their catalog to feature in your own publication ads directed to consumers. The catalog house will provide you with the name of the firm or supplier of the article so you can contact them and establish sales relations and terms with them. In most cases, a drop-ship arrangement will be instituted. This works out well at times, particularly when the item is still novel; however, since the very same catalog is sold to scores of mail order concerns, each of which distributes it to his prospects and customers, the novelty of the items listed soon wears off. It is not uncommon for a consumer to receive three identical catalogs, each with a different company imprint. This happens most frequently during the pre-Christmas gift-buying season.

Such catalog houses generally sell mailing lists of prospective consumers at so much per thousand. Most catalog houses claim that the names they sell you will not be supplied to other firms. Even so, as explained elsewhere, buying consumer lists is generally a gamble, for it may be necessary to test several lists before you find one that shows a profit. Meanwhile, you dissipate your funds on circulars, postage, and the lists themselves.

Experience has shown that such canned catalogs are most effective when they supplement your own mailing pieces or when used as stuffers with your own shipments of merchandise, ordered as a result of publication advertising.

In the long run, it is generally more advantageous to prepare your own catalog to be sent out to your own fresh list of customer names, acquired through publication advertising. Your catalog can grow as you acquire more and more products. At first it may be a single sheet affair, then develop to four or eight pages, until it matures into a real catalog.

A Partial List of Catalog Houses

Selective Books, Inc.
P.O. Box 1140
Clearwater, FL 33517

Specialty Merchandise Corp.
9401 De Soto Avenue
Chatsworth, CA 91311

Wilshire Books
12015 Sherman Rd.
No. Hollywood, CA 91605

R&D SERVICES
Box 644
Des Moines, IA 50303

Emkay Distributing Co.
309 W. 6th St.
Cleveland, OH 44113
(sample catalog $1.00)

Mail Order Associates
120 Chesnut Ridge Rd.
Montvale, NJ 07645

SOME OF THE LEADING
MAIL ORDER HOUSES

Would you like to have your product pictured and described in someone else's catalog without cost, and place yourself in a position to receive considerable business as a result? The firms listed here are likely to offer you this opportunity. Just send them a letter with a description of your item and indicate that it would be appropriate for listing in their mail order catalog. Offer them a free glossy photo to reproduce in their catalog, if they are interested. Also state your discount to them on any sale of your merchandise that results. There should be a separate discount offer on a direct sale, where they stock your merchandise, and on a drop-ship arrangement, where you ship the product to their customers, using the addressed labels which they provide.

The following names are but a few of the thousands of mail order houses, large and small, which distribute catalogs and in all likelihood would include a listing of your product if it appeals to them. Bear in mind the sales of catalog houses run into billions of dollars. For a list of 4,000 active mail order houses, consult or purchase the *Mail Order Business Directory* published by B. Klein Publications, P.O. Box 8503, Coral Springs, FL 33065 or R & D Services, Box 644, Des Moines, IA 50303.

The mail order houses listed here differ from the list in the preceding chapter in that the firms do not usually sell their catalogs to other firms for name imprinting. Their business is not to make a profit on printing but on the sale of merchandise—which may include yours—as a result of the distribution of their catalog.

Advance Home Products
2654 W. 19
Chicago, IL 60608

A.W. Wells Mail House
505 W. Coleman Ave.
Hammond, LA 70401

Aldens, Inc.
5000 W. Roosevelt Rd.
Chicago, IL 60650

Bazar Francais
666 Ave. of the Americas
New York, NY 10019

Ambassador International Inc.
711 W. Broadway Rd.
Tempe, AZ 85282

Bodine's
2552 Greenmount Blvd.
Baltimore, MD 21216

Cape Cod Quilt Club
P.O. Box 431
Taunton, MA 02780

Country Club Products
622 W. 67th St.
Kansas City, MO 64103

Walter Drake & Sons
4510 Edison Ave.
Colorado Springs, CO 80915

Fidelity Products
705 Pennsylvania Ave., So.
Minneapolis, MN 55426

Foster & Gallahar
6523 N. Galena Rd.
Peoria, IL 61614

Francis-Morris Gifts
75 Henry St.
Brooklyn, NY 11201

Galco Sales Co. Inc.
7120 Harvard St.
Cleveland, OH 44105

Gump's
1784 Union
San Francisco, CA 94123

The Herchow Collection
P.O. Box 340862
Dallas, TX 75234

Hop Home Parties Inc.
Avon, CT 06001

I. Lehrofft Co.
560 Belmont Ave.
Newark, NJ 07108

J.A.M. Sales
919 N. 6th St.
Phoenix, AZ 85504

Jeret Corporation
P.O. Box 1357
Sarasota, FL 33578

J.C. Penney Co.
11220 S. Michigan
Chicago, IL 60640

Lana Lobell
225 W. 34th St.
New York, NY 10001

L. Luria and Son Inc.
980 S.W. 1st Street
Miami, FL 33130

Louis Perloff
733 Walnut Street
Philadelphia, PA 19106

Mascene Dorte
14 Belle Place
Matawan, NJ 07747

Miles Kimball Company
41 W. 8th Ave.
Oshkosh, WI 54901

Misheke
R.R. 4
Waseca, MN 56093

Signet Club Plan
265 Third St.
Boston, MA 02142

S.J. Wegman Co.
35 Wilburst
Lynbrook, NY 11563

Spencer Gifts, Inc.
Spencer Bldg.
Atlantic City, NJ 08411

Sunset House
111 Sunset Blvd.
Beverly Hills, CA 90213

Taylor Gifts
335 E. Conestoga Rd.
Wayne, PA 19087

Two Brothers, Inc.
808 Washington Ave.
St. Louis, MO 63101

How to get rich

How can you get rich some day? Make a hit record . . . a killing on the stock market . . . or invent a gadget like the hula hoop?

For most of us, these are just dreams. But have you ever stopped to think that there *is* a way to get rich—possibly only one sure way? Most fortunes, as you know, are made by people who own their own business.

Perhaps you've thought of starting a small business of your own . . . a franchised drive-in, or maybe a service business. Trouble is, you need $10,000 to $15,000 to get started and even then it's a gamble—with slim chance of ever making really big money.

But there is *one* business which could make you rich—almost overnight. And the beauty of it is, you can start on a shoestring during your spare time, even while holding your regular job.

Cash by Mail

The business is Mail Order—and it's fabulous! Come up with a 'hot' new item . . . and WHAM!

It strikes like a bolt of lightning! Suddenly, you are deluged with cash orders from all over the country . . . MORE MONEY than you could ever make in a lifetime!

Like the Vermont dealer who ran one ad in Sports Afield Magazine. His ad pulled 22,000 orders—over A HALF MILLION DOLLARS IN CASH!

There is no other business where you can make a fortune so quickly!
● A beginner from Newark, N.J. ran his first small ad in House Beautiful—offering an auto clothes rack. Business Week reported that his ad brought in $5,000 in orders. By the end of his first year in Mail Order, he had grossed over $100,000!
● Another beginner—a lawyer from the midwest, sold an idea by mail to fishermen. Specialty Salesman Magazine reveals, "he made $70,000 the first three months!"

Proof

It's a fascinating business! Running ads in newspapers and magazines . . . mailing gift catalogs . . . getting cash orders in your daily mail—steady as clockwork.

There is no other business where you can start on a shoestring and pyramid your profits—*without investing in merchandise!* One husband and wife mail order team took in $40,000 selling one item. They obtained FREE ads in national magazines . . . didn't invest a cent in merchandise, and even got the supplier to ship all orders for them!

These exceptional cases are absolute proof that *you can get rich* in your own Mail Order business. Very rich.

Even a U.S. Gov. Report stated: "A number of one-man Mail Order enterprises make up to $50,000!"

Pick up any magazine. Notice how the same mail order ads are repeated . . . month after month? That's concrete proof! You know those ads wouldn't be repeated over and over again—*unless* they were bringing in big cash profits to their owners.

The Secret

The secret of getting rich in Mail Order lies in *financial leverage*. It's a little-known, almost secret method—using other people's capital to make money for you!

You can get thousands of dollars worth of advertising in big national magazines—without investing your own money! And you don't have to write a single ad. Tested and proven ads are prepared for you by experts. Reinvest the profits from your first successful ad—to get more, larger ads, and the profits begin to snowball! It's like building a chain of stores . . . each new store puts more money in *your* pocket.

You mail out beautiful catalogs which offer hundreds of dollars worth of fine, quality gifts—yet you don't

The thrill of receiving money in your mail is one you'll never tire of!

invest one cent of *your* own money in merchandise! Your catalogs are printed with your name and address, so all orders come to you. Everything is "drop-shipped" for you, and there's up to *100% mark-up!* You pocket the cash profits immediately—even before the orders are shipped to your customers!

Repeat orders alone, just from mail-

ing catalogs, could bring you a steady income for the rest of your life!

Yes, Mail Order is the fastest-growing, most profitable business in America! And now, with more people moving to the suburbs . . . the population explosion . . . and the expanding teen-age market . . . we are on the verge of the BIGGEST BOOM in Mail Order history!

Now, with the help and backing of Mail Order Associates, Inc., of Montvale, N.J., you can follow the same proven steps to Mail Order success—using the 'secret' of financial leverage!

Start Now

We supply you with beautiful gift catalogs throughout the year. All products are drop-shipped for you, with up to 100% mark-up! You get free samples of top-selling mail order items, plus monthly trade reports on 'hot' new products . . . tested, successful ads are sent to you monthly. You get advertising directories, postal laws, complete courses, expert guidance — EVERYTHING you need to practically guarantee YOUR SUCCESS. Why? Because *our* business depends upon *your* success. It's mutually profitable!

A recent feature article in Income Opportunities Magazine stated, "Mail Order Associates Inc., offers the most comprehensive Mail Order program ever offered to beginners." They go on to say, "This could be the opportunity you've been looking for. A chance to get in on the ground floor in a little known business which we believe is on the verge of a new boom."

Free

We are now accepting a limited number of charter members in our new Mail Order Program. No previous experience is required but you must be over 21.

If you are sincerely interested in starting a profitable business on your own . . . if you can see the tremendous advantages which Mail Order offers . . . then ACT NOW!

Mail the coupon today, or simply send your name and address on a postcard. No salesman will call. We will send you a free book—gift catalog, reprints of feature articles, plus complete facts about our program. Write to:

**Mail Order Associates, Inc., Dept. 194
Montvale, New Jersey 07645**

**Rush Coupon for
FREE BOOK!**
plus reprints of Mail Order articles

**Mail Order Associates, Inc., Dept. 104
Montvale, New Jersey 07645**

Please rush complete details on your Mail Order Program. I understand everything is free and there is absolutely no obligation. I am over 21.

Name ....

Address ....

City .... State .... Zip ....

This is a good example of how a catalog house makes a package deal bid for business from those persons who contemplate entering the mail order field. Notice the effective coupon which shouts FREE BOOK in reverse type and illustrates the book "How to Make Money."

PUBLICITY—HOW AND WHEN TO USE IT

The use of free editorials as a money-saving instrument for making mail order sales is recommended in certain situations. It is particularly effective when a new product is being introduced and the company desires widespread publicity without a heavy advertising expenditure. A publicity program can be instituted prior to, or simultaneous with, an advertising campaign.

Such a publicity program entails sending photos and releases (write-ups) to editors of publications, selected on the basis of their readers' age, sex, income, buying habits. Such factors would determine the type of reader apt to purchase the particular item featured. It is necessary to distribute in quantity, to at least 100 publications, to produce a worthwhile response. Realistically, only a small percentage of editors put these releases in editorials. To do so, the editors must like the product, think it will interest their readers, and they must, of course, have available space.

A great many editors will first favor their regular advertisers with free write-ups. Other publications offer their advertisers a free editorial for each paid ad or for every two ads, or some other similar arrangement. Notwithstanding, there are numerous publications which will give free editorials without prior advertising commitments. It is their hope that if the editorial produces sales, the sponsoring company will be encouraged to use the publication for paid advertising.

Considerable Sales Could Follow

Thus, if only a few editors use the publicity material they receive, sales will generally follow in sufficient quantity to make the publicity program worthwhile. Such results are sometimes phenomenal, when a publication with a circulation in the millions gives a free write-up. In such cases, sales often amount to thousands of dollars in earnings. Sometimes the story about the inventor of a product or its development is so unique that a publication will run a feature story about it. One good editorial will generally more than pay for the whole publicity program. Such a campaign involves writing an interesting and persuasive release (see examples on the following page), printing it, selecting a special list of suitable publications for the product, making glossy photos of the item (8 inches x 10 inches or 5 inches x 7 inches), addressing labels, envelopes, mailing, and postage. Be sure you type releases in double or triple space. It is best to key each release so that the source of orders and inquiries can be traced.

It would pay any firm promoting a new mail order product to study whether it lends itself better to a publicity or an advertising program or a combination of both. Oftentimes, the professional advice of an advertising or publicity expert is worth a moderate fee.

Sample Publicity Release—1.

New Vibrating Cushion Builds Health

Here at last is a highly efficient body-conditioning device for people who don't have the time or money for expensive health programs. Hospital-tested, it works its wonders in a number of health-building ways—stimulating body tone, controlling weight, improving blood circulation, conquering fatigue.

Made of polyurethane, this new all-purpose Contour Vibrating Aid Foam Cushion weighs only 3 pounds but can support up to 300 pounds. It comes equipped with an internal electric motor, batteries, and a switch which controls its vibrations. The body fits perfectly into its three-dimensional slope form. Flip the switch, and it gets to work, toning up tired muscles. The rhythmic vibrations help trim hips, thighs, tummy, and waist when used for calisthenics or isometric exercises a few minutes every day.

This Contour Aid Cushion also serves to aid blood circulation. Many people find its form-fitting design ideal for improving posture. It is also utilized as a kind of health bed to relax in. The cushion, which measures only 22 inches by 22 inches, can easily be stored in a closet, and taken out any time someone wants to use it. Send $26 or write for further details to All Aids Household Products, Dept 7, P.O. Box 136, Brevoort Station, Brooklyn, NY 11216.

Sample Publicity Release—2.

Housewife's New Utility Aid

Life can be made a little easier with this UTILITY AID, the worksaver. At times, cleaning gets many women down—even those who like housework. Messy pots are piled in the sink ceiling high and caked-on food makes cleaning almost impossible. Housewives clean floors and there's still dirt in the corners of the room which has to be scraped out. Here is where this Super Tool comes in handy. It's more than a sponge, more than a brush, more than a scraper—it's all of these things rolled into one. Everything you need is right there, all in one amazing UTILITY AID. On one end, the sturdy scraper clears away the toughest dirt, on the other end, the bristle brush and sponge tackle more delicate problems like cleaning fabrics, plastics, and even pets. The UTILITY AID scrapes and brushes away dirt from those tough-cleaning problem areas like pots and pans, walls, floors, dishes, and even fishbowls. Send only $1.50 to ALL AIDS HOUSE-HOLD PRODUCTS, Dept. 99, P.O. Box 136, Brevoort Station, Brooklyn, NY 11216.

At this price, you can afford to have a few SUPER TOOLS around the house to help out wherever there is dirt that refuses to budge.

Note that the language used in the preceding examples is in tone with the style generally employed by publication editors. Although enthusiastic, it is necessarily more restrained than the high pressure sales talk used in mail order advertisements and sales literature.

A PARTIAL LIST OF CONSUMER MAGAZINES ACCEPTING PUBLICITY RELEASES

AIR PROGRESS—7950 Deering Ave., Canog Park, CA 91304

AMERICAN AGRICULTURIST—Box 369, Ithaca, NY 14850 (New Products Editor)

AMERICAN BABY INC.—575 Lexington Ave., New York, NY 10022 (Best Buys for Baby Editor)

AMERICAN LEGION MAGAZINE—P.O. Box 1055, Indianapolis, IN 40206

AMERICAN RIFLEMAN—1600 Rhode Island Ave., N.W., Washington, DC 20036 (New Products Editor)

ARMY TIMES—475 School St., S.W., Washington, DC 20024 (Editor)

BABY TALK—185 Madison Ave., New York NY 10016 (Baby Shop Talk Editor)

BACKPACKER—One Park Ave., New York, NY 10016

BEST SELLING HOME PLANS—201 Kinderkarnack Rd., Oradell, NJ 07649

BETTER HOMES & GARDENS—1716 Locust St., Des Moines, IA 50336 (Shopping By Mail Editor)

BOATING—One Park Ave., New York, NY 10016 (Editor)

BOWLING MAGAZINE—1020 Church St., Evanston, IL 60201

BOYS LIFE—1325 Walnut Hill Lane, Irving, TX 75062

BRIDE'S MAGAZINE—350 Madison Avenue, New York NY 10017 (Gifts for Bridesmaids Editor)

CAR CRAFT—8490 Sunset Blvd., Los Angeles, CA 90069 (New Products Editor)

CAR & DRIVER—One Park Avenue, New York, NY 10016 (New Products Editor)

CARS—P.O. Box 567, Mt. Kisco, NY 32019

CARS AND PARTS—P.O. Box 482, 911 Vandermark Rd., Sidney, OH 45365

CATS—445 Merrimac Dr., Port Orange, FL 32019

CATHOLIC DIGEST—2115 Summit Ave., St. Paul, MN 55105 (Shopping Editor)

CHANGING TIMES—1729 H Street N.W., Washington, DC 20036 (New Products Editor)

CHATELAINE—481 University Avenue, Toronto 2, Ontario, Canada (New Products Editor)

CHICAGO TRIBUNE MAGAZINE—435 North Michigan Avenue, Chicago, IL 60611 (Editor)

CHRISTIAN LIFE—396 St. Charles Rd., Carol Stream, IL 60187

CO-ED—730 Broadway, New York, NY 10003 (Editor)

COLUMBIA—78 Meadow St., New Haven, CT 06507 (Shopping with Laure Editor)

CONSUMER DIGEST—5705 N. Lincoln Ave., Chicago, IL 60659 (Managing Editor)

CRAFT'S MAGAZINE—P.O. Box 1790 News Plaza, Peoria, IL 61656 (New Products Editor)

DIVERSION—60 East 42nd St., New York, NY 10156 (Editor)

EAGLE MAGAZINE—2401 West Wisconsin Avenue, Milwaukee, WI 53233 (Eagle Easy Shopper Editor)

EBONY—820 South Michigan Avenue, Chicago, IL 60605 (Editor)

ELKS MAGAZINE—425 West Diversey Parkway, Chicago, IL 60614 (Family Shopper Editor)

ESQUIRE—2 Park Ave., New York, NY 10016 (Editor)

EXPECTING—685 Third Ave., New York, NY 10017

FAMILY CIRCLE—488 Madison Avenue, New York, NY 10022 (The Shopping Editor)

FAMILY HANDYMAN—1999 Shepard Rd., St. Paul, MN 55116 (Editor)

FAMILY WEEKLY—1515 Broadway, New York, NY 10036 (Weekend Shopping Editor)

FARMER—1999 Shepard Road, St. Paul, MN 55116 (New Products Editor)

FATE—500 Hyacinth Place, Highland Park, IL 60035 (Editor)

FIELD & STREAM—1515 Broadway, New York, NY 10036 (Sportman's Shopper Editor)

FLOWER & GARDEN—4251 Pennsylvania Avenue, Kansas City, MO 64111 (Market by Mail Editor)

FLYING MAGAZINE—One Park Avenue, New York, NY 10016 (New Products Editor)

FORTUNE—Time & Life Building, Rockefeller Center, New York, NY 10020 (Editor)

GENTLEMENS QUARTERLY—350 Madison Avenue, New York, NY 10017 (Gentlemens Showcase Editor)

GLAMOUR—350 Madison Avenue, New York NY 10017 (Glamour Aisle Editor)

GOLF—380 Madison Avenue, New York, NY 10017 (The Golf Shopper Editor)

GOLF DIGEST—495 Westport Avenue, Norwalk, CT 06856 (Golfers Shopping Guide Editor)

GOOD HOUSEKEEPING—959 8th Avenue, New York, NY 10019 (Gallery of Gadgets Editor)

GOURMET—1560 Lexington Ave., New York, NY 10022 (Garden of Eating Editor)

GRIT—208 West 3rd Street, Williamsport, PA 17701 (New Products Editor)

GUN WORLD—34249 Camino Capistrano, Capestrano Beach, CA 92624 (New Products Editor)

GUNS AND AMMO—8490 Sunset Boulevard, Los Angeles, CA 90069 (New Products Editor)

GUNS MAGAZINE—591 Camino de la Reina, San Diego, CA 92608 (Shopping with Guns Editor)

HARPER'S BAZAAR—1700 Broadway, New York, NY 10019 (Shopping Bazaar Editor)

STEREO REVIEW—One Park Avenue, New York, NY 10016 (New Products Editor)

HIT PARADE—Charlton Bldg., Derby, CT 06418 (Editor)

HOME—600 Madison Avenue, New York, NY 10022 (Editor)

HOOSIER FARMER—130 East Washington Street, Indianapolis, IN 46204 (Editor)

HORTICULTURE—300 Massachusetts Avenue, Boston, MA 02115 (Shop the Easy Way Editor)

HOT ROD MAGAZINE—8490 Sunset Blvd., Hollywood, CA 90028 (New Products Editor)

HOUSE & GARDEN—350 Madison Avenue, New York, NY 10017 (Shopping Around)

HOUSE BEAUTIFUL—1700 Broadway, New York, NY 10019 (Window Shopping)

INCOME OPPORTUNITIES MAGAZINE—380 Lexington, New York, NY 10017 (Editor)

JET—820 N. Old Oak Blvd., Middlebury Heights, OH 44180 (Editor)

KANSAS FARMER—1500 Old Oak Blvd., Middleburg Heights, OH 44130 (Editor)

KIWANIS MAGAZINE—3636 Woodview Trace, Indianapolis, IN 46268 (Editor)

LADY'S CIRCLE—21 West 26th Street, New York, NY 10010

LADIES HOME JOURNAL—Three Park Avenue, New York, NY 10016 (The Journal Store)

LET'S LIVE MAGAZINE—444 N. Larchmont Boulevard, Los Angeles, CA 90004 (New Products Editor)

MADEMOISELLE—360 Madison Avenue, New York, NY 10017 (Country Editor)

McCALL'S NEEDLEWORK—625 Seventh Avenue, New York, NY 10019 (New Products Editor)

MECHANIX ILLUSTRATED—1515 Broadway, New York, NY 10036 (Home & Shop Products Editor)

MODERN BRIDE—One Park Avenue, New York, NY 10016 (Wedding Gifts Editor)

MONEY-MAKING OPPORTUNITIES—11071 Ventura Boulevard, Studio City, CA 91604 (Editor)

MOOSE MAGAZINE—676 St. Clair, Chicago, IL 60611 (Moose Home Shopper Editor)

MOTHERS TODAY—841 Lexington Ave., New York, NY 10017 (Baby Buys Editor)

MOTOR BOATING AND SAILING—224 West 57th St., New York, NY 10019 (What's New Editor)

MOTOR TECH—224 W. 57th St., New York, NY 10019

MOTOR TREND—8490 Sunset Boulevard, Los Angeles, CA 90039 (New Products Editor)

NATIONAL GUARDSMAN—1 Massachusetts Avenue, N.W., Washington, DC 20001 (Editor)

NAVAL AFFAIRS—1303 New Hampshire Ave., N.W., Washington, DC 20086

NEWSWEEK—444 Madison Avenue, New York, NY 10022 (What's New)

NEW YORK TIMES—229 West 43rd Street, New York, NY 10036 (Editor New & Useful Home Section)

NEW YORK MOTORIST—28 East 78th Street, New York, NY 10021 (New Products Editor)

OHIO MOTORIST—P.O. Box 518, Cleveland, OH 44101 (New Products Editor)

ORGANIC GARDENING & FARMING—33 East Minor Street, Emmaus, PA 18049 (Market Place Editor)

OUTDOOR LIFE—380 Madison Avenue, New York, NY 10017 (Shopping for Indoor & Outdoor Editor)

PARADE—750 Third Avenue, New York, NY 10017 (Parade of Progress Editor)

PARENTS—685 Third Avenue, New York, NY 10017 (Shopping Scout Editor)

POTENTIALS IN MARKETING—731 Hennepin Avenue, Minneapolis, MN 55403 (Editor)

POPULAR COMMUNICATIONS—76 N. Broadway, Hicksville, NY 11801 (New Products)

POPULAR ELECTRONICS—One Park Avenue, New York, NY 10016 (New Products Editor)

POPULAR HOT RODDING—12301 Wilshire Blvd., Los Angeles, CA 90025 (Editor)

POPULAR MECHANICS—224 West 57th Street, New York, NY 10019 (Editor)

POPULAR PHOTOGRAPHY—One Park Avenue, New York, NY 10016 (What's New Editor)

POPULAR SCIENCE—380 Madison Avenue, New York, NY 10017 (New Aids for Living New Tools Editor)

PRAIRIE FARMER—2001 Spring Road, Oak Brook, IL 60521 (Editor)

PREVENTION—33 East Minor Street, Emmaus, PA 18049 (New Products Editor)

PROGRESSIVE FARMER—Box 2581, Birmingham, AL 35209 (Progressive Shop Editor)

RADIO-ELECTRONICS—200 Park Avenue South, New York, NY 10003 (New Products Editor)

RAILROAD MODEL CRAFTSMAN—Fredon-Springdale Rd., Fredon, NJ 07860 (Merchandise Depot Editor)

RETIREMENT LIFE—1533 New Hampshire Ave., Washington, DC 20036 (New Products Editor)

ROAD & TRACK—1499 Monrovia Avenue, Newport Beach, CA 92663 (New Products Editor)

THE ROTARIAN—1600 Ridge Avenue, Evanston, IL 60201 (Peeps at Things to Come Editor)

RUNNER'S WORLD—P.O. Box 366, Mountain View, CA 94043 (New Products Editor)

SAGA—355 Lexington Ave., New York, NY 10017 (Saga in the Shops Editor)

SCIENCE 84—1101 Vermont Ave., Washington, DC 20005 (New Ideas & Gadget Editor)

SCIENCE DIGEST—888 Seventh Ave., New York, NY 10106 (Editor)

SCIENCE & MECHANICS—380 Lexington Avenue, New York, NY 10017 (What's New)

SCIENCE NEWS—1719 N Street N.W., Washington, DC 20036 (New Products Editor)

SEVENTEEN—850 Third Avenue, New York, NY 10022 (Shop Wise Editor)

SKI—380 Madison Avenue, New York, NY 10017 (Ski Shopping Guide Editor)

SKI X-C—One Park Avenue, New York, NY 10016 (Shopping with Skiing Editor)

SKIN DIVER—8490 Sunset Boulevard, Los Angeles, CA 90069 (Editor)

SOUTHERN LIVING—820 Shades Creek Parkway, Birmingham, AL 35209 (New Products Editor)

SPARE TIME MAGAZINE—5810 W. Oklahoma Avenue, Milwaukee, WI 53219 (Editor)

SPORTS AFIELD—250 West 55th Street, New York, NY 10019 (Shopping Afield Editor)

SPORTS CAR—1765 Newhopem, Fountain Valley, CA 92708 (New Products Editor)

SPORTS ILLUSTRATED—1271 Avenue of the Americas, New York, NY 10020 (Weekend Shopper Editor)

SUCCESSFUL FARMING—1716 Locust Avenue, Des Moines, IA 50311 (Editor)

TEEN—8490 Sunset Blvd., Los Angeles, CA 90069 (New Products Editor)

TODAY'S LIVING—390 Fifth Avenue, New York, NY 10018 (Editor)

TRAILER LIFE—29901 Agoura Rd., Agoura, CA 91301 (Editor)

TRAVEL & LEISURE—1350 Avenue of the Americas, New York, NY 10019 (Editor)

TOWN & COUNTRY—717 Fifth Avenue, New York, NY 10022 (Counter Points Editor)

TRAVEL HOLIDAY—Travel Blvd., Floral Park, NY 11001 (Editor)

V.F.W. MAGAZINE—9 East 41st St., New York, NY 10017 (Reader's Shop by Mail Editor)

VOGUE—350 Madison Avenue, New York, NY 10017 (Shop Hound Editor)

WALLACES FARMER—2001 Spring Rd., Oak Brook, IL 60521 (Products Editor)
WOMAN'S DAY—1515 Broadway, New York, NY 10036 (Editor)
WOODSMEN OF THE WORLD MAGAZINE—1700 Farnam Street, Omaha, NB 88102 (New Products Editor)
WORKBENCH—4251 Pennsylvania, Kansas City, MO 64111 (New Products Editor)
YACHTING—One Park Ave., New York, NY 10016 (Waterfront News Editor)

SEND YOUR PUBLICITY RELEASE TO FEATURE AND SYNDICATED COLUMNISTS

Here is a partial list of columns which might do you much good because they are syndicated and are therefore distributed far and wide to newspapers and read by millions. These columnists are on the alert for new products to write about. Many will describe your offerings in full detail and will also include price; others will merely suggest where a person should write for full information.

When sending your releases with photoprint to these columns, you might state that you are prepared to answer such inquiries. For a more complete list of feature writers and syndicates, consult *The Working Press of the Nation* at your local library. The book is published by the National Research Bureau, Inc., 221 North LaSalle St., Chicago, IL 60601.

Better Homemaking	Newspaper Enterprise Association 20 Park Ave. South, Suite 602 New York, NY 10017
Boating	United Press International 220 E. 42nd St. New York, NY 10017
Business Today	Bell-McClure Syndicate 230 West 41st Street New York, NY 10036
Camera News	AP News Features 50 Rockefeller Plaza New York, NY 10020

Fashions	United Press International 220 East 42nd Street New York, NY 10017
Hobbies	AP News Features 50 Rockefeller Plaza New York, NY 10020
Homemaking Helps	King Features Syndicate 235 East 45th Street New York, NY 10017
Household Hints	King Features Syndicate 235 East 45th Street New York, NY 10017
Interior Decorating	AP News Features 50 Rockefeller Plaza New York, NY 10020
It's New to Me	Chronicle Features Syndicate 870 Market Street San Francisco, CA 94102
It's New	Columbia Features 36 W. 44th St. New York, NY 10016
Male Corner (fashions)	General Feature Syndicate 826 14th St. Brooklyn, NY 11230
Pet Doctor	AP News Features 50 Rockefeller Plaza New York, NY 10020
Science Newsfeatures	AP News Features 50 Rockefeller Plaza New York, NY 10020
Touching Home	Chicago Tribune New York Syndicate Inc. 220 East 42nd Street New York, NY 10017
Wife Preserves	King Features Syndicate 235 East 45th Street New York, NY 10017

Women's Corner	Chicago Tribune New York Syndicate Inc. 220 East 42nd Street New York, NY 10017
Working Girls *Notebook*	Chicago Tribune New York Syndicate Inc. 220 East 42nd Street New York, NY 10017
Young Mother's *Page*	Plus Business Features 545 Fifth Avenue New York, NY 10017
Your Business *and Mine*	Chicago Tribune New York Syndicate Inc. 220 East 42nd Street New York, NY 10017
New Products	American Way Features Inc. 128 Lighthouse Dr. Jupiter, FL 33458
	AP News Features 50 Rockefeller Plaza New York, NY 10020
	Associated Press 50 Rockefeller Plaza New York, NY 10020
	The Caraba Corporation Box 40 Maplewood, NJ 07040
	Chronicle Features 870 Market St. San Francisco, CA 94102
	City Desk Features 110-45 71 Rd. Forest Hills, NY 11375
	College Press Service 2629 18 St. Denver, CO 80211
	Columbia Features 36 W. 44th Street New York, NY 10036

New Products

Feature News Service
2330 S. Brentwood Blvd.
St. Louis, MO 63144

Field Newspaper Syndicate
Box 19620
Irvine, CA 92714

Fine Press Syndicate
Box 1383
Radio City Station
New York, NY 10019

Independent News Alliance
200 Park Ave.
New York, NY 10166

Jeffrey Lee Syndicate
2 Holly Drive
New Rochelle, NY 10801

Liberation News Service
17 W 17th St.
New York, NY 10011

Mc Naught Syndicate
60 E. 42nd St.
New York, NY 10017

Midcontinental Paulus
Feature Syndicate
Box 1662
Pittsburgh, PA 15230

Newspaper Enterprise Association
200 Park Ave.
New York, NY 10166

OPS (Oceanic Press Service)
Box 4158
North Hollywood, CA 91607

Pacific News Service
604 Mission St.
San Francisco, CA 94105

Press Wire Services
Box 2P
144-45 35th Ave.
Flushing, NY 11354

New Products

Sawyer Press
Box 46-578
Los Angeles, CA 90046

Singer Communications
3164 W. Tyler Ave.
Anaheim, CA 92801

Sioux City Journal
Sioux City, IA 51102

Sipa News Service
59 E. 54th St.
New York, NY 10022

Transworld Feature Syndicate
142 W. 44th St.
New York, NY 10036

United Press International
200 East 42nd Street
New York, NY 10017

Universal Press
4400 Johnson Dr.
Fairway, KS 66205

Zodiac News Service
54 Mint St.
San Francisco, CA 94103

TRADE MAGAZINES USE PUBLICITY RELEASES ALSO

The following are some of the countless trade journals, particularly the larger ones, which are known to give editorial mention to new items. The *Business Directory* of *Standard Rate and Data Service*, available in many libraries, lists thousands of other similar publications.

While some will actually print a firm's name and address, others as a matter of editorial policy, will not, but in lieu of this they ask their readers to fill out a Reader's Service Card. Those cards which pertain to your product are then sent to you for you own follow-up. It is not uncommon for a publication to forward from 500 to 1,000 inquiries relating to a single product.

Your release, as in the case of consumer publications, should be accompanied by a photo of the product. The number of inquiries converted into sales is contingent, in large measure, on the amount of "sell" injected into your follow-up literature. It will be to your advantage to send your releases to the New Products editor.

ADVERTISING AGE—740 N. Rush St., Chicago, IL 60611

AUDIO-VISUAL COMMUNICATIONS—25850 Hawthorne Blvd., Torrance, CA 90505

AIR CONDITIONING, HEATING AND REFRIGERATION NEWS—P.O. 2600, Troy, MI 48007

AIR FORCE MAGAZINE—1750 Penn. Ave., N.W., Washington, DC 20006

AMERICAN CLEAN CAR—500 N. Dearborn Street, Chicago, IL 60610

AMERICAN CITY & COUNTRY—Bershire Common, Pittsfield, MA 01201

AMERICAN DRUGGIST—655 West 57th Street, New York, NY 10019

AMERICAN DYE STUFF REPORTER—50 West 23rd St., New York, NY 10010

AMERICAN GLASS REVIEW—1115 Clifton Avenue, Clifton, NJ 07013

AMERICAN HAIRDRESSER—100 Park Avenue, New York, NY 10017

AMERICAN LAUNDRY DIGEST—500 N. Dearborn St., Chicago, IL 60610

AMERICAN MACHINIST—1221 Avenue of the Americas, New York, NY 10020

AMERICAN TEACHER—11 Dupont Circle, N.W., Washington, DC 20036

ARCHITECTURAL DESIGN, COST & DATA—1041 East Green St., Pasadena, CA 91106

ARCHITECTURAL RECORD—1221 Avenue of the Americas, New York, NY 10020

ARMY—2425 Wilson Blvd., Arlington, VA 22201

AUDIO TIMES—135 West 50th St. New York, NY 10020

AUTOMATIC MACHINING—228 N. Winton Rd., Rochester, NY 14610

AUTOMATION IN HOUSING—P.O. Box 120, Carpinteria, CA 93013

AUTOMOTIVE NEWS—965 E. Jefferson Avenue, Detroit, MI 48207

AUTOMOTIVE FLEET—2500 Artesia Boulevard, Redondo Beach, CA 90278

BAKING INDUSTRY—301 East Erie St., Chicago, IL 60611

BANK SYSTEMS & EQUIPMENT—1515 Broadway, New York, NY 10036

BEVERAGE WORLD—150 Great Neck Rd., Great Neck, NY 10021

BILLBOARD—1515 Broadway, New York, NY 10036

BOATING INDUSTRY—850 Third Ave., New York, NY 10022

BOWLERS JOURNAL—875 N. Michigan Ave., Chicago, IL 60611

BRAKE & FRONT END—11 S. Forge St., Akron, OH 44304

BROADCASTING—1735 DeSales St., N.W., Washington, DC 20036

BUILDING DESIGN & CONSTRUCTION—P.O. Box 5060, Des Plaines, IL 60018

BUILDING SUPPLY NEWS—5 S. Wabash Ave., Chicago, IL 60603

CARPENTER—101 Constitution Ave., N.W., Washington, DC 20001

CERAMIC INDUSTRY—1350 Touhy Ave., Des Plaines, IL 60018

CHEMICAL ENGINEERING—1221 Avenue of the Americas, New York, NY 10020

CHEMICAL & ENGINEERING NEWS—1155 Sixteenth Street N.W., Washington, DC 20036

CHEMICAL EQUIPMENT—13 Emery Ave., Randolph, NJ 07869

CHEMICAL WEEK—1221 Avenue of the Americas, New York, NY 10020

CHRISTIAN BOOKSELLER & LIBRARIAN—396 E. Charles St., Wheaton, IL 60187

COINAMATIC ACE—5 Beckman St., Rm 401, New York, NY 10038

CREDIT AND FINANCIAL MANAGEMENT—475 Park Ave. S., New York, NY 10003

DAIRY RECORD—5725 E. River Rd., O'Hara Plaza, Chicago, IL 60631

DATAMATION—875 Third Ave., New York, NY 10022

DENTAL MANAGEMENT—7500 Old Oak Blvd. Cleveland, OH 44130

DENTAL SURVEY—757 Third Ave., New York, NY 10017

DRILLING—4703 West Lovers Lane, Dallas, TX 75209

DRUG TOPICS—680 Kinderkamack Rd., Oradell, NJ 07649

DRUG MERCHANDISING—481 University Ave., Toronto MSW AA5W 1A7 Toronto, Ont., Canada

DRYCLEANING NEWS—70 Edwin Ave., Waterbury, CT 06708

DUN'S BUSINESS MONTH—875 Third Ave., New York, NY 10022

ELECTRICAL WHOLESALING—1221 Avenue of the Americas, New York, NY 10020

ELECTRONIC PRODUCTS—645 Stewart Ave., Garden City, NY 11530

ELECTRONICS—1221 Avenue of the Americas, New York, NY 10020

FARM CHEMICALS—37841 Euclid Ave., Willoughby, OH 44094

FARM & POWER EQUIPMENT—9701 Gravois Ave., St. Louis, MO 63123

FARM STORE MERCHANDISING—2501 Wayzata Blvd., Minneapolis, MN 55440

FEED MANAGEMENT—Sandstone Bldg., Mount Morris, IL 61054

FISHING TACKLE TRADE NEWS—Box 70, Wilmette, IL 60691

FOOD & DRUG PACKAGING—120 W. Second St., Duluth, MN 55802

FOUNDRY—1111 Chester Ave., Cleveland, OH 44114

FURNITURE PRODUCTION—804 Church Street, Nashville, TN 37203

GIFT & DECORATIVE ACCESSORIES—51 Madison Ave., New York, NY 10010

GOLF—380 Madison Ave., New York, NY 10017

GOLF INDUSTRY—1545 N.E. 123rd St., North Miami, FL 33161

GOVERNMENT PRODUCT-NEWS—1111 Chester Ave. W., Cleveland, OH 44114

GOVERNMENT EXECUTIVE—1725 K St. N.W., Washington, DC 20006

GRAPHIC ARTS MONTHLY—875 Third Ave., New York, NY 10022

HARDWARE AGE—Chilton Way, Radnor, PA 19089

HARDWARE MERCHANDISER—7300 N. Cicero, Lincolnwood, IL 60646

HARDWARE RETAILING—770 High Rd., Indianapolis, IN 46224

HEALTH FOODS RETAILING—390 Fifth Ave., New York, NY 10018

HEATING/PIPING/AIR CONDITIONING—2 Illinois Center Bldg., Chicago, IL 60601

HEATING AND PLUMBING PRODUCT NEWS—30 Emery Ave., Dover, NJ 07801

HANDLING & SHIPPING MANAGEMENT—1111 Chester Ave., Cleveland, OH 44114

HOME AND AUTO—7500 Old Oak Blvd., Cleveland, OH 44130

HOME CENTER MAGAZINE—300 W. Adams, Chicago, IL 60606

HOUSEWARES—7500 Old Oak Blvd., Cleveland, OH 44130

HYDRAULICS & PNEUMATICS—1111 Chester Ave., Cleveland, OH 44114

INCENTIVE MARKETING—633 Third Ave., New York, NY 10017

INDUSTRIAL EQUIPMENT NEWS—250 West 34th St., New York, NY 10119

INDUSTRIAL HEATING—1000 Killarney St., Pittsburgh, PA 15234

INDUSTRIAL MACHINERY NEWS—2916 Southfield Rd., Southfield, MI 48086

INDUSTRIAL PHOTOGRAPHY—475 Park Ave. S., New York, NY 10016

INDUSTRY WEEK—1111 Chester Ave., Cleveland, OH 44114

INFOSYSTEMS—665 Hitchcock Bldg., Wheaton, IL 60189

IN-PLANT PRINTER—P.O. Box 368, Northbrook, IL 60062

INSTRUCTOR—7500 Old Oak Blvd., Cleveland, OH 44130

INSTRUMENT & APPARATUS NEWS—Chilton Way, Radnor, PA 19089

INTERIOR DESIGN—850 Third Ave., New York, NY 10022

IRON AGE—Chilton Way, Radnor, PA 19089

JEWELER'S CIRCULAR-KEYSTONE—Chilton Way, Radnor, PA 19089

JOBBER RETAILER—P.O. Box 5417, Akron, OH 44313

JOBBER TOPICS—7300 N. Cicero Ave., Lincolnwood, IL 60646

JOURNAL OF FOOD PROTECTION—Box 701, Ames, IA 50010

JUVENILE MERCHANDISING—370 Lexington Ave., New York, NY 10017

LABORATORY EQUIPMENT—13 Emery Ave., Randolph, NJ 07869

LAWN CARE INDUSTRY—7500 Old Oak Blvd., Cleveland, OH 44130

LAWN AND GARDEN MARKETING—P.O. Box 12901, Overland Park, KS 66212

MACHINE & TOOL BLUE BOOK—Hitchcock Bldg., Wheaton, IL 60189

MAINTENANCE SUPPLIES—101 West 31st St., New York, NY 10001

MANUFACTURING ENGINEERING—P.O. Box 930, Dearborn, MI 48121

MARINE ENGINEERING—345 Hudson St., New York, NY 10014

METAL PROGRESS—Metals Park, OH 44073

MINING ENGINEERING—Littleton, CO 80127

MINING/PROCESSING EQUIPMENT—13 Emery Ave., Randolph, NJ 07869

MODERN CASTING—Golf and Wolf Rds., Des Plaines, IL 60016

MODERN GROCER—370 Lexington Ave., New York, NY 10017

MODERN JEWELER—P.O. Box 2939, Shawnee Mission, KS 66201

MODERN HEALTHCARE—740 North Rush St., Chicago, IL 60611

MODERN MACHINE SHOP—6600 Clough Pike, Cincinnati, OH 45244

MODERN OFFICE PROCEDURES—111 Chester Ave., Cleveland, OH 44114

MODERN PLASTICS—1221 Ave. of Americas, New York, NY 10020

MODERN PHOTOGRAPHY—825 Seventh Ave., New York, NY 10019

MODERN TIRE DEALER—P.O. Box 5417, Akron, OH 44313

MOTOR—555 West 57th St., New York, NY 10019

MOTOR AGE—Chilton Way, Radnor, PA 19089

MUSIC TRADE MAGAZINE—P.O. Box 432, Englewood, NJ 07631

NATIONAL JEWELER—1515 Broadway, New York, NY 10036

NATIONAL PETROLEUM NEWS—950 Lee St., Des Plaines, IL 60016

NATIONAL PROVISIONER—15 W. Huron St., Chicago, IL 60610

NEW EQUIPMENT DIGEST—1111 Chester Ave., Cleveland, OH 44114

OFFICE—1200 Summer St., Stamford, CT 06904

OFFICE PRODUCTS DEALER—Hitchcock Bldg., Wheaton, IL 60189

OFFICE PRODUCTS NEWS—645 Stewart Ave., Garden City, NY 11530

OFFICE WORLD NEWS—645 Stewart Ave., Garden City, NY 11530

PHOTO MARKETING—3000 Picture Place, Jackson, MI 49201

PHOTO WEEKLY—1515 Broadway, New York, NY 10014

PLANT LOCATION—345 Hudson St., New York, NY 10013

PLASTICS WORLD—221 Columbus Ave., Boston, MA 02116

PLAYTHINGS—51 Madison Ave., New York, NY 10010

POLICE CHIEF—13 Firstfield Rd., Gaithersburg, MD 20878

POOL & SPA NEWS—3923 West 6th St., Los Angeles, CA 90020

POULTRY TRIBUNE—Sandstone Bldg., Mount Morris, IL 61054

PRECISION METAL—1111 Chester Ave., Cleveland, OH 44114

PRINTING EQUIPMENT NEWS—801 Milford St., Glendale, CA 91209

PRINTING NEWS—468 Park Ave. S., New York, NY 10016

PRINTING VIEWS—8328 N. Lincoln Ave., Skokie, IL 60077

PRODUCTION ENGINEERING—1111 Chester Ave., Cleveland, OH 44114

PRODUCT MARKETING—124 E. 40th St., New York, NY 10016

PRODUCTS FINISHING—600 Main St., Cincinnati, OH 45202

PROGRESSIVE ARCHITECTURE—600 Summer St., Stamford, CT 06904

PROGRESSIVE GROCER—1351 Washington Blvd., Stamford, CT 06902

PROFESSIONAL CAR-WASHING—8 Stanley Circle, Latham, NY 12110

PUBLIC WORKS MAGAZINE—200 S. Broad St., Ridgewood, NJ 07451

QUALITY PROGRESS—230 West Wells St., Suite 7000, Milwaukee, WI 53203

RADIO-ELECTRONICS—200 Park Ave. S., New York, NY 10003

RETAIL LUMBERMAN—4901 Main St., Kansas City, MO 64112

SAFETY JOURNAL—P.O. Box 4189 Anderson, SC 29622

SAVING & LOAN NEWS—111 E. Wacker Dr., Chicago, IL 60601

SCHOOL ARTS MAGAZINE—50 Portland St., Worcester, MA 01608

SCHOOL PRODUCT NEWS—1111 Chester Ave., Cleveland, OH 44114

SERVICE STATION MANAGEMENT—560 Lee St., Des Plaines, IL 60016

SMALL WORLD—393 Seventh Ave., New York, NY 10001

SCIENCE—1515 Broadway, New York, NY 10036

SPORTING GOODS DEALER—1212 N. Linbergh St., St. Louis, MO 63166

SPORTS MERCHANDISER—1760 Peachtree Rd., N.W., Atlanta, GA 30357

SUPERMARKETING—1515 Broadway, New York, NY 10036

SUPERMARKET BUSINESS—25 W. 43rd St., New York, NY 10036

SUPER SERVICE STATION—7300 N. Cicero Ave., Chicago, IL 60646

SWIMMING POOL AGE & SPA—6255 Barfield Rd., Atlanta, GA 30328

TELEPHONY—55 W. Jackson Blvd., Chicago, IL 60604

TEXTILE INDUSTRIES—4170 Ashford-Dunwoody Rd., Suite 420, Atlanta, GA 30319

TEXTILE WORLD—1175 Peachtree St., N.E., Atlanta, GA 30361

TIRE REVIEW—11 S. Forge St., Akron, OH 44304

TOOLING AND PRODUCTION—5821 Harper Rd., Solon, OH 44139

TOY AND HOBBY WORLD—124 East 40th St., New York, NY 10016

TOYS TRADE NEWS—7500 Old Oak Blvd., Cleveland, OH 44150

VARIETY—154 West 46th St., New York, NY 10036

WATER CONDITIONING & PURIFICATION—P.O. Box 42406, Tucson, AZ 85733

WATER & WASTES DIGEST—380 Northwest Hwy, Des Plaines, IL 60016

WELDING DESIGN & FABRICATION—1111 Chester Ave., Cleveland, OH 44114

WHOLESALER—135 Addison Ave., Elmhurst, IL 60126

WIRE JOURNAL—1570 Boston Post Rd., Guilford, CT 06437

WOOD & WOOD PRODUCTS—300 W. Adams St., Chicago, IL 60606

WOODWORKING & FURNITURE DIGEST—Hitchcock Bldg., Chicago, IL 60606

YOUR CHURCH—198 Allendale Rd., King of Prussia, PA 19406

LEGAL STEPS

You can avoid legal technicalities by operating under your own name either from your home address, a post office box number, or from the address of a firm that operates a mail pickup service. If you adopt a company or other trade name, bear in mind that in most states it is necessary to register the assumed name with the county clerk. A small fee is required. Operating under a trade name does not reduce your responsibility to creditors. If more capital is required, it is often good policy to take in a partner who will share costs, financial responsibility, and profits with you. Of course, when setting up a partnership, the arrangement should be in writing. A corporation is a more formal type of business. It requires a charter by the state—shares of stock—a board of directors and officers. Stockholders share in the profits in proportion to their stock holdings. Liability is generally limited to the original investment. In short—creditors cannot claim a stockholder's personal wealth, as in the case of individual ownership or partnership. If you plan to organize a corporation, you will need a lawyer to draw up the papers.

Whether you are an inventor or purchasing an invention, you may have to protect yourself by looking into certain government regulations—depending on the type of product and its distribution. The following departments have issued regulations which must be observed if you wish to stay out of trouble: Post Office, Federal Trade Commission, Food and Drug Administration, Copyright Office (Library of Congress). Then, to be sure, there is the Patent Office. If you wish to protect an invention by means of a patent, better consult a patent attorney. In most cases, one need not concern himself with government regulations if he is on the level with the public, offering honest merchandise at a fair price, making no false claims, and is ready to return merchandise if the customer is dissatisfied. Certain mail order products such as cosmetics, medicinals, food products, and aphrodisiacs are more likely to be scrutinized by governmental agencies and Better Business Bureaus.

GIVE HER 1, 2, 3, 4, OR 5
EYE POPPING RINGS
for Christmas
They Cost Little Enough!

Here is an eyeful of delightful gold-tone rings to glorify her pretty fingers. This mad, mod, marvelous jewelry is the new look which every girl craves for. Cleverly realistic, colorful glass eyes (including cat's eyes) are magnificently mounted. Perfect for stocking stuffers, too! Guaranteed to arouse interested stares and green-eyed envy. A full hand of fun and beauty. Expertly crafted in wide choice of styles. Packed individually in elegant ring display boxes. Rush your order with check or money order to:

Regularly $2.98 — $1.95 each —
SPECIAL FOR THE HOLIDAYS—
ALL 5 for $5.00!

G. SCHOEPPER, Dept. DN
STORE
128 West 31st St., bet. 6th & 7th Ave.
New York, N.Y. 10001

Here is a three-fold appeal to insure sales. It makes a Christmas gift appeal; it satisfies the demand for popular modern rings, and finally it attracts those interested in bargains.

This *Wall Street Journal* ad was designed to appeal to males in the high income category, especially sportsman. Since animal heads and animal rugs are used to decorate homes as well as offices, the same ad with a slight change in the heading could effectively run in the Shelter Magazines such as *Home Beautiful* and *House & Garden.*

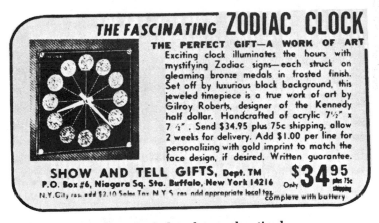

This clock has been advertised during the period when Zodiac products have been in great demand. The advertisement appeared in the magazine section of the *New York Times.*

A MAIL ORDER CHECK LIST TO HELP AVOID COSTLY ERRORS

There are many guideposts to success in mail order advertising. Here are 120 suggestions culled from the experience of mail order advertisers, agencies, and media. Not all of them will apply to any one mail order operation, but those that do apply will prevent serious mistakes and oversights.

Company

1. Select a short easily remembered company name.
2. Give a homey, informal touch to the company setup.
3. Use a mailing address that can handle a large volume of mail (not the address of another company, unless you are one of the principals).

Product

4. Choose a good product of acceptable quality.
5. Select something that people need.
6. Try to select a product in considerable demand or an unusual item difficult to get from individual retailers who can't afford to carry it because of the small local demand. However, on a nationwide scale this demand can add up to a sizable amount.
7. Market an item which is newly popular with large groups of people such as ex-GIs, Canasta players, television fans.
8. Try to obtain an exclusive arrangement with the source of your product, thus reducing competition.
9. Choose a product generally in short supply but available to you.
10. Pick a product that will lead up to switching consumers to new, succeeding or alternate items.
11. If supplies become low, switch products.
12. The product must not be too costly to make in small quantities at first (no expensive dies).
13. Brand-new merchandise has an edge over standard catalog items.

Line

14. Develop a line of merchandise—you'll probably never get rich on one item.
15. Use a succession of items.
16. Promote a variety of products.
17. Sell services as well as products.

Samples

18. Offer samples if possible, particularly if the products need to be examined to be appreciated.
19. Don't make samples superior to actual merchandise; the customer will become suspicious and irritated, and further sales to him lost forever.

Packaging

20. Use colorful, imaginative packaging.
21. Make sure the packaging is practical, durable, and of the proper size.
22. Keep a ready supply of merchandise available proportionate to product orders (unless you deal with a dropship supplier).

Shipping

23. Compare transportation rates (mail, United Parcel, freight, etc.) and use the cheapest.
24. Prepay postage in most cases, especially on low-priced items.
25. Watch shipping weight so that a slight excess doesn't raise mailing costs.
26. Your address label should have complete legible information.
27. Guarantee postage so that the post office will notify addressee.

Supplier

28. Try nearby suppliers first.
29. Be aware that a reliable supplier is the keystone of a mail order operation.

30. Make sure that he will guarantee his output for quality and volume.
31. Will he make small deliveries at first and step up production as needed?

Purchases

32. Buy at a price which allows for your proper markup but keeps your supplier in business.
33. Price merchandise fairly.
34. Figure in prepaid postage where possible.
35. Use round numbers on low-priced products—preferably one coin or one bill (not odd-cent prices) for convenience in remitting.
36. Offer a cash refund; allow for this cost, too.
37. Determine your break-even point acurately.
38. Allow for all costs: unit cost of product; cost of depositing checks; wrapping; transportation; postage; damage; rejects; replacement; C.O.D. costs; refusals; bad debts; normal business overhead.
39. Determine the correct ratio of selling price to cost of product.
40. Don't limit yourself to low-priced merchandise, especially if markup is too small to be profitable.

Advertising

41. Have enough capital to advertise continually or don't even start in business.
42. Start with small ads, classifieds, if necessary.
43. If you have a sure seller, buy large advertising space.
44. Suit your advertising to the medium to appeal to its readership.
45. Base your budget and schedule on ad pull by months.
46. Don't be afraid to experiment; vary ad size, copy, and appeal. Check and double-check to find right advertising slant and selling appeal.
47. Try split-run testing if available.
48. Use special gimmicks, such as gift appeals, holidays, quantity discounts.
49. Base your advertising budget on the number of inquiries needed to make the ads pay.
50. Remember that the power of one ad over another may vary as much as 25 to 1.

51. The conventional selling cost by mail is 15 percent compared with 3 to 4 percent for retailers; but only repeat orders make mail order profitable.
52. Repeat a successful ad until you reach a point of diminishing returns.
53. Get editorial mentions in the shopping sections of publications.

Copy

54. Use a practical how-to-approach.
55. Write tight copy.
56. Except for prestige advertising, white space is less important than copy.
57. Write copy for a mass market and write as you speak.
58. Use unstylized selling copy.
59. Prepare copy carefully to suit each medium.
60. Avoid tricky phrases; be sincere; don't exaggerate.
61. Use the YOU approach.
62. Convince the reader that you are dependable and reliable.
63. Make it easy for the prospect to act—give simple, specific directions.
64. Don't attempt institutional or goodwill copy; just sell!
65. Analyze readership studies to develop copywriting techniques.
66. Use all space effectively. Sell your line in the unused spaces of other products, book jackets, direction sheets, packages, boxes, wrappers and letters.
67. Use short testimonials to plug products and company.
68. Play up local or regional fame, like well-known fruit areas, Williamsburg craft shops, Southern delicacies.
69. Guarantee both the product and customer satisfaction; offer return privilege.
70. Offer something free as a premium or bonus.
71. Key all ads to test pull.
72. Check and double-check copy for possible omissions, ambiguous statements, confusing directions.

Art

73. Use appropriate illustrations—selling pictures, not art for art's sake.
74. Be sure to include a photo or a clear drawing with the detailed copy, particularly if product is complicated.

75. Bold headlines and layout outpull cheesecake illustrations.

Media

76. Consult other mail order operators and agencies on the best media to use.
77. Make sure your merchandise is advertised in the best media for your product.
78. For a quick return and an early check on copy pull, use newspapers for pilot tests; for the long pull, use magazines.
79. Try new media.
80. Use direct mail for follow-up.
81. Build a mailing list from your inquiries and customers.
82. Rent lists from reputable houses, mail order advertisers, or agencies.
83. Rent your lists to noncompeting mail order companies and direct mail houses.
84. Keep your mailing lists restricted as much as possible to more promising prospects.

Agencies

85. Use an agency that's sold on mail order and really wants the account. The return will be small until the account begins to pay off for both of you.
86. Inquiries and sales will give you quick proof of the agency's effectiveness.
87. Avoid agencies with clients and products that are competitive with yours.
88. Expect to pay cash in advance and offer references; agencies are wary of mail order credit.
89. Agency commissions are generally 15 percent, but may vary because of the greater risk involved with mail order accounts.
90. An agency may net more than 4 percent on mail order accounts compared with 2 to 3 percent on other accounts.

Customer Payment

91. Cash, money order or checks, preferably not C.O.D.
92. Accept checks—few bounce.
93. Obtain the necessary papers to legalize those checks made out to any possible variation of your company name.

94. On most C.O.D. orders it is wise to ask for an advance deposit to increase the number of paid orders.
95. Prepay postage on C.O.D. orders to avoid nondelivery, and bill customer for postage.
96. Avoid the phrase "Bill me" in coupon or order form.

Complaints

97. Remember: The customer is always right.
98. Take care of complaints quickly; make replacement or adjustment immediately.
99. Don't be afraid to write a courteous letter of explanation.

Refunds

100. Make immediate refunds at no cost to customer.
101. Adjust overpayments quickly.

Follow-up

102. Repeat business is vital to success; keep the customer sold.
103. It takes a long time to build customer confidence in buying by mail.
104. Be prompt and courteous in answering inquiries. Ship orders, explain delays, make adjustments, and refund money quickly.
105. Personally sign all correspondence.
106. Follow up initial sale with mailing pieces, folders, catalogs, brochures.
107. From time to time mail new price lists to customers to encourage business.
108. Ask satisfied customers to submit names of friends, neighbors, relatives, and business associates as potential customers; offer a bonus for this.
109. Continue to offer a product and to work good mailing lists until they are no longer profitable. Then try them again later.
110. Be ready to answer all sorts of by-product mail, offers, inquiries, deals.
111. Watch out for tricky offers (for example, worthless space and catalog listings), in return for free products.

Keeping Records

112. Based on a keying system, keep accurate records of the pull of each ad, showing the relative effectiveness of various combinations of headline, art, copy, medium.

Catalogs

113. Mail order catalog-making is a science.
114. Offer catalogs if your line is big enough, but charge a small sum or restrict distribution to active customers. Paying for the catalog increases its value to the customer and saves you money as well.

Other Means of Distribution

115. Chances are that wholesale and retail trade will gradually replace mail order volume on some items.
116. Let retailers take orders from displayed samples of items; then fill the orders by mail.
117. If you let a retailer promote your item heavily in his market, be prepared for a drop in mail order sales.
118. If you want a retailer to carry your item, don't give him concentrated mail order competition in his own market.

Miscellaneous

119. Don't be surprised if there are ups and downs depending on the season, time of the month or competition.
120. Don't expect many returns after the first six months, but don't be surprised if orders or inquiries trickle in for years.

(The information in the foregoing check list is based on an article which originally appeared in Printer's Ink, Nov. 10, 1950, Copyright 1950 Decker Communications, Inc. to whom grateful acknowledgement is made.)

NOTES

NOTES

NOTES